Seashores

An Ecological Guide

Seashores
An Ecological Guide

Julian Cremona

CROWOOD

First published in 2014 by
The Crowood Press Ltd
Ramsbury, Marlborough
Wiltshire SN8 2HR

www.crowood.com

© Julian Cremona 2014

All rights reserved. No part of this publication may be reproduced or transmitted in any form or by any means, electronic or mechanical, including photocopy, recording, or any information storage and retrieval system, without permission in writing from the publishers.

British Library Cataloguing-in-Publication Data
A catalogue record for this book is available from the British Library.

ISBN 978 1 84797 804 2

Dedication
To Brenda

Acknowledgements

Over the eighteen years spent as Head of Dale Fort Field Centre my knowledge and understanding of marine ecology was extensively increased, modified and corrected by the staff and people I met: Dr Steve Morrell and Phil Wensley in particular. As work colleague and friend, John Archer-Thomson has been a constant source of inspiration and help which has continued after my recent retirement. He has provided valuable assistance in the writing of this book and allowed two of his photographs to be included. Photographing under the microscope is a great skill which I have struggled with and I thank Mike Crutchley for coming to the rescue. He has provided a number of his superb plankton images as well as two mollusc radula. Dr Robin Crump has always been a great friend and I thank him for his help with lichens, echinoderms and for many other areas of his expertise. I particularly enjoy marine insects but identification is difficult as they are so small and my thanks go to Dr Joe Botting and Dr Tristan Bantock of britishbugs.org.uk. You could not ask for a more tolerant 'field assistant' than my wife Brenda, who has been by my side in some of the worst climatic conditions possible. I could never be where I am today without you.

Graphic design, layout and illustrations: Peggy Issenman, Peggy & Co. Design
Printed and bound in Malaysia by Times Offset (M) Sdn Bhd

CONTENTS

	Introduction	7
1	**Elements of the Coast**	8
	Basic principles	8
	The ecosystem	8
	Abiotic factors	10
	The tides	10
	Wave action and types of shore	12
	Biotic factors	13
	Primary production	16
	Consumers	20
	Nutrient flow and decomposition	23
2	**Rocky Shores**	24
	Part 1: The communities	24
	Cliffs and sea-bird colonies	27
	Splash zone community	33
	Upper shore community	38
	Middle shore community	44
	Lower shore community	54
	Laminaria zone: the transition from littoral to sub-littoral	64
	Part 2: Ecology of the shore	72
3	**Plankton**	85
	Introduction	85
	Phytoplankton	85
	Zooplankton	88
	Plankton blooms	92
4	**Sediment Shores**	94
	Part 1: The communities	94
	Upper and middle sandy shore communities	97
	Lower sandy shore communities	101
	Estuarine and muddy shore communities	106
	Part 2: Ecology of sediment shores	114

5	**Salt-marsh**	**122**
	Part 1: The communities	122
	Lower salt-marsh – pioneer zone	125
	Salt-marsh creek community	134
	Upper salt-marsh community	137
	Part 2: Ecology of the salt-marsh	142
6	**Sand Dunes**	**148**
	Part 1: The communities	148
	Embryo dune – the pioneer zone	150
	Yellow dune community – mobile dunes	152
	Grey dune community – fixed dunes with shell sand present	158
	Grey dune community – fixed dunes with silica sand	160
	Slack community – damp alkaline slacks	163
	Slack community – damp acidic slacks	165
	Part 2: Colonization and succession of sand dune communities	167
7	**Shingle**	**171**
8	**Threats and Conservation**	**176**
	Introduction	176
	Pollutants	176
	Climate change, invasive and alien species	178
	Direct action on the shore	179
	Marine conservation	180
	Glossary	181
	Reference and Further Information	183
	Appendix: Classification of the Organisms Discussed in this Book	184
	Index	188

INTRODUCTION

Where would you like to go on holiday? When asked people often say 'sea, sand, and sun'. Where did this love for the seaside begin? The early Britons were certainly coast dwellers. The wild woods prevented the crossing of the land and protection was often best on promontory headlands where we see the remains of Bronze and Iron Age forts. Domestication of the coastal vegetation, like carrots and cabbage, gave us the veggies we have today. Scavenging between the tides provided a host of limpets and other shellfish, a delicacy still sought in many diets. The seashore was part of our evolution, fixed in our blood before the great forests were cut down and we moved inland.

The Victorians brought us back with railways. We went in our thousands to escape the grime and drudge of industrialization, to sit on a beach and experience a natural world. However, the Victorians' love of exploration caused some to leave the deckchair and bathing machine to beachcomb. Soon people wanted to know more and finding weird and amazing creatures gave birth to identification books. Amazing and quite stunning books appeared, the like of which we may never see again. One example was the three leather-bound volumes of *Phycologia Britannica* published in 1846, a complete coverage of British seaweeds, all with painted colour plates. The first modern book of the seashore was *Collins Guide to the Seashore* by Barrett and Yonge in 1958. Remaining in print for several decades, it was the standard by which all identification books were judged.

Today we are served with a diversity of identification books to help satisfy the question, 'What is it?' There is a plethora of excellent guides filled with colour illustrations of the many hundreds of species from the common to the very rare, typically ordered from the simple to the complex – seaweeds at the start going through to fish at the end. This book, too, may help you answer the 'What is it?' question, as it covers the key species that are most likely to be encountered. Here, however, species are approached from the community perspective, since organisms are not solitary beings, so the first aim is to identify the community. Each shore type is divided into two parts: the first part helps with that identification and breakdown of the community; the second looks at the ecology of the whole. Each community begins with photographs of what may be encountered, with bulleted information on those species followed by a breakdown of additional plants and animals. There will always be some overlap between communities, so be prepared to find what you are after nearby.

In this way the book aims to interpret the role of populations and communities within their environment; answering different questions about adaptations to where they live, why they live where they do, and how they interact and feed.

The scientific names of species given in this book were correct at the time of writing. However, the nomenclature and classification of organisms is constantly being reviewed and may change. The book is aimed at the layman, student and naturalist. It is easy to dip into and text has been kept short and succinct. Exploring the seashore is one of the most absorbing pastimes within which we can indulge ourselves. I hope this book helps in your enjoyment.

Chapter 1
ELEMENTS OF THE COAST

Basic principles

Ecology is concerned with the relationship between living things and their external environment. Animals also have an internal environment consisting of tissue fluid which bathes the body cells. Higher organisms, e.g. mammals, can regulate this fluid (called homeostasis) within narrow limits but amongst the lower invertebrates there is a lessening of control and a greater dependence on the conditions within their external environment. For example, sea anemones have no control over water loss or the water entering their tissue fluid. They must live in an aquatic environment whose concentration (osmotic potential) matches that of their tissue fluid so that water loss will equal water gain, referred to as isotonic. As well as water they must obtain glucose, protein, salts, oxygen and gametes or reproductive cells from the environment. This is the fundamental relationship between any organism and its environment. Each organism has its specific needs for survival and to understand an organism it is important to understand its external environment, including the interactions that occur with other species.

The ecosystem

No organism is independent; we are all part of an ecological system. The life on planet earth is known as the biosphere and is built like a jigsaw puzzle, made of pieces or units called ecosystems. A tropical rainforest, a moorland or a rocky seashore are examples of ecosystems although the environment you see is called the habitat within which the ecosystem occurs. The actual system is not a tangible item but a theoretical relationship between four interacting components all occurring within the habitat:

- The abiota – the physical and chemical features determining the system.
- The biota – the populations and communities of organisms.
- An *input* or source of energy (e.g. solar energy, which powers a system through photosynthesis); in order to be sustained each system will have a minimum or annual amount of energy requirement – an 'energy budget'.
- An *output* or flow of nutrients, including the cycle of decomposition (e.g. nitrogen and carbon cycles).

Fig. 1.1
An eroding rocky coast and an exposed sandy beach with waves breaking off-shore. Pembrokeshire.

Fig. 1.2
A very sheltered rocky shore at low tide. Western Scotland.

Fig. 1.3
Moderately exposed rocky shore of soft limestone. Flamborough Head.

Fig. 1.4
Sediment shore of sand and mud deposits. Mussel beds encrusted with barnacles in the foreground. Moray Firth, Scotland.

Fig. 1.5
A sand bar and extensive sand dunes in the background have produced sheltered conditions for a salt-marsh to develop, dominated by Cord Grass and Eel Grass. Holy Island, Northumberland.

Elements of the Coast   9

Fig. 1.6
High and low spring tide in a sheltered bay. The black band on the rocks is a tar lichen *Verrucaria maura* marking the tidal limit whilst the pale region below is of barnacles.

Abiotic factors

The abiota are the total of all the factors affecting an ecosystem and will determine the presence and development of an organism. These may be termed abiotic or limiting factors. A rabbit and a fish are both backboned creatures and yet they live in totally different habitats because the abiota are so different in each case. This may be an extreme example of very different abiota but it is to these factors that organisms have evolved and adapted to over time. They are the environment in which the organism must live. Abiotic fluctuations may bring organisms close to their lethal limits from environmental stress. Temperature is one such factor; imagine how that could affect your survival. You will operate within an ideal range, which as we know often varies even between individuals; as temperature approaches the extremes of your tolerance so you feel increasingly uncomfortable and stressed: this is environmental stress.

Ecosystems usually have several primary limiting factors that may in turn control secondary ones. On the seashore tides and wave action are of primary importance. The latter will be significant in determining the type of seashore, e.g. rocky or sand shores. Tides have a huge effect on the creatures living on any shore and an understanding of them is required in order to interpret the ecology.

The tides

Typically on Atlantic coasts, twice a day the water rises and falls vertically across the edge of the land. These tides are of two types: neap tides and spring tides. The latter has nothing to do with the seasons but is related to the greater rise and fall than on a neap tide. There are areas of coast where the number of tides seems to double with a secondary rise and fall, e.g. near Southampton. This usually relates to local geography, in this instance the presence of the Isle of Wight, where a

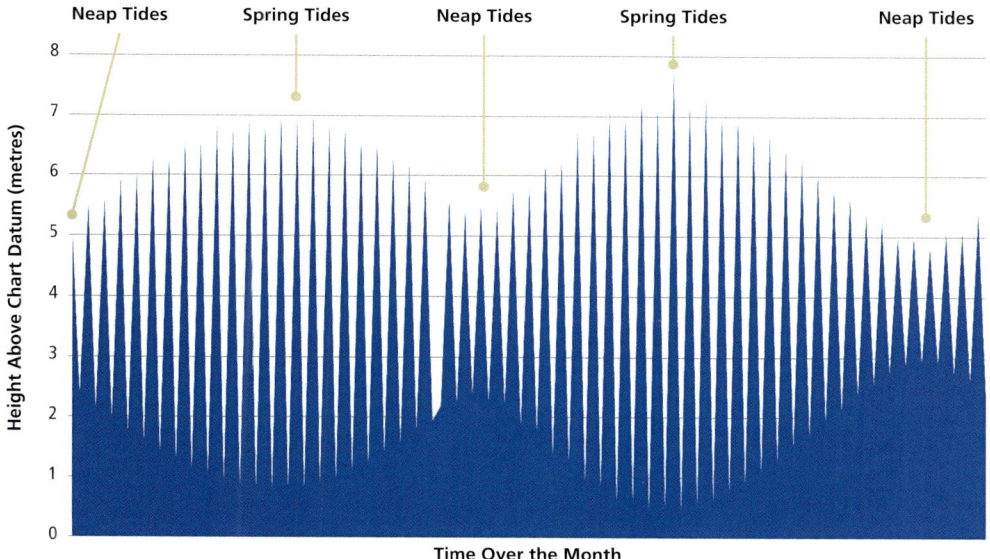

Fig. 1.7
Tidal Range at Milford Haven over the month of September 2013. Blue indicates the position of the seawater. At one point it almost reaches 8 metres before a decline to minimal movement at the end of the month.

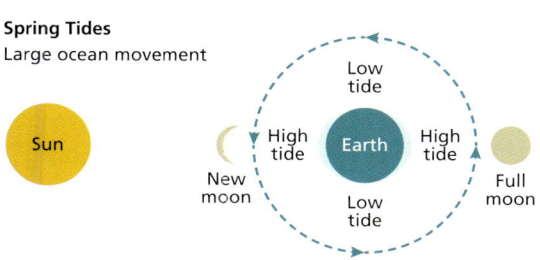

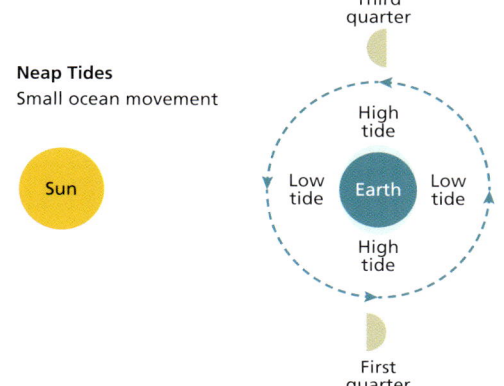

Fig. 1.8
Tides are the result of a gravitational pull caused by the sun and moon on the earth. The peak spring tides occur when the sun, earth and moon are in alignment but as the moon rotates away from this the gravitational pull becomes less. At the quarters position it is at its least and neap tides occur.

falling tide can 'bounce' back off the land. In other cases around the world the two daily tidal movements may be uneven, e.g. in Singapore, where the first tide of the day may have an extensive range but is then followed by one of minimal movement. This demonstrates that tides are very sensitive to local conditions.

Both the moon and sun exert a gravitational pull on the earth's surface but it is the former, closer body that has the most effect. It is this pull that causes the oceans to move and the water to rise and fall. The tidal range varies as the moon moves on a 28-day cycle around the earth. When the three bodies – earth, moon and sun – are in alignment the moon shows in the sky as either a full or new moon. This alignment creates the greatest pull and therefore tidal movement: the spring tide. These high tides will peak at the full or new moon but for a few days either side the effect will be similar. As the moon continues to orbit the earth it moves to a new alignment, at right angles with the sun and earth. With the influence of the sun counteracting the moon, which

appears as a quarter in the sky, the tidal movement is at its least: the neap tide. Fig. 1.7 shows the position of the water over a 28-day period. Initially the tide goes from neap to spring and then back to neap again. However, spring and neap tides vary over the course of the year as the heavenly bodies vary in their alignment.

Tidal ranges vary from place to place as well as from day to day. Dorset has a range of 1–2 metres whilst in the Channel Islands it is 5–10 metres. Local tide tables give us a prediction of the daily high and low tides with a time and the height in metres. The reference point for these heights is called 'chart datum' which may be thought of as the lowest tide (on average) in an area. On rare occasions every few years the tide may dip just below chart datum, especially if the atmospheric pressure is high and the wind is blowing away from the land. These are two influences affecting the prediction of tides. Conversely, high spring tides coupled with low pressure and on-shore winds may cause flooding inland as the sea rises above the predicted height.

Elements of the Coast

Fig. 1.9
24-hour tidal movement for Milford Haven. The blue line represents an example of a spring tide whilst the red is for neap tides.

Fig. 1.9 shows the tide heights over a 24-hour period. The spring tide uncovers well into the lower shore and at high tide wets the upper shore, here going higher than 7 metres. Values from a week later show that we are now in neap tides with the vertical movement much less. At low neap tide the water has barely uncovered any of the lower shore or covered the upper shore. In this example an organism living on the upper shore at 6 metres will be submerged in seawater for only a few hours every other week, when a spring tide occurs. Likewise in the lower shore, a creature is only uncovered during spring tides.

This is why tides are such an important limiting factor on seashores. The rise and fall of the tide creates an environmental gradient of water supply up and down the habitat. At the top there is least water, the driest region of the shore. Moving down the shore the humidity and chance of drying out becomes less and less until organisms are permanently under water. The terms immersion and emersion refer to, respectively, being in or out of the water. Emersion is not a commonly used word except on seashores and refers to the organisms being uncovered by the tide and exposed to desiccation or drying out. As a primary factor the tide influences a number of secondary ones like temperature as water creates a more stable environment. Out of water the creatures are more likely to freeze in winter or bake in the sun during summer. The abiotic factors relevant to each type of shore are given in the respective chapters.

Wave action and types of shore

The area between the high and low water marks is specifically known as the littoral region. Below this, where it is very rare for emersion to occur is called the sublittoral. Conversely the area above high water is the supralittoral where it is rare to find submerged organisms. This area can receive seawater from crashing waves and is more commonly known as the splash zone.

The extent of all of these regions is strongly influenced by the amount of wave action present. It is the interaction between the geology and waves that determines the coastline. A wave is a wind-induced oscillation of the water surface, its energy continuing until expended or deflected by an object. Two wave types can be identified on the coast: first the pounding, destructive or eroding wave that removes material leaving hard rocky areas; and secondly the spilling, constructive or depositing wave which creates the soft coastline. A surfer wishing to survive chooses the second type, usually occurring where the beach consists of a shallow off-shore region. As the waves travel across the shallow area so the water drags along the bottom causing the wave top to spill over and gradually the energy is lost until the water reaching the shore is gentle and deposits sand or shingle. Seashores that have strong wave action are referred to as exposed shores, thus 'exposure' relates to the amount of wave action rather than the time emersed.

Elements of the Coast

Fig. 1.10
Destructive wave action.

Fig. 1.11
Constructive wave action; energy has dissipated on the shore and sand is deposited.

Wave action will therefore determine the substrate and type of shore that develops. Eroding waves scour the land, revealing hard, rocky shores. These show a wide range of exposure from sheltered sea lochs to extreme, wave-worn headlands and islands facing into the open Atlantic. With the lessening of the wave energy so a grading of shores from shingle through sand and fine silt deposits to create soft mud in very sheltered conditions. There is an almost endless variation of shores along the coast with rocky outcrops providing shelter for sand and mud to deposit between boulders. This does cause immense variation on seashores where such overlap in conditions occurs. It is not uncommon to find sheltered spots on exposed shores and vice versa.

Biotic factors

Upon first sight of a habitat the assemblage of creatures may look rather chaotic, but there is structure. Groups of individuals of the same species living in the same area and free to interbreed will be termed a population. Even a quick look at the habitat shows a range of species and this means there will be more than one population present. Groups of populations in the same area and free to interact will be known as a community. This interaction could mean they are feeding on each other, a prey–predator relationship. It could also mean that different populations compete with each other for the same food or space (known as inter-specific competition). Competition may occur within a population.

Fig. 1.12
Close-up of a cliff-top plant community.

Usually, there is a dominant species in the community which we recognize as an indicator species of the environmental conditions. Marram grass gives its name to the marram community typical of wind-blown sand. A number of communities may live within an ecosystem: not a random mix of species but an orderly distribution of communities changing along the gradient of limiting factors. As the conditions change so the communities overlap with each other, producing biological bands of communities called zones. On the rocky shore there is a fairly static zonation, unchanged spatially from year to year although variation in populations can occur within it. Dynamic zonation is typical of the plants of sand dunes and salt-marsh where a succession of communities replace each other in time. This is termed ecological succession.

A population will exhibit a niche; put in its simplest form this is the role played by a population within its community but it is a rather abstract concept. Firstly, the niche will be defined by the upper and lower limits of the abiota. Think of yourself and what your boundaries are with regard to one factor, e.g. temperature. Perhaps you find your ideal working temperature is 20°C but you could survive at 36°C in midsummer and just about cope down to 0°C. Unless action is taken, outside these temperatures you find it lethal; thus your potential niche for temperature is within the range 0–36°C, although your optimal niche is somewhere in the middle. At the extremes of your potential niche you will only be able to do a few functions and you will be more susceptible to disease and stress. Your reproductive capacity would be impaired. That is just one of many abiotic factors determining an organism's tolerance limits and if they are operating close to the edge of a number of tolerances they probably will not survive. Once all these factors are taken into consideration the optimal niche for an organism can be deduced and identified within a habitat.

Bladder Wrack *Fucus vesiculosus* is a common and widespread brown seaweed. It can tolerate around six hours of emersion and drying but must have water every day. This makes it difficult for it to exist in the upper shore region. Light will be considered later but that too is an important factor and the lower shore has least light on the shore. It seems ideally placed in the middle shore. Searching this area on a rocky shore you may find varying amounts and possibly none. Why, if this is the ideal niche? It could be due to other abiota but is most likely due to inter-specific competition, probably with Knotted Wrack *Ascophyllum nodosum* or even barnacles. Alternatively, the young sporeling stage of the seaweed's development could have been eaten by limpets. This alone with feeding would be examples of biotic factors. Abiotic factors may determine the parameters of a niche but biotic factors also modify it. Understanding the realized (actual) niche of a population requires details of both types of factor.

An organism's tolerance on the abiotic range can be remarkably limited in some species but extensive in others. Bladder Wrack has a wide tolerance of wave action and so it can be found, in theory, across a range of exposed and sheltered shores. The seaweed derives its name from

Fig. 1.13
Bladder Wrack is adaptable to differing degrees of wave action.
Left, sheltered shore with air bladders; right, 'bladderless' form on a very exposed shore.

Fig. 1.14
Knotted Wrack in sheltered conditions is out-competing the Bladder Wrack.

the small air bladders that help it float to reach the light. A possible drawback is that this increases the surface area and in areas of exposure to wave action a large surface area will increase the chance of being ripped from the rocks and lost. Bladder Wrack is an adaptable organism, changing its growth form according to the wave action and a quick look at the number of bladders is an indication of the wave energy. In very sheltered conditions it has huge numbers, declining gradually with increased exposure – Bladder Wrack can even be found in bladderless form! By contrast the Knotted Wrack is typical of sheltered conditions and not adaptable. Wave action destroys the fronds and it becomes stunted or lost completely. Typically the middle shore on sheltered rocky coasts is dominated by heaps of Knotted Wrack which out-competes the Bladder Wrack. The latter grows for around three years after which it dies whilst the former can survive for twenty years. This means that if they both grow together, then after three years the Knotted Wrack continues to spread and shade the rocks, preventing any Bladder Wrack establishing again. The niche of Bladder Wrack is large enough that it can easily grow where it does not get that competition.

Biotic factors therefore reduce the size of a species niche. The more competitors or predators, the smaller the niche becomes. The larger the potential niche is at the start the better it is for the population as the biota will vary with the shore. Some species are known to have huge tolerances to, say, wave action and could potentially be found on any shore but have a limited presence as they are poor competitors with minimal resistance to grazing, e.g. Thongweed *Himanthalia elongata*.

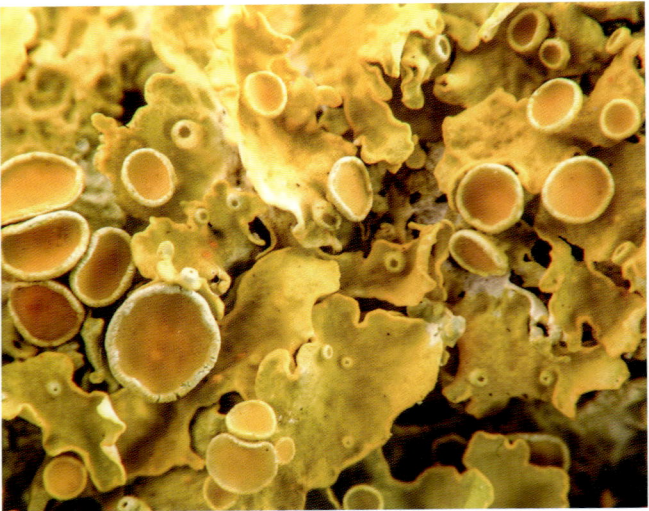

Fig. 1.15
Symbiosis: yellow lichen *Xanthoria parietina* surviving in the splash zone through symbiosis.

Fig. 1.16
Symbiosis: Snakeslock Anemone *Anemonia viridis* in a rockpool. The green colour is an alga, *zooxanthellae*, photosynthesizing inside the animal cells with both organisms benefiting.

Symbiosis is a phenomenon whereby two organisms work collaboratively, helping each other when possibly on their own each species might not survive. In cases of symbiosis the niche expands in size. The lichens, which dominate the splash zone, are an example of a fungus that has a symbiotic alga living amongst its tissue. This inhospitable region of the shore is akin to a desert, dry and salty. If it was not for symbiosis it is unlikely they would survive here; by working together the population can expand and grow.

Primary production

For life to exist energy must be fixed to produce organic matter. This primary production is done by organisms known as producers or autotrophs. Typically, we think of green plants trapping sunlight, using that energy to split water molecules and combine the hydrogen formed with carbon dioxide to make carbohydrates – a process called photosynthesis. One look at a rocky shore at low tide reveals a shortage of higher plants but large numbers of colourful seaweeds. The term 'green plant' is confusing. The green refers to the pigment chlorophyll that is the catalyst for photosynthesis and is present inside the seaweed. The green colour is masked by other pigments and is often only seen as the organism dies and loses these other colours. 'Plant' is a rather generic term. In strict biological classification, seaweeds are not plants but members of the primitive algae which scientists categorize in a different kingdom to the plants. Algae are the most important primary producers on the planet. Being simple in structure they can grow very quickly and far exceed the biomass generated by crops on land.

Fig. 1.17
Seaweed colour on the lower rocky shore. The green Sea Lettuce is in a minority, dominated by the red and brown algae. The red pigment has been bleached out in *Mastocarpus* appearing as yellow tips.

So why are they not green on the seashore? There are some, simple green types, often higher up the shore, but the dominant colours are varying shades of red and brown. The primary wavelengths of light are red, green and blue. Chlorophyll, to do its job of photosynthesis, uses the red and blue light energy. The leaves of grass and most other land plants have absorbed the red and blue light but the unused green is reflected away; this is the reason we see these plants as green. The problem for aquatic plants is that most light is reflected away from the water surface. Some light does enter the water but the three colours do not pass evenly downwards. A seaweed attached in the middle shore may have metres of water above, covering it at high tide. As depth increases there is less and less light. Even if the water is clean and clear, after 10–15 metres conditions are

Fig. 1.18
Mature reproductive conceptacles of the Spiral Wrack.

very dim with little light for photosynthesis. Blue and, especially, red light quickly diminish with depth; green light reaches the deepest. This means that in seawater there is reduced light and much of it will be green. In the lower shore this will be particularly so and that is where many red seaweeds grow. They have pigments with the ability to absorb green and blue light and when we look at them, out of the water, we are seeing them in an environment where there is red light but as they are not adapted to absorb it they show up red.

To carry out photosynthesis they also need basic nutrients and water. When covered by the tide this is not a problem. Algae absorb nutrients direct throughout their surface, either by diffusion or active transport. Terrestrial flowering plants have roots with complex transport systems into stems and leaves; this is not the case with algae, where the bulk is made up of the fronds that connect through a stem-like stipe to an attachment point on the substrate. This base is the 'holdfast', layers of cells which grow out across and into the surface of the hard substrate. This is why seaweeds dominate rocky shores where rooted plants could not anchor themselves. Algae are a diverse group of organisms and this is reflected in the holdfast – from a simple flat plate to the tangled mass found in the kelps – enabling them to hold on in rough conditions. The method of sexual reproduction involves gametes produced in small swellings, conceptacles, on their fronds, a bit like sperm and eggs, which swim through the water for fertilization. The result is a spore which may commence growing on a hard substrate such as the rocky shore. The seaweeds that we encounter on the shore are called macro-algae whilst many, especially in the plankton, are microscopic species. The seaweeds, particularly on a sheltered shore, may form huge amounts of biomass, a potential food source for the animals on the shore. Yet few directly eat the seaweeds. We will see that even with flowering plants on salt-marshes and sand dunes that there are few grazers of living macro plants on the coast. One reason is that many are unpalatable. The Flat Periwinkle *Littorina obtusata* may be found nibbling on the edge of Pepper Dulse *Osmundea pinnatifida* and other seaweeds in the middle shore, but grazers like this tend to be the exception. The basis of the littoral food web is biofilm, an aggregate of micro-organisms.

Biofilms are found on any surface where there is moisture, from swimming pools to the top of a mountain range, from the surface of a moss to the film that covers your teeth before you brush them clean. Biofilms develop quickly and all have features in common. Essentially, they are a biodiverse mixture of micro-organisms that are dynamic and adapt to conditions and changes in the environment. You can remove some material by scraping the surface of a rock on the shore to look at under the microscope. However, the best method is to fix clear plastic or glass plates to a rock in the middle shore and allow colonization to take place, removing them at intervals to observe changes under the microscope. The dynamic nature of biofilms means that they are changing with time, a process called succession.

Within minutes a bare surface attracts bacteria that may come and go. During this time they secrete a variety of chemicals such as polysaccharides that begin to coat the bare surface. Over a matter of hours more bacteria are attracted and after a day or so the bacteria are now permanent residents. They are now secreting a profusion of chemicals such that a matrix of layers build. The biofilm

Fig. 1.19
Limpet grazing on biofilm in a rockpool. The dark trail is where the limpet has rasped away the biofilm which becomes quickly recolonized by bacteria and the biofilm quickly regenerates.

becomes a complex 3D structure of holes and tunnels. This initial bacterial layer is now ripe for colonization by micro-algae called diatoms. These are found in the plankton but a specific group of benthic (those living on a surface) diatoms now attach themselves and multiply. Great strings of these continue the building of the mesh along with cyanobacteria. These are a type of photo-synthesizing bacterium, an ancient group that were some of the earliest forms of life on earth. The mesh traps detritus, small particulate organic matter, much of which has been derived from the seaweeds. Wave action especially erodes the surface of the seaweeds and generates detritus. So the macro-algae become incorporated into the food web via the biofilm. With so much microscopic food available it is inevitable that tiny single-celled animals (protists like ciliates) and rotifers, appear in the biofilm quite early on in the succession process. After some weeks the biofilm can consist of a complex community which is ever changing with conditions. Samples taken just a few centimetres apart can be quite different in composition. In addition to the organisms present, quantities of inorganic matter like sand particles will also become trapped in the matrix. That in turn will alter the construction to encourage a different group of protists to arrive, increasing the biodiversity yet further.

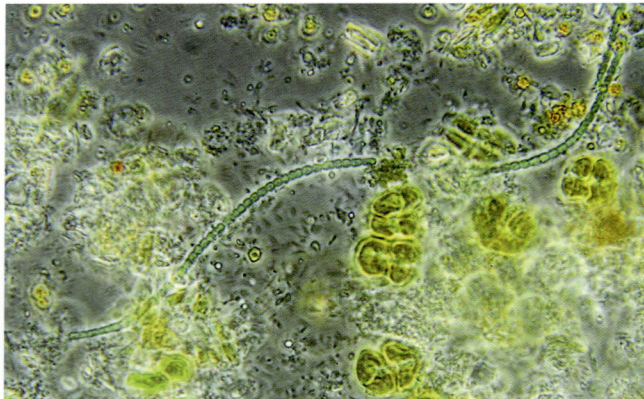

A

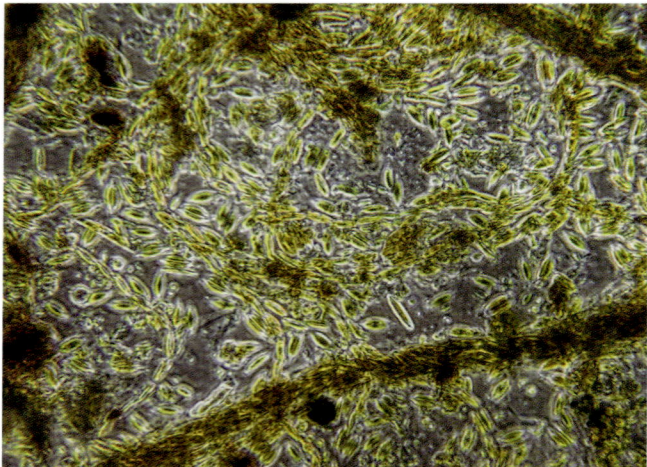

B

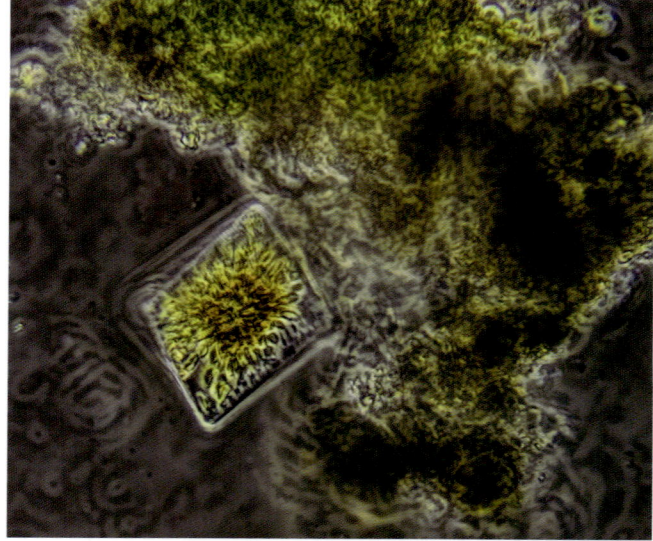

C

Fig. 1.20
Examples of biofilm magnified around ×100–200.
(A) Small, dark, elongated dots are bacteria in the early stages of development. Through the middle is a chain of cyanobacteria. Diatoms and detritus form the rest of the film. (Photo: MC)
(B) Bacteria and strings of diatoms with some detritus.
(C) *Striatella*, a benthic diatom living in biofilm, attached to detritus from seaweed.

A

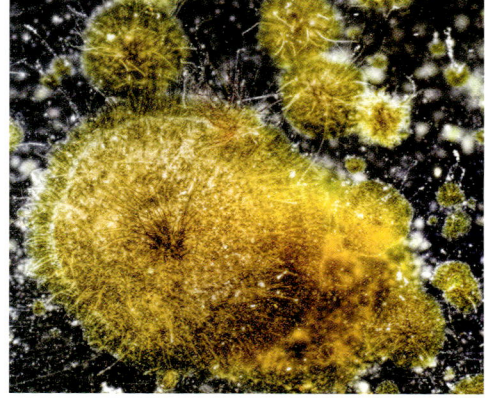
B

Fig. 1.21
Biofilm and developing macro-algae, magnified ×10.
(A) Sporelings from the large seaweeds begin to grow within the biofilm, developing flat, plate-like holdfasts. Once developed they begin to grow strands of cells vertically. These are mainly brown weeds with a red alga in the foreground.
(B) The same but looking down on the developing seaweed. These circles are the developing holdfasts, a rich food source for limpets.

Fig. 1.22
The substantial holdfast of kelp *Laminaria digitata*.

Fig. 1.23
After a storm. Even with the strong holdfast and stipe, seaweeds become dislodged in strong, autumnal winds and contribute extensively to the dead organic matter in the ecosystem. The large holdfast in the foreground is of a mature *Laminaria hyperborea*.

Biofilm components like the bacteria change over time and it has been demonstrated that this is not an entirely passive process. They communicate between themselves and after a while can direct groups of bacteria to break away into the water and disperse. This dynamic process will generate detached clumps that form an important food source for suspension feeders like barnacles. With such complex bacterial communities in the biofilm they are being investigated for a range of products in the medical industry. A common global marine bacteria on rocky surfaces is *Pseudoalteromonas* which has been shown to produce anti-bacterial chemicals that fight off rivals and can kill *Staphylococcus*.

Biofilm does not just form on rock surfaces but on the macro-algae themselves. When it appears that grazers like periwinkles and topshells are feeding on a seaweed they are in fact consuming biofilm. Biofilm needs water to develop and so will be influenced by the tide. Towards the top of the shore, where water is at a premium, biofilm is dominated by cyanobacteria. In some places this may discolour the rocks forming a distinct, dark band on the shore where it mixes with tar lichens, *Verrucaria* species. The microscopic nature means that only after it has been grazed and removed by an animal can the presence of biofilm be noticed. It is easily overlooked and yet plays a major role in understanding the coast. The dynamic and complex structure is not just in the biodiversity but in the variety of organic chemicals secreted to hold the structure together. If it was not for this many seaweeds would struggle to become attached to a rock as biofilms help the young seaweed become established.

Elements of the Coast 19

Fig. 1.24 Chemosynthesis. Close-up of the mud surface on a sheltered sediment shore where the thin, brown, aerobic mud has been scraped away to reveal black anaerobic (anoxic) mud beneath. Ancient, anaerobic sulphur bacteria thrive creating the black sulphide layer.

A discussion of primary production would not be complete without a mention of chemosynthesis. At the beginning of life on earth photosynthesis was not a process found in these early forms. The first chemical reactions to trap energy used hydrogen sulphide as a source of hydrogen to make carbohydrates. The by-product was the sulphide. The descendents of bacteria that evolved this process are still with us, living on the coast where oxygen is not present, for example in the mud of sheltered sediment shores and salt-marshes. Break through the pale brown surface and just below will be the blue-black sign of the sulphur bacteria. The dark colouration is the sulphide and the strong smell of bad eggs is hydrogen sulphide.

Primary production on a rocky shore reaches its maximum in the lower shore where there is greater diversity and biomass of algae. For sand dunes, shingle and salt-marshes, where producers are dominated by flowering plants, it is the reverse. Biofilm needs water to develop and follows a similar pattern to the macro-algae with production declining towards the upper shore, lichens dominating the splash zone. Autotrophs are also influenced by environmental conditions; for example, increased wave action causes a drastic reduction in productivity.

Consumers

Consumers are the animals within the biota. In a traditional food web these are split into trophic levels of herbivore and types of carnivores. On the shore the line between them blurs. Many crabs will be carnivorous and are detritivores. Fish like the blenny eat barnacles but also seaweeds and those that filter material from the water column could be consuming anything – detritus, planktonic plants and animals. The nutrition and specific methods of feeding are discussed later but we can identify at this stage three basic groups: grazers, suspension feeders and predators.

Grazers

These consumers can be divided into four functional groups. The first is the group that collects biofilm, like the topshells. Their tongue or radula has tiny teeth that sweep the biofilm from rocks and macro-algae, making no impression on the rock surface. The second group have slightly larger teeth and consume more by raking the surface. This can leave marks on rocks after biofilm removal and will allow them to cut away small amounts of macro-algae. These rakers are dominated by the periwinkles, amphipods and isopods. All manner of sizes of the latter two are easily found on seaweeds. The Rough Periwinkle *Littorina saxatilis* is found on the upper shore and splash zone where it grazes the biofilm, cyanobacteria and fine tar lichen.

Limpets are an important grazing type in the third category, the abraders, having teeth that are tipped with hard iron oxide. In one species, the Blue-rayed Limpet *Patella pellucida*, clear marks can be seen left behind on the kelp (Fig. 1.22). The abundant Common Limpet *Patella vulgata* is a very important grazer across rocky shores. They consume huge quantities of biofilm, which contain very young stages of developing macro-algae, such as the young holdfast cells on the rock surface. Limpets could be likened to rabbits found in terrestrial environments. Rabbits crop the vegetation close to the ground consuming everything including very young developing bushes and trees. Once the vegetation grows beyond a specific size it will be ignored and continues to grow tall. In this way rabbits maintain grassland and in high numbers prevent the growth of bushes and woodland. Large populations of limpets consume the young stages of macro-algal growth and keep the macro-algae cropped down leaving large areas of rock devoid of large seaweeds. A drop in limpet density (if they are eaten by oystercatchers, for example) allows some young seaweed to keep growing beyond the size available to limpets. Now patches of Bladder Wrack and other macro-algae develop on the rocks. Limpets can leave abrasion marks on the rock and they do consume particles of the surface with the biofilm. Chitons and sea urchins fit this category as well.

The fourth group of grazers are those that cut macro-algae, such as a few fish species and the small spider crabs, *Macropodia* species. The crabs can be quite small, living in fringe weeds within lower shore pools. As well as cutting small fragments of weed to eat they also stick pieces on to their carapace to camouflage themselves.

Elements of the Coast

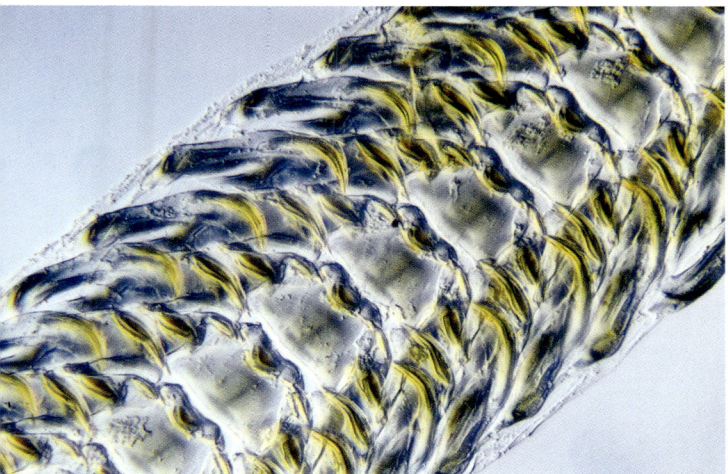

Fig. 1.25
Radula surface of the Edible Periwinkle *Littorina littorea*, a raker, magnified ×100 to show the complex of small hooks for collecting biofilm. (Photo: MC)

A

B

Fig. 1.26
Radula of the Common Limpet, an abrader. (A) A side view to show the hardened teeth embedded in mucosa. (B) A closer view of a central tooth. (Photo: MC)

Fig. 1.27
Decorator crab *Macropodia*.

Fig. 1.28
A small grazing amphipod. Also, Spiral Worm *Laeospira corallinae*, a suspension feeder attached to *Corallina* a red seaweed. The worm has its tentacles extended, feeding.

Elements of the Coast   21

Fig. 1.29 Close-up of the head of a Velvet Swimming Crab *Necora puber*, a voracious carnivore.

Fig. 1.30 Grey Sea Slug *Aeolidia papillosa* feeding on a Beadlet Anemone *Actinia equina*, also a carnivore.

Suspension feeders

Through various methods these animals filter seawater either internally (e.g. mussels) or externally (e.g. barnacles) for suitable microscopic food, both animal and plant plankton, along with bacteria-laden detritus. Suspension feeders form a substantial group including sponges, sea mats, sea squirts and many sedentary marine worms.

Predators

Seabirds are the most visible of the top predators moving down to feed with the tide. With the returning tide the birds roost in the splash zone to digest the food and await the tide change. As the birds finish feeding they are replaced by fish swimming in to feed with a rising tide. Other predators have to remain on the shore. Sedentary or sessile ones like sea anemones have limited mobility and use stinging as a means of collecting prey. Crabs will hide under rocks and algae or in pools when the tide is out. Primarily carnivorous, they can be opportunistic, feeding on dead material as well by cutting up food with the claws (the chelae). Holding it in one chela it uses the other to cut pieces to place in its mouth. Some like the stone crabs *Xantho* species have very powerful chelae. The common name of 'sea slug' does not do justice to the beautiful and diverse nudibranchs. These delicate looking molluscs can be an army of small carnivores feeding on hydroids, ascidians and sea mats.

Elements of the Coast

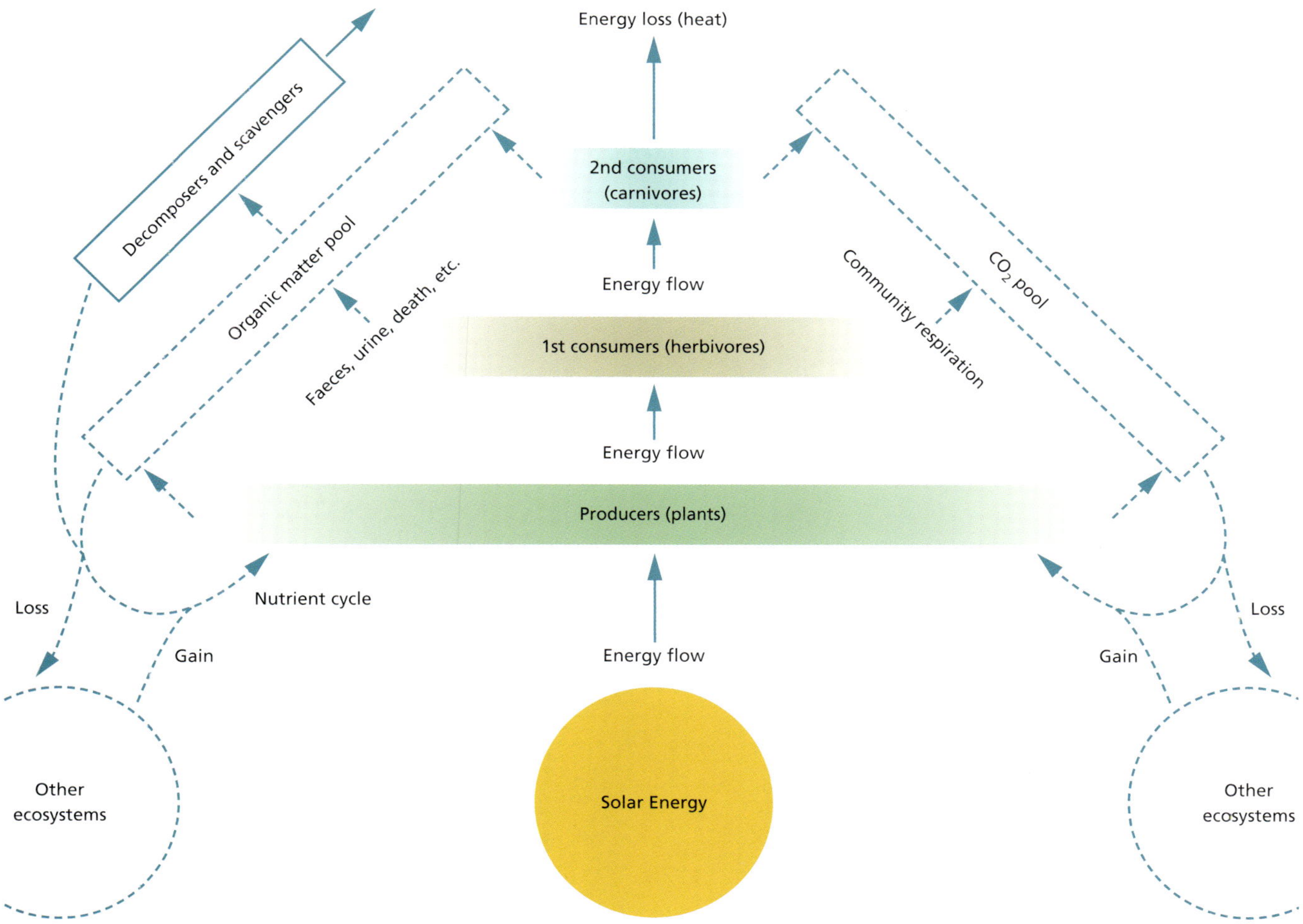

Fig. 1.31
A summary of the ecosystem.

Nutrient flow and decomposition

The final component of the ecosystem to consider is the flow of nutrients. Closely linked with primary production is the need to provide the autotrophs with sufficient nutrients such as nitrogen needed for protein production. Most comes from nutrient recycling (e.g. nitrogen, carbon and phosphorus cycles). Animals like the crabs and shrimps eat dead organisms, breaking them down into smaller pieces of organic matter. Dead seaweed soon breaks down physically into smaller and smaller pieces. This particulate material or detritus is decomposed further by bacteria, fungi and protists present in the seawater and biofilm. The detritus (DOM – dead organic matter) is sometimes referred to as 'marine snow' as it constantly drifts down through the water column. It is a valuable food source and animals, e.g. barnacles, that feed on it are called detritivores. (Similar situations occur in fresh water.) The eventual breakdown products will be molecules small enough to be dissolved in the water, which can be taken up by algae during primary production.

DOM has sources throughout the marine system with plant material washing off salt-marshes and coming down estuaries from the land. Each tide arrives on the shore bringing dead material from the sea, depositing it in rockpools and the strandline. Tidal movements may also flush much of the nutrient away. This flow of essential nutrients between ecosystems can be quite finely balanced. For example, a cow may fall over the cliff, adding nutrients to the seashore, whilst land birds often feed on the upper shore in winter, taking nutrients back to the land.

Fig. 1.32
Grey Atlantic seals are important top carnivores around the coast.

Chapter 2
ROCKY SHORES

Fig. 2.1
Rocky shore on a high energy coast at low spring tide on a calm day.

Part 1: The communities

Introduction

This is an environment like no other. The biodiversity range alone, which cuts across every kingdom and most major species groups, makes it unique. This is reflected here by being the largest chapter in the book and is in two parts. The first part is divided into the main communities of the rocky shore, starting at the top of the shore and working down to the lowest regions; each community is broken down into its relevant and typical species to understand their role. The second part looks at the ecology of the communities within the ecosystem as a whole.

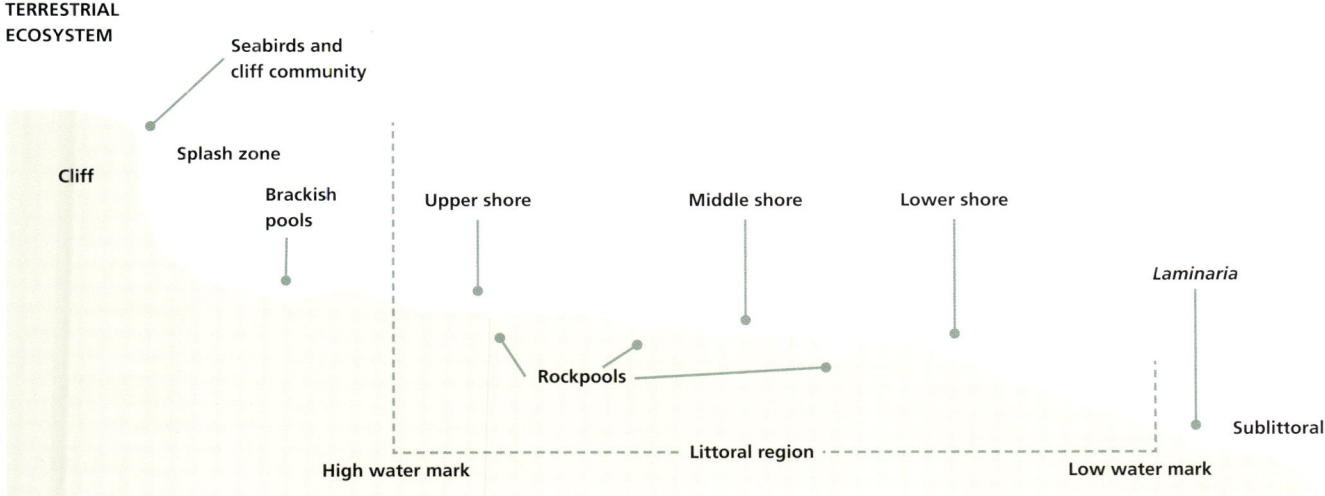

Fig. 2.2
Profile of a typical rocky shore.

Fig. 2.3
Sabellaria alveolata, a tube worm, creates extensive reefs on rocky shores where clean, coarse sand is available.

Fig. 2.4.1
Oval Piddock *Zirfaea crispata* outside its rocky burrow.

The substrate

This type of shore consists of eroding rock surfaces, which may be colonized by algae and attached invertebrates. Although referred to as hard shores, there will be varying degrees of hardness based on the geology. Soft rocks may have animals that have burrowed into them, e.g. the Piddock, whilst hard rocks are easier for algae to attach. Limestone erodes into complex shapes, affording shelter of a different variety from that of harder granites whilst sandstones can crack and provide only temporary attachment for life. The angle at which the rock strata lie will affect the shore: upright strata may produce deep gullies and long rockpools whilst flat strata produce platforms of rock with broader, shallower rockpools. Boulders and large stones will increase the shelter afforded to animals, resulting in a greater diversity of life.

Fig. 2.4.2
Rock Pipit. This common and insignificant looking is typical of rocky seashores where it feeds on insects, small crustaceans and seeds washed up in the strandline.

Rocky Shores 25

The sheltered areas of the shore will have small deposits of sand and even finer material like silt. These may form distinct beds between rocks although most stones and boulders will trap these deposits underneath. If this includes dead organic matter, oxygen levels can plummet as it decays. Sand will encourage colonization by animals more typical of depositing shores, e.g. Lugworm. Rocky shores with a plentiful supply of coarse, clean sand nearby may have a marine worm, *Sabellaria alveolata*, creating extensive colonies and reefs down through the lower shore.

Problems and features of living here

Attachment to the rock

For rooted, vascular plants, attachment is impossible and so colonization of the rock is dominated by algae. These can be very diverse in colour and size. The larger seaweeds, like the kelps and wracks, are of the brown types and may dominate a shore. They display a trend of becoming larger species and individuals passing from the upper to the lower shore. Red seaweeds are generally the smaller, more delicate varieties and have the greatest biodiversity. Green seaweeds may be abundant or dominant but are represented by a few species.

Obtaining nutrients

Algae obtain their minerals and other essential nutrients from the seawater using active transport over their thin surface. This delicate layer offers minimal protection against water loss or cell damage. The latter can result in massive tissue loss which puts detritus into the water.

Wave action

This has a modifying influence: if severe it will limit the communities' ability to survive and individual species may show considerable variation in growth, e.g. Bladder Wrack and the Common Limpet.

Light for photosynthesis

When the tide is out the rate of photosynthesis may stop in the immersed algae (water being an essential component in photosynthesis). When covered by water the light is filtered by the seawater so that only some wavelengths pass through.

Points of special interest

The tides create an environmental gradient from the splash zone through to the lower shore which leads to distinct bands of communities called zones. Biodiversity is high with examples of a wide range of animal species. There will be representatives of all the main classes from very primitive sponges through crustaceans and molluscs to echinoderms, fish and even mammals like seals. Some groups are only found here whilst others, e.g. insects, have lower variety than on land. Diversity is greatest in the lower shore, which is more hospitable, although competition will be high. The reverse is the case in the upper shore.

Practical issues and precautions

Seaweeds are slippery when wet and seemingly bare rock can be worse because of slimy cyanobacteria. Always check the tide tables carefully and with the tide returning make sure that your access to leave the shore has not been cut off by rocky outcrops. You should always avoid working beneath a cliff as rock falls can occur at any time. Waves are not consistent and on a high energy coast there will be occasional ones that reach high on to the shore, easily dislodging people. If you turn over a rock looking for life beneath, always turn it back again carefully, as leaving it exposed will kill all the life beneath.

Cliffs and sea-bird colonies

Vegetation

Vegetation on cliffs will be cropped and pruned by the intensity of wind action producing a very low-growing plant community. In May the dull, dense greenery blooms with the most intense diversity of colour and profusion. The plants compete for space developing huge soft cushions of Thrift *Armeria maritima* and Kidney Vetch *Anthyllis vulneraria*. The former may dominate the cliffs with a root system that can penetrate the narrowest of rocky crevices to grasp a tenacious hold on the cliff helping to bind the rocks together. Within this network many other species grow, like the Spring Squill *Scilla verna*, a close relative of the Bluebell that also occurs on some western cliffs in the UK. The stability will depend very much on the extent of the slope. Invariably there is intense grazing at the top of the cliff by rabbits, which allow only closely cropped grasses such as fescue to grow. Thrift and plantains are rabbit-'resistant'; Sea Beet *Beta vulgaris* var. *maritima* and Rock Samphire *Crithmum maritimum* are not but do have a high tolerance of salt. The community living here is a very specialized one, particularly with the guano from the sea-birds. Sea Campion *Silene uniflora* cannot

Fig. 2.5
Cliff and sea-birds community.

Problems of life on the cliffs for the vegetation

- Erosion and instability. These may be increased by the action of sea-birds.
- High salt content in the soil.
- High uric acid/nitrogen content from the sea-birds' droppings.
- The soil is very shallow and will be leached away, the minerals staining the cliff rock.
- Grazing by rabbits at the top.
- Strong, desiccating wind action.

Rocky Shores 27

Fig. 2.6
Cliff-top in May. The dominant flower is the Thrift, a common salt-tolerant plant found in other coastal habitats. The white flower is Sea Campion with the blue Spring Squill and Kidney Vetch interspersed.

Fig. 2.7
Cliff-top in May. On an exposed Atlantic cliff is the Prostrate Broom, perfectly adapted to the strong winds. Spring Squill and Kidney Vetch are also present.

Fig. 2.8
Spring Squill.

Fig. 2.9
Sea Campion forms thick tussocks especially near seabirds.

tolerate grazing but is prolific around guano-covered cliffs. It will typically be found around the entrance of Puffin burrows. Wind will stunt growth and increase the problem of transpiration. Many of the plants are semi-succulent, storing water, and have some tolerance to salt.

Sea-birds

These are the top carnivores of the coastal ecosystem. Most nest in colonies on inaccessible cliff faces, on both mainland and off-shore islands, safe from mammal (ground) predators such as foxes and rats. In several ways sea-birds are different to land species. Many only come onto land to breed, staying away at sea for the rest of the time. A big difference is in the vast colonies, often of many thousands of birds, making some of the greatest spectacles on earth, of both sight and smell. Each species

Fig. 2.10
Rock Samphire is a common cliff and shingle species, much collected in the past as food. Here it grows across splash zone lichens, in particular the bright *Xanthoria ectaneoides*.

Fig. 2.12 Great Black-backed Gull carrying off a rabbit.

Fig. 2.13 Herring Gull.

Fig. 2.14 Herring Gull nest.

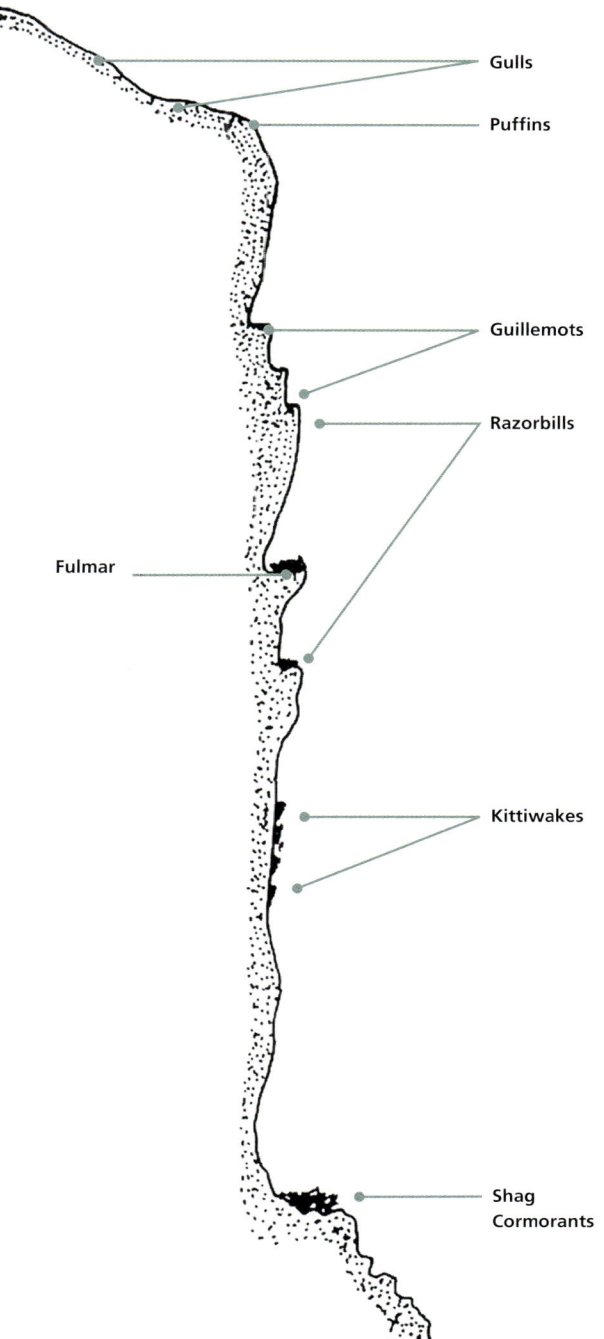

Fig. 2.11
Sea-bird cliff profile with potential nesting niches.

of sea-bird has its own distinct nesting behaviour and location on the cliff. This helps to avoid inter-specific competition for space. Where populations co-exist on the same sea-bird cliffs a zonation occurs, often spatially separating them, although the actual arrangement depends on the availability of nesting niches, e.g. ledges and grassy slopes. Soft rocks will crumble and are unsuitable nesting sites.

Gulls

Great Black-backed Gull *Larus marinus*: the pink, flesh-coloured legs are a characteristic feature along with its bulky, strong build. This is the largest European gull with jet black wings and a yellow beak with distinct orange spot, which acts as a trigger for the chicks. Found in all cliff-top nesting gulls, chicks tap the spot to stimulate the adult to regurgitate food from the crop. It takes four years to reach sexual maturity. These are true maritime gulls, found only around the coast, and they even stay at sea during the winter. This is the top predator and will feed on large prey like puffins, swallowing them whole. They do not form large colonies but nest amongst other gulls.

Herring Gull *Larus argentatus* and Lesser Black-backed Gull *Larus fuscus*: these are closely related and of similar medium size. The latter has a slate grey back rather than a truly black one and yellow legs, while the Herring Gull is very much paler with pink legs. They nest on flattish ground at the top of the cliff or partly inland on islands. The nesting period starts at the end of April and runs through to August, with the nest made from seaweed,

Rocky Shores

Fig. 2.15 Lesser Black-backed Gull.

Fig. 2.16 Kittiwake nesting with chicks.

Fig. 2.17 Guillemots.

Fig. 2.18 Razorbill.

Fig. 2.19 Puffin with sand eels.

grass and flotsam. It takes three years to reach sexual maturity when they produce three or four eggs. At this time they are strongly territorial and happily eat a neighbour's egg or chick if is not guarded. The diet is varied: birds may be carnivores or scavengers. Feeding on waste tips has caused a decline in the Herring Gull due to food poisoning derived from sun-warmed black bin liners breeding botulism bacteria.

Kittiwake *Rissa* tridactyla: this is the only cliff-ledge nesting gull, forming noisy colonies down the vertical cliff. They build a deep nest with plentiful amounts of guano to glue it to the cliff. They have an extra toe for holding on and usually face into the cliff, particularly the young. Behaviour is adapted to survive cliff ledge life with quick appeasement to prevent fights. The chick remains by the nest until ready to fly, whilst other gull chicks leave the nest shortly after they hatch. Also the adult does not have the orange spot on the beak but a red throat. This encourages the chick to put the beak down the throat to stimulate food regurgitation. Food passes straight into the chick without the risk of being lost down the cliff. Adults feed at or just below the water surface.

Auks

The wings of auks are characteristically short which provides for excellent swimming and diving to chase fish, mainly sand eels. Guillemots can dive to almost 200 metres although typically feed at 90 metres. For Razorbills this is 150 metres and 45 metres, respectively.

Guillemot *Uria aalge*: these nest in dense colonies on bare cliff ledges. They are easily panicked by gulls, especially the Great Black-backs. This is a deliberate ploy by the gull, hoping to dislodge eggs or reveal the presence of chicks. The eggs are adapted by being pointed at one end so they roll in circles and not over the edge.

Razorbill *Alca torda*: associated with the Guillemot colonies, but Razorbills are not normally found in large numbers, occupying small ledges. Black plumage and a large beak distinguish the Razorbill from the Guillemot, more chocolate brown with a dagger-like beak.

Puffin *Fratercula arctica*: the smallest of the three auk species, living in burrows near the top of the cliff where more soil is available. On arrival in spring they take over burrows from rabbits. The colourful beak takes several years to develop and expands with age. It is well developed for catching sand eels with the top and bottom opening parallel, rather than like scissors. As they swim the head is moved from side to side through a shoal of

Fig. 2.20
Fulmar.

Fig. 2.21
Fulmar populations increased in the nineteenth century with the whaling industry. Fulmars feeding on a dead whale (Iceland, 1980).

Fig. 2.22
Shag on its nest.

Fig. 2.23
Cormorant drying its wings.

Fig. 2.24
Cormorant feeding.

Fig. 2.25
Gannet with chick.

sand eels and so they are stacked up in the beak with head to tail alternating. Ten to twenty fish at a time can be in the beak when it lands to feed the young.

Fulmar

Appearing superficially like a gull, Fulmar *Fulmarus glacialis* is a member of the petrel family, birds that are primarily scavengers, feeding at the water surface and on offal. Populations grew in density at the time of whaling in the north Atlantic. Unlike the gulls there is no black on the wings, which Fulmars hold out straight, gliding and sweeping low over the water. Above the beak there is a double tubular 'nostril', typical of petrels. This may be used to assess wind speed but no one knows for sure. On land they are awkward: their legs are bent forward so they are unable to stand like gulls. Nesting singly on ledges they only start to breed when eight years old, producing one egg. They feed the chick for around three months, at which time it is twice the adult weight, and the parents desert, leaving it to fend for itself. They can live for fifty years.

Shag and Cormorant

These similar, large black birds are common along the coast although the latter often moves inland, along estuaries. The Shag *Phalacrocorax aristotelis* is smaller with a greenish sheen on the feathers. The Cormorant *P. carbo* has a white patch on the chin. Both make large, smelly nests near the base of a cliff but away from spray, which would cool and kill the chicks. The large nests are constructed of seaweed and sticks stuck with guano. Three or four eggs can be laid early in the year but once left by the parents the juveniles can take several months before they fly. These birds catch large fish by diving. Feathers are not waterproofed and they spend long periods drying wings. It is thought that this behaviour helps to increase their temperature, assisting gut enzyme action to speed up digestion of the large fish.

Gannets

Gannet *Morus bassanus* is the largest European seabird at 180cm. Gannets usually nest on off-shore islands where huge colonies of up to 70,000 pairs exist. They can be seen from the shore, feeding on large fish, e.g. mackerel, which they dive from a height to catch.

Fig. 2.26
Splash zone community.

Fig. 2.27
Splash zone on a wave-exposed shore. The pale zone of barnacles is within the upper and middle shores.

Problems of living in the splash zone

- There is a high salt content from sea spray drying on the rocks.
- The temperatures are extreme from night to day, winter to summer.
- Very little water is available; desiccating coastal wind.
- On the strandline, the dumping of dead organic matter has a shading effect despite acting as a nutrient source.
- Uric acid (guano) from sea-birds, deposited on rocks, has a 'burning' effect on vegetation.

32   Rocky Shores

Fig. 2.28
Grey lichen, *Tephromela atra*.

Fig. 2.29
Orange lichen, *Caloplaca*.

Splash zone community

Vegetation

Orange lichens: *Xanthoria* species
These leafy lichens have raised orange fruiting bodies in the centre. The orange pigment (parietin) is in the upper surface layer to protect lower, algal cells (constituting 7 per cent of cellular material) from extreme sunlight. Therefore, it tends to be pale on north-facing or shaded slopes. It releases spores throughout the year. *Caloplaca marina* is an encrusting lichen with a knobbly surface.

White and grey lichens
Ochrolechia parella is a dense, encrusting form with raised fruiting bodies the same colour as the rest of the lichen. *Tephromela (Lecanora) atra* is similar but has black fruiting bodies.

Green, fruticose lichen
Sea Ivory *Ramalina siliquosa* forms dense, brittle, strap-like projections of grey-green colour. Tiny granular pieces on these straps are called soredia and are a method of vegetative reproduction. They contain fungal and algal tissue and become dispersed by the wind.

Black Tar Lichen *Verrucaria maura* (agg)
A black, encrusting lichen.

Thrift or Sea pink *Armeria maritima*
This has probing roots and is able to penetrate crevices of rock for water and gives stability to the zone. It can survive in a minimum of soil with seeds developing in the humus of dead lichen. The narrow leaves reduce surface area slowing water loss. It is salt tolerant and also associated with salt-marshes.

Succession in the splash zone

Lichens are the first colonizers of bare rock. Lichens are slow growing but long lived. As they grow the action of acids and expansion of their cells cause a slow break-up of the rock into tiny fragments. Along with dead, organic matter, this produces a raw soil that is colonized by mosses. These continue the weathering of the rock and as humus collects in crevices, so the seeds of salt tolerant flowering plants, e.g. Thrift, germinate. These plants have strong, penetrating roots that anchor well into rock faces, which helps to stabilize loose surfaces. This mini-succession is called a lithosere and can be found on mountain rocks with non-salt tolerant species. In this zone the Thrift sere is usually the climax.

Species of the splash zone and cliff

Lichens

This region, above the tidal littoral zone, is one of the most inhospitable environments on our planet and consequently has a low biodiversity. Lichens are well adapted for the conditions and have become dominant.

The key to survival here is their symbiotic nature. The bulk of a lichen is the fungus with threads of the mycelium forming the attachment to the rock, amongst the top of which are algal cells near the light for photosynthesis. The water is provided by the fungus, which has the ability to store up to 35 times its volume when water is available. The alga is the smaller component (<10 per cent) and photosynthesizes to provide both with food. Lichens can be slow growing depending on the environment and species, making some very long lived.

Even a cursory glance at the splash zone shows the zone to be divided into further sub-zones. Best seen on a steep slope, the area around high water mark for spring tides displays an encrustation of Black Tar lichen *Verrucaria maura*: the 'black' zone. This grades into an 'orange' zone dominated by *Caloplaca* species which further grades into a mixture of older lichens making the 'grey' zone. The latter has a predominance of white and grey species like *Ochrolechia* and *Tephromela* species, both crusty types, although the fruticose varieties of *Ramalina* and the more terrestrial leafy lichen *Xanthoria* species do well here.

This sub-zonation is linked with tolerance to saltwater but there are also biotic reasons. Just appearing at the bottom are small snails, Rough Periwinkle *Littorina saxatilis*. They graze on micro-organisms attached to the rock like cyanobacteria and lichen. The tar lichens are tolerant of this and quickly regrow whilst the slow-growing forms like *Ochrolechia* cannot withstand the grazing and disappear. The periwinkles are at their upper limit due to the problem of desiccation and stop their upward movement around the *Caloplaca* area. Hence the white and grey lichens survive at the top where there are no grazers. Also in this area small mosses grow like the *Schistidium* species. Given time these mosses along with organic matter derived from old lichens create pockets of humus within which plants can become established. This is the start of a lithosere (see box).

Salt-tolerant lichens form an important community between the tidal zone and the clifftop flowering plants. The lichens are very susceptible to pollution and can be used to monitor sulphur dioxide in the air. Splash zone lichens are killed by oil pollution and some of the detergents used to disperse spillages. There may be a higher diversity on exposed shores as there is more spray wetting the rocks as well as a greater splash zone area. Exposed shores also have a different group of lichens, possibly through less competition for space. Amongst the orange lichen *Caloplaca* grows a very fine, furry,

Fig. 2.30
Zonation of lichens and two periwinkle species in the splash zone.

Fig. 2.31 Small Periwinkle, *Melaraphe neritoides* with *Lichina confinis*.

dark-tufted lichen called *Lichina confinis*, whilst nearer the middle shore *Lichina pygmaea* is found. Both these species are erect lichens constituted from strands of cyanbacteria wrapped in fungal mycelia.

Prasiola stipitata is a very small, flattened green alga often found in the splash zone where sea-birds roost and water collects. The guano from the birds will be high in nitrate; most organisms could not tolerate this but *Prasiola* and some lichens are able to cope and form dense patches on the rock. Although small the algal tufts quickly merge to form the green slime where water collects in crevices along with bird guano. This is a very tolerant alga, both of fresh water and high salt content.

Flowering plants

The plants surviving here depend on their ability to cope with the salt and desiccation, coupled with the almost total lack of soil. Thrift is well adapted to deal with all of this and grazing. Sea Plantain grows here and, like Thrift, can survive extreme conditions; both are members of tundra communities. To avoid water loss, the leaves of these plants may be narrow and succulent, thus reducing the surface area. Around the stomata of the leaves may be a dense covering of hairs, helping to retain moisture by reducing transpiration.

Molluscs

Black or Small Periwinkle *Melaraphe neritoides*, is one of the few marine animals found in the splash zone. Up to 6mm in length they graze on encrusting lichens and microscopic algae. For a seashore creature they tolerate extreme temperatures, e.g. 46°C, they can lower their metabolic rate when times are hard and are tolerant of highly variable salinity. Most marine organisms excrete waste nitrogen as ammonia but use water to flush it from the body. By synthesizing uric acid this periwinkle excretes it as a solid, preventing water loss. It has a modified gill cavity, lined with capillaries, which acts like a lung to breathe air. Living in crevices, the female sheds egg capsules only at high spring tides during the autumn and winter when the sea is roughest. The larva lives within plankton and when metamorphosis occurs, settles in the barnacle zone. Using responses to light and gravity it migrates up to the splash zone. Other than the planktonic larva phase tying it to the shore this organism is one of the best adapted to survive on land.

Fig. 2.32
Bristle tail *Petrobius*.

Insects and other animals

The species found in this area have mostly evolved from terrestrial habitats. Few insects have adapted to life on the seashore; one that has is the primitive Marine Bristletail *Petrobius maritimus* which grows up to 10mm in length. A fast moving, mainly nocturnal scavenger with large compound eyes it has biting mouthparts with long palps and sharp mandibles (closely resembling those of crustaceans). However, it is believed to be mainly a lichen feeder. It can rove to the top of cliffs and down into the upper shore. The slightly scaly body makes it difficult for a predator to grip and it is adept at sudden jumping with a flick of the abdomen. For rapid movement it needs warmth, absorbing this from the sun-heated rock. At other times it will hide in crevices. *Strigamia maritima* is a centipede occasionally seen in the splash zone feeding on small insects.

After strong wind and high spring tides, huge piles of seaweeds accumulate above the upper shore. This strandline is essentially the world's largest compost heap and can be several metres deep in decaying wracks and kelp. Small white maggots in these heaps are just part of the astounding biodiversity living in this very specialized community. Strandlines are unique: each continent has its own distinctly evolved, endemic family group of fly species. Flies and micro-organisms recycle the dead and dying algal heaps. In the northern Atlantic, genera like *Orygma*, *Coelopa*, *Fucellia* and *Thoracochaeta* dominate although all are referred to as seaweed flies. What is remarkable is the speed with which the fly maggots, in a unique interaction with the micro-organisms, recycle huge amounts of algal biomass to soluble products that become recycled back into the ecosystem. Without these highly specialized flies, able to eat dead, salty seaweed, seaweed primary production would be unavailable to other organisms (discussed in the previous chapter).

In addition to the seaweed flies, crustaceans called Sand-hoppers are also found underneath the decaying seaweed. Several types exist, including *Orchestia gammarella* and *Talitrus saltator*, the latter mainly associated with sandy shores (see Chapter 4). Growing up to 20mm in length, they occur usually above the high tide mark under debris by day. They are nocturnal feeders on freshly stranded algae, retreating to humid places by day to avoid desiccation. The behaviour is geared to day:night rhythms as well as tidal ones. They flex their abdomens rapidly to escape predators, hence the name of Sand-hopper.

See also *Ligia*, *Anurida* and *Littorina saxatilis*.

Fig. 2.33
Seaweed Fly *Fucellia*.

Fig. 2.34
Sandhopper on seaweed in the strandline.

Fig. 2.35
Oystercatcher nest in the splash zone.

Rocky Shores 37

Upper shore community
(north-facing and moderately sheltered to wave action)

Fig. 2.36
Upper shore community.

Notes

- The rock in the above photo is Old Red Sandstone and where it is free from macro-algae shows up red/brown in colour and is covered in microscopic biofilm with cyanobacteria. The former will have young stages of developing macro-alga such as the Spiral Wrack.
- This zone shows a sub-zoning of algae, with the Channel Wrack at the top and Spiral Wrack slightly lower down. The latter has slightly less ability to survive desiccation so its upper limit is not as high as the Channel Wrack. The lower limit of the latter is determined by being out-competed by the Spiral Wrack.
- This can also be seen in the tar lichens, with the black at the top and green at the bottom.
- *Catanella* is found only on north-facing shores where there is less sunlight. This is high up on the shore for red algae to grow. It is replaced by *Lichina* on exposed shores.
- This is the upper limit of barnacles and at this height is mainly the *Chthamalus* species.

Problems of living in the upper shore

- Drying out: only 1–2 hours' immersion due to the tides.
- Short time for algae to absorb nutrients from the water, thus slow growth and poor productivity.
- Wide variation in temperature possible, affecting metabolism.

Lichen

- Black Tar lichen *Verrucaria maura* is ingrained matt-black lichen, covering the bare rock.
- Green Tar lichen *V. mucosa* has a greenish sheen and is found lower down the shore.
- Terrestrial species capable of tolerating brief periods of saltwater cover.
- Edible to grazing animals after softening by water.
- Probably not one species but an aggregation of several.

Channel Wrack *Pelvetia canaliculata*
- Up to 16cm, bushy growth.
- Highest level brown alga, indicating high-water mark.
- Rolled fronds reduce water loss, trapping water face downwards.
- Fatty (oily) layer over cell slows desiccation.
- Thick cell wall (1.2 microns) which shrinks with drying.
- With less water available, it survives lower nutrient level than other brown alga, leading to slow growth.
- Survives up to 95 per cent water loss but rapid recovery of metabolism when tide returns (e.g. photosynthesis in 20 minutes). It is therefore a stress-tolerant alga, well adapted to niche at the top of shore.

Spiral or Twisted Wrack *Fucus spiralis* up to 35cm
- Slightly lower level than *Pelvetia*, but with much overlap.
- Spiralling traps water and slows evaporation but not so effective as *Pelvetia*.
- Thinner cell wall but lacks the oiliness of *Pelvetia*, hence the slightly lower level.
- Faster growth than *Pelvetia*; where overlap between the two occurs, *Fucus* out-shades the other and dominates.
- Shows better stress-tolerance than other wracks that are found further down the shore.

Catanella caespitosa
- A red alga rarely found high up the shore as strong sunlight bleaches out the delicate pigments, but remaining in the shade of other weeds and on north-facing (shaded) shores it survives.
- It is replaced by *Lichina* on wave-exposed shores.

Gutweed *Ulva* species
- Green and tubular although flattened and twisted.
- Survives extremes of temperature from −21° to 40°C, with optimum around 17°C.
- Dries quickly but recovers very fast after exposure by the tide.
- Can exist in any zone as it has no specific niche on the shore, growing wherever it can survive grazing, e.g. shell apex of grazing limpets.

Barnacles
- Barnacle larvae in the plankton are attracted by the presence of adult barnacles to ensure they congregate in large numbers together. However, the whiplash of any seaweed nearby may prevent them from settling.
- The white calcareous plates grow out and undercut the algal holdfast (competition).
- Some are tolerant of high temperatures, e.g. *Chthamalus* (50°C or more).
- Tolerant of desiccation by being able to close the aperture at low tide, sealing it in place to reduce water loss.
- They have a low metabolic rate (i.e. slow heart rate and respiratory movement).
- Can breathe atmospheric air at low tide, trapping an air bubble with its plates.
- Excretion continues at low tide; faecal pellets and shed exoskeleton are pushed out of the plates.
- Death leaves a micro-habitat for colonization, e.g. by Small Periwinkles.

Rough Periwinkle *Littorina saxatilis* (agg, i.e. not just one species)
- Grazer on biofilm and lichens, often leaving radula marks.
- It has a high temperature tolerance: at 36–38°C it crawls into crevices and becomes inactive.
- In extremes of desiccation and temperature it cements itself to rock, respiring without oxygen for up to a week.
- The gills are reduced, with oxygen absorbed directly into soft tissue around the mantle cavity; they are capable of surviving one month out of water.
- The adults mate and some forms retain the eggs (viviparous); seawater is then not needed for fertilization or a planktonic life.
- It excretes insoluble uric acid to help conserve water.

Common Limpet *Patella vulgata*
- Their shell prevents water loss and clamps down on the rock at low tide allowing them to survive the desiccation of the zone. They become more dominant in the middle shore but can survive all the tidal zones.

Species of the upper shore

Lichens and biofilm

Submergence of the upper shore, even for a brief period, eliminates all the splash zone lichens except for the marine-adapted tar lichens. These form a very distinct dark band at the top of any rocky shore. They grow flush with the rock and reproduce and disperse with a fruiting body called the perithecia. These are tiny, bowl-shaped structures in or on the surface. The microscopic biofilm dries quickly here and is dominated by cyanobacteria, a photosynthesizing bacterium type of organism, which – along with the lichen – are the main source of food available to grazers. In the lower area of the zone on exposed shores the lack of competition from Wracks may allow the growth of a fruticose lichen, *Lichina pygmaea*. These can form large, black and bushy patches raised over a centimetre from the rock surface where there is a dominance of barnacles. Unlike typical lichens, instead of algae forming the symbiont with fungus it is a more primitive cyanobacteria, often *Calothrix*, which grows in the biofilm. With the ability to hold moisture, and with its dense nature, a perfect micro-habitat is formed for tiny animals including marine insect larvae. See *Lasea* and *Neobisium* below.

Seaweeds

Channel Wrack *Pelvetia canaliculata*: a hermaphrodite seaweed, having both male and female structures on the same frond. Conceptacles ripen in summer with the release of gametes in September to coincide with the high spring tides. The settlement of sporelings occurs at this time but little development occurs until late winter. They take twelve months to mature. Having both sexes on the same plant increases the chances of fertilization on the upper shore where the tide does not give a long period of immersion. Light is a factor in allowing good settlement of spores as it stimulates the growth of rhizoids which anchor the young plant to the rock.

Spiral or Twisted Wrack *Fucus spiralis*, like *Pelvetia* above, is also hermaphrodite. No other species of *Fucus* is, however. The frond shows variation in its shape from one shore type to another and will be greatly affected by salinity and wave action. It also hybridizes (crosses) with *F. vesiculosus* under certain conditions. Specimens at the bottom of the zone are less able to tolerate stress. This is due to individuals adapting (acclimatizing) to the stresses over a period of weeks. This is not genetic and is similar to drought hardening.

The frond is not always twisted and the swollen tips are reproductive structures (Fig. 1.18). In extreme wave action the species does not exist although on some exposed shores a shortened, dwarf variety grows, a form called *nanus*.

Fig. 2.37
Lichina pygmaea colony.

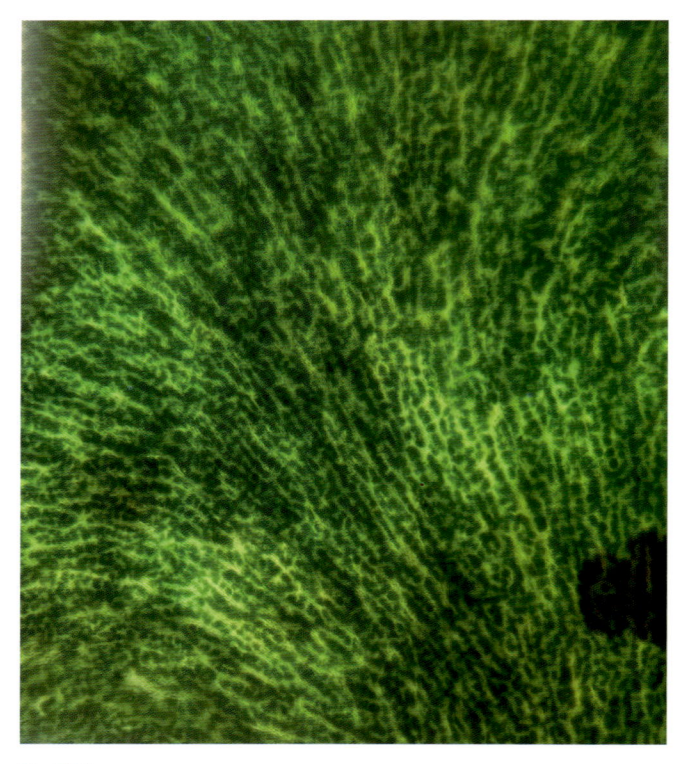

Fig. 2.38
A single strand of *Lichina pygmaea* magnified ×60 showing the cyanobacteria inside.

Fig. 2.39
Channel Wrack *Pelvetia canaliculata*.

Fig. 2.40
Spiral Wrack *Fucus spiralis*.

Fig. 2.41
Diagram to show the three main barnacles.

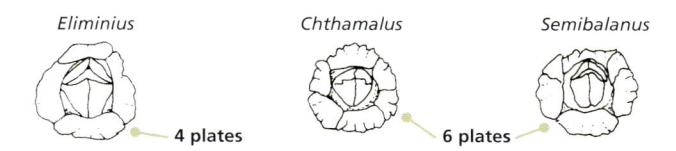

Eliminius — 4 plates

Chthamalus

Semibalanus — 6 plates

Gutweed *Ulva* species is a long, green tubular alga found in shallow pools and hanging over ledges. It grows rapidly, starting life as two sheets of cells which fuse to form a tube. This inflates with oxygen as it photosynthesizes to keep it afloat at the surface. A maximum standing crop can be produced in only two weeks. It is very tolerant of environment change, e.g. salinity, and can be the dominant alga growing where fresh water runs across the shore or within brackish pools. It is good indicator of diluted seawater. It is an early colonizer of bare rock and after grazing is quick to recolonize. After pollution incidents, such as an oil spill which would kill grazers, a 'green flush' occurs when the alga covers the shore. The scientific name used to be *Enteromorpha*.

Barnacles

The outer surface comprises four or six calcareous plates, depending on the species, which are cemented to the rock. These plates continue to grow with the animal inside and help to prevent water loss. Internal fertilization takes place, from another barnacle less than 3.5cm away, necessitating a very long penis. Eggs are retained inside the shell cavity until hatching into planktonic larvae, which aids dispersal. They feed and go through six changes in the plankton before settling on the shore, usually near to a group of existing adults, to which they are attracted chemically. Adults feed on detritus and plankton when covered by seawater. The plates open to let the hairy legs move outside to filter through the water in a combing fashion. When the barnacles are left exposed, those individuals in regions of high humidity, e.g. in a small crevice, may use a small hole (the micropyle) to take in air to assist respiration. Intense grazing by periwinkle and limpets may clear the rocks of algae, assisting larval settlement. As they are cemented to the rock they form a distinct part of the zone and in the absence of wracks, such as in exposed conditions, they form a distinct pale band or biological zone on the shore. (See Plankton, Chapter 3.)

Fig. 2.42
Barnacle *Chthamalus* with an empty pupa case of the marine midge *Clunio*. Black spots are the lichen *Collemopsidium*.

Fig. 2.43
A feeding barnacle showing the hairy legs groping through the water.

Fig. 2.44
Rough Periwinkle *Littorina saxatilis*.

Fig. 2.45
Laver *Porphyra umbilicalis*.

Molluscs

Rough Periwinkle *Littorina saxatilis*: natural selection in this most variable of regions has produced a group, complex or aggregation of species, largely because it is geographically widespread and abundant. With low intraspecific competition and a low density of crabs as predator, it may be that this common species has adapted out to fill the variety of niches available. Having internal fertilization and no planktonic larva reinforces local differences in relatively isolated populations. The group experiences considerable variation which makes clear field identification impossible; the debate on the number of different species often changes between biologists.

Currently, it is thought that three species exist: *L. saxatilis*, *L. compressa* and *L. arcana*. The first of these is the most abundant and widespread including in estuaries and salt-marsh. They give birth to live young and live up to six years whilst the other two species lay eggs on the shore and survive to four or five years. Roughness of the shell can increase with wave action, possibly for extra strength and grip when washed into crevices. Those found amongst boulders and stones may lack the grooves on the shell completely. Colour variation is common and adds further confusion in identification but this is thought to be a local variant. For example, a red-orange form can be found locally on certain shores of old red sandstone. This may aid camouflage but it may also be due to a colour change caused by an internal trematode parasite. The mollusc is a secondary host for the fluke, *Microphallus*, whose eggs are consumed with its food. The periwinkle is eaten by birds, particularly gulls. Feeding on the periwinkle will infect them with the fluke which lays eggs that pass out with the bird faeces, once more into the cycle contaminating the food of the periwinkle. As well as a possible colour change the parasite alters behaviour, e.g. climbing to the top of stones (more likely to be eaten by birds), and makes them more susceptible to extremes of temperature. If dislodged and washed down the beach they are like all periwinkles and will migrate back; an important adaptation to maintain their position in the zone.

Additional species of the upper shore

Seaweed

Laver *Porphyra umbilicalis* is a flat, sheet-like red alga, found on the surface of rocks but also on sand and gravel. Mainly purple but the seaweed can change pigments in the cells (chromatic adaptation) to suit its position on the shore. Hence it can be very pale purple, even red or green. It absorbs a wide range of the light spectrum and as an early colonizer of rock surfaces it shows no particular zoning on the shore. The alga functions best at low temperature and will be most abundant in winter and spring but can occur at any time. Although it is likely to dry out at low tide it has the ability to recover very quickly afterwards. This is a highly nutritious seaweed and is eaten by humans – particularly in South Wales as laver bread – and can be purchased fresh or in tins.

Arthropods

Sea Slater *Ligia oceanica* grows up to 25mm or even longer, coming out mainly at night and thus avoiding predators and desiccation. As nocturnal scavengers they will feed on anything washed in by the tide but will also be carnivorous, catching and eating small arthropods including young Sand-hoppers. They have large compound eyes. The two appendages at the end of the body (uropods) are sensory like the antennae. They are fast-moving animals without modified gills, which means that they need periodic immersion in seawater. Unlike periwinkles in this region, ammonia is excreted, not uric acid. This too puts pressure on the need for water, to remove the nitrogenous waste. To adapt to the latter

Fig. 2.46
Marine Springtail *Anurida maritima* feeding on a dead barnacle.

Fig. 2.47
Marine Springtails floating in the surface tension.

Fig. 2.48
Sea Slater *Ligia oceanica*.

Fig. 2.49
Pseudoscorpion *Neobisium maritimum*.

Fig. 2.50
Lasea rubra bivalves amongst *Lichina pygmaea*, ×4 magnification.

they suppress their protein metabolism to reduce the amount of waste. Sometimes they are found with very pale regions of the body, where shedding of the exoskeleton has occurred.

Marine Springtail *Anurida maritima* is one of the few insects living on the seashore. The maximum length is 4mm and typically will be much less. Easily overlooked as individuals crawling over the rocks and barnacles in summer months, they can form dense groups clustered in the surface tension of small rockpools. Their blue-black colouration is due to a very dense covering of hair, like velvet, which repels water. Unlike most springtails, they cannot spring but can disperse in air bubbles with the tide. This dispersal can take them to salt-marshes where they crawl over the mud surface looking for food. Like *Ligia* they are scavengers but are also partial to fresh meat when they can get it. They find food by smell and any small dead creature will soon be swarming with them.

Marine Pseudoscorpion *Neobisium* maritimum: at just 2–3mm in length this arachnid is easily overlooked and yet is widespread and common, living in crevices within the upper shore. It is probably a mixture of scavenger and carnivore with the ability to spin silk cocoons to survive in as well as lay eggs and tolerate the daily cover of the tide.

Bivalve mollusc

Lasea rubra is the most abundant bivalve mollusc on the seashore, but it is difficult to find! Up to 2mm in length, it lives in large numbers amongst the *Lichina pygmaea* and empty barnacle shells, usually in clusters, attached by a single byssus thread. As a bivalve it is a suspension feeder and can react very fast to the incoming tide so that no time is lost to feed whilst covered. It is negatively phototactic, i.e. it moves away from light, keeping it within its habitat and crevice. The muscular foot is very long to enable the rapid response. It is a hermaphrodite with possible self-fertilization and has no planktonic larva, useful when living high on the shore.

Middle shore community
(moderately sheltered to wave action)

Fig. 2.51
Middle shore community.

Notes
- This community is moderately sheltered to wave action.
- The photograph was taken after the brown wrack seaweed was pulled back.
- The larger wracks provide shelter for smaller species beneath.
- These wracks grow larger than those in the upper shore; thus biomass is greater here.
- Serrated Wrack is on the upper limit of its niche here and specimens may be far from perfect.
- The Beadlet Anemone has withdrawn its tentacles as it is out of water.

Bladder Wrack *Fucus vesiculosus*
- It has pairs of air bladders aiding buoyancy towards the light.
- Many variants develop in response to salinity and wave action, e.g. bladderless form.
- It grows rapidly after establishment (length 20–75cm); those on the edge of the distribution range may remain small.
- Breaking strain 45.5 kg/cm^2.
- Tolerant of fresh water, intolerant of desiccation.
- Cell wall thickness 0.69 microns.
- Replaces *Ascophyllum* lower down and in wave-exposed places.

Serrated Wrack *Fucus serratus*
- This is a small piece at the upper end of its range and is more typical in the lower shore.
- It is eaten by Flat Periwinkles.

Pepper Dulse *Osmundea pinnatifida*
- Red alga, 2–10cm.
- The flattened, branched frond is variable in colour depending on exposure to light, becoming bleached to yellow-white in strong light.

Problems of living in the middle shore

- Species are covered for half of the day by the tide so desiccation problems are less severe than on the upper shore.
- Variable temperatures and humidity.
- Light intensity reaching algae is poor at high tide.
- Better availability of seawater provides more nutrients and so better growth of algae although this means possible competition and predation.

Irish Moss *Chondrus Crispus*
- A red seaweed growing to around 20cm, but variable in colour and shape.
- Although mainly a lower shore species it survives in damp places and pools in the middle shore; may be confused with *Mastocarpus* found around the kelp zone.
- Can out-compete Bladder Wrack.

Green Tar Lichen *Verrucaria mucosa*
- Like the black form this is probably a mixture of species that are difficult to distinguish.

Purple Topshell *Gibbula umbilicalis*
- Herbivore, 1–2cm, grazing on biofilm.
- Separate sexes release gametes into water for external fertilization. Planktonic larva.
- Hollow spiral through shell; a horny plate, the operculum, closes across the shell opening to reduce water loss at low tide.

Common Shore Crab *Carcinus maenas* and Edible Crab *Cancer pagurus*
- Carnivores (e.g. eating periwinkles) and scavengers.
- *Cancer* has a pie-crust edge; *Carcinus* has five points on the carapace side, near the eyes.
- They are very mobile and can avoid some environmental stress by sheltering under large algae and stones. *Carcinus* is very adaptable and copes with varying salinity and temperature.

Flat Periwinkle *Littorina obtusata*
- Herbivore, 1cm, one of the few to feed directly on seaweed as well as biofilm. Gill breather.
- Periwinkle with least tolerance (of all the periwinkles) of temperature and humidity variation.
- The smooth, rounded shell blends with bladders of *Fucus*. Numerous colour variations (polymorphism) give camouflage at different seasons as algae varies.
- The eggs are laid in a gelatinous mass (prevents drying) on *Fucus* where they hatch into small periwinkles (no larval form) direct on to the foodplant.
- A second, very similar species, *L. fabalis* can occur here but is normally on the lower shore and is smaller.

Beadlet Sea Anemone *Actinia equina*
- Size 2–6cm, the example here is contracted; common under stones, ledges and seaweed where it is humid.
- Copes with desiccation by retracting the tentacles inside, which reduces surface area; mucus secreted over the surface further reduces water loss. This adaptation allows it to survive high on the shore.
- A carnivore feeding upon crustaceans and small fish.
- Gaseous exchange is by diffusion.
- Primitive animal, attaches to hard surfaces but can move very slowly.

Common Limpet *Patella vulgata*
- Size: up to 4cm.
- Herbivore, feeding on microscopic algae attached to rock surface. May prevent the growth of larger seaweeds.
- Adhesion to the surface by muscular foot and the secretion of a chemical.
- Hold on rock: 75 lbs/in^2.
- Clamping down at low tide prevents drying out. Water is drawn in to the gills via a hole above the head.
- Reduced metabolism when uncovered by tide.

Orange Sponge *Hymeniacidon*
- An irregularly shaped organism that grows in damp crevices under the seaweed.
- May be more abundant in the lower shore.
- Surprisingly tolerant of desiccation for a sponge and so can be quite visible.

Under more sheltered conditions expect the Knotted Wrack to be present.

Fig. 2.52
Knotted Wrack *Ascophylum nodosum* on a sheltered shore. Some epiphytic, red alga *Vertebrata lanosa* present.

Fig. 2.53 Knotted Wrack *A. nodosum* cut by wave action, providing easier attachment for the *V. lanosa* epiphyte which is well developed.

Knotted or Egg Wrack *Ascophyllum nodosum*
- Typically up to 2 metres or more in length.
- Single, large air bladders float the fronds towards the light for maximum photosynthesis.
- The mean breaking strain of 37.6 kg/cm^2 is lower than many wracks and limits the species to more sheltered shores. The more the wave action the shorter and cut it becomes, probably due to the large surface area. Damaged tips are common.
- Longevity is high, living for fifteen years or more; it thus competes favourably with other algae by forming a blanket over the rocks in extreme shelter. Little can grow below it and so it may dominate sheltered shores.
- It is unpalatable for most animals and tolerant of shading.
- Cell wall thickness is 1.02 microns.
- A small amount of a red alga, *Vertebrata lanosa*, is attached.

Species of the middle shore

Seaweeds

Knotted or Egg Wrack *Ascophyllum nodosum* is the longest lived but least adaptable of the brown algae. Strong wave action cuts off fronds and so is a good indicator of sheltered shores where it will dominate. Sexes are separate and reproductive structures fall off after the release of spores. This produces a weak thallus allowing the entry of spores from the red alga *Vertebrata lanosa* (until recently known as *Polysiphonia lanosa*). Growth of this epiphyte may increase the chance of being torn off the rocks (heavier weight and increased surface area). Air bladders grow one a year for each frond length. Colonization beneath this wrack by other algae is difficult.

Bladder Wrack *Fucus vesiculosus*: swollen conceptacles form at the tip of the frond and release spores in spring and summer; afterwards they decay and are lost. They live for about three years and grow 0.5cm per week. They may become colonized by other algae, e.g. *Ectocarpus*. Bladder Wrack needs a high light intensity to grow well. The millions of spores released are rarely able to complete development as limpets consume them early on. These grazers will limit Bladder Wrack considerably if their population density is high. Bladder Wrack adapts well to variable wave action, reducing the number of bladders to limit surface area and size with increasing wave action. This is a very widespread species, found in some form on the majority of rocky shores.

Pepper Dulse *Osmundea pinnatifida*, a red alga, is the most common of what are known as the fern-weeds; it grows to 8cm although usually much less. *O. osmunda* is fairly common and grows to 20cm. They both have separate sexes and vary in colour from purple to dark red-brown. Pepper Dulse has been used as a spiced alga and has been commonly eaten in the past. The seaweed can generate dense stands across open rocky areas in the middle and lower shore where it can compete favourably with the fucoid algae. In sunny areas it can become bleached and shows up white or yellow. This is especially so higher up the shore, where it is also short; the longest varieties are found in the lowest areas of the shore. It is perennial and during the summer acts like a turf on which many other seaweeds grow, e.g. *Ceramium* and *Leathesia*. Under the flat fronds small animal species thrive.

Fig. 2.54
Bladder Wrack floating.

Fig. 2.55
Pepper Dulse *Osmundea pinnatafida* with green *Ulva*.

Fig. 2.56
Beadlet Anemone *Actinia equina* in a rockpool.

Fig. 2.57
Beadlet Anemone just released from a parent, approximately a millimetre long.

Sea anemones

The Beadlet *Actinia equina* is the most tolerant anemone species and is found from the upper shore down to the lower region. It can survive out of water by withdrawing its tentacles into the body, when it then appears as a dark red blob stuck to the rock. The Snakeslock *Anemonia viridis* cannot retract its tentacles and is restricted to rock pools. Tentacles will increase the surface area for water loss. The Beadlet can also secrete mucus over the surface of the body to restrict water loss. They are carnivores, catching prey by stinging them with nematocysts that paralyse the prey. Triggered to fire by proteins on the food surface, they feel sticky to the touch as they fire the 'harpoons' into the skin. Around the top edge of the Beadlet column are blue spots called acrorhagi used for defence containing dense clusters of nematocysts. Anemones are territorial. Beadlets nudge each other aggressively over days and the loser will be expelled from the immediate area. Anemones exhibit both asexual and sexual reproduction although asexual is the most seen in the Beadlet. Any individual can create buds on the inside of the body and then 'spit' them out in large number. These tiny clones may attach nearby and adults can recognize their own and are less aggressive towards them. Once adult they are thought to live for twenty years or more. Snakeslock form large colonies where clones are produced through splitting in half.

Fig. 2.58
Common Shore Crab *Carcinus maenas* female with eggs.

Fig. 2.59
Hatching eggs of Shore Crab.

Crabs

They have separate sexes and mate when the female has recently shed the exoskeleton (a process called ecdysis) so the cuticle is still soft. The female then carries the 800,000 eggs underneath the abdomen. A zooea larva hatches to live in the plankton (Figs. 3.25 and 3.26). The chance of survival is minimal – hence the large egg number. The Edible Crab is migratory, living and spawning off shore. When the larvae settle as young crabs on the seashore they feed and mature there, moving down into deeper water as they become adult. This avoids competition for food with young and adults occupying different sites. Crabs live for up to four years, carrying out ecdysis as necessary for growth. Soft 'peeler' crabs are those that have just shed their exoskeleton. The Shore Crab is very variable in colour and most tolerant to variable salinity and temperature and will hunt over most of the shore.

Molluscs

Common Limpet *Patella vulgata*: there are several similar-looking limpets on the shore but this species is the most widespread and not restricted to any one zone. Those higher up the shore can suffer from desiccation stress whereby an accumulated effect over several days in summer can lead to death. The muscular foot clamps down on the surface by creating a vacuum as well as the secretion of a 'superglue' of mucopolysaccharides. They can graze the biofilm both at high and low water, for the latter more at night. As discussed earlier, the lengthy radula has iron-oxide hardened teeth that abrade the surface to graze, often leaving marks on the rock. It is a very important herbivore in restricting the growth of algae; often the only algae and lichen to be found in the area is that growing on the shell where the radula cannot

Fig. 2.60
Edible Crab *Cancer pagurus*.

reach. This helps to prevent desiccation at low tide and dissuades predators.

Limpets can roam up to 2 metres whilst grazing but always come back to the same spot (called 'homing'). On arrival back they rotate the shell and grind it into rock producing a good fit, further improving the seal to prevent water loss. When they die, a scar is left on the rock.

Shell shape is variable with wave action, tending to be more flattened in sheltered conditions and domed in wave action. All manner of forms exist on the same shore where localized patches of shelter and exposure occur. The cause of variation is unclear; it may be due to the indirect effect of muscles pulling down to hold on in wave action, affecting the angle at which shell is secreted. Sexes are separate but as in many molluscs they often begin life as males changing to a female. Spawning in the autumn is triggered by a reduction in water temperature to around 11°C. The larvae live in the plankton for

Fig. 2.61
Common Limpet *Patella vulgata* with two limpet home marks on the rock.

Fig. 2.62
The underside of a limpet showing the large muscular foot and head.

Fig. 2.63
Limpet grazing marks left on the rock.

Fig. 2.64
Male limpet releasing sperm into the rockpool for external fertilization. (Photo: JA-T)

barely two weeks before settling on the shore. Longevity varies with shores, such that on sheltered ones large individuals up to seventeen years old are found, whilst the high energy shores have higher densities but individuals barely survive five years, possibly due to having a higher metabolism. Limpets are very important as prey and are a foundation species. Oystercatchers can eat one every five minutes; they are over a third of the food consumed by Dogwhelks and three-quarters of Clingfish food.

Fig. 2.65
Group of Edible Periwinkle *Littorina littorea*.

Rocky Shores

Fig. 2.66
Flat Periwinkle *Littorina obtusata*, brown form.

Fig. 2.67
Flat Periwinkle, yellow form.

Fig. 2.68
Eggs of Flat Periwinkle.

Fig. 2.69
Underside of Purple Topshell *Gibbula umbilicalis*.

Fig. 2.70
Underside of Common Topshell *Osilinus lineatus*.

Periwinkles and Topshells are quite different types of grazer. Both have a horny plate attached to the back of the foot, which acts like a trap door, closing the shell aperture when it retracts. In periwinkles this is teardrop shaped but in topshells it is circular. The latter are more colourful molluscs. Edible or Common Periwinkle *Littorina littorea* is one of the most widespread species found on all seashores, even on sediments. Numbers may be low on shores dominated by *Ascophyllum*, partly because this grazer actively avoids eating it and also because the fronds harbour *Carcinus*, the prime predator of molluscs. Elsewhere it is a prolific feeder on biofilm and the young stages of *Ulva* species (Fig 1.25). Like limpets the grazing will influence seaweed growth and with the elimination of these green algae a wider diversity of other species, like *Chondrus*, occurs. The heavy shell protects against drying and mechanical damage along with the horny plate (the operculum). Fertile eggs are released into the water and the larvae swim in the plankton. It settles out on the shore and migrates up the beach, guided by responses to gravity and light. Gills are present but they can breathe for a period out of water.

Flat Periwinkles *Littorina obtusata* and *L. fabalis* show a wide range of colour forms and are almost impossible to tell apart. They primarily live on *Fucus* species, especially the Bladder Wrack in *L. obtusata* and Serrated Wrack in the *L. fabalis* although this is not rigid. *L. fabalis* is limited to the lower shore whilst the other is on both the middle and lower. It is thought that *L. obtusata* was the original species, taking two years to slowly reach sexual maturity, laying eggs on the wrack, hatching then into a larva to live in the plankton before settling back on a shore. In the lower shore predation from crabs is at its height and there is a clear problem of periwinkles surviving two years to produce offspring. Possibly in evolution there was an advantage for a mutant form to put less energy into growth but to reproduce early, after just six months. This could be the reason *L. fabalis* is successful in the lower shore. The two species display the two classic strategies for life survival, called 'K species' and 'r species' strategies, respectively. (Put simply, in life finite resources are available to a species. Humans (and *L. obtusata*) are K species as they develop slowly, have a long life span and produce a small number of offspring; r species, like *L. fabalis*, put most energy into the pro-

Fig. 2.71
Ceramium, a filamentous red alga.

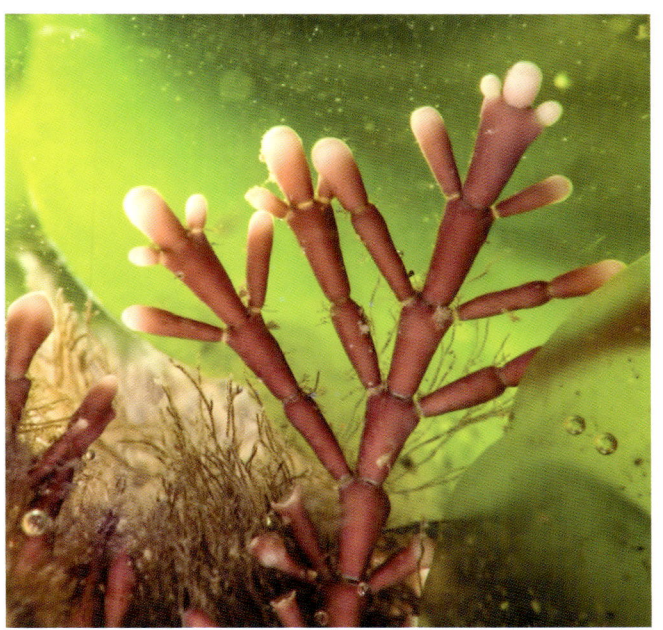

Fig. 2.72
Corallina, a calcareous red alga.

duction of offspring rather than growth and longevity.) The colour forms help with camouflage, depending on whether they are viewed from above or below. Yellow is difficult to see from below whilst brown stands out. The reverse is true from above.

Purple Topshell *Gibbula umbilicalis* is the most abundant topshell and is typical of the middle shore. The larger Toothed Topshell *Osilinus lineatus* appears in smaller numbers but exists higher up the shore, possibly as it is more temperature-tolerant. This latter species is extending its range northwards and has also increased its reproduction to almost any month of the year (both possibly linked with climate change). When turned over, a small hole is visible in the shell of *G. umbilicalis* whilst the other has a small bump on the side of the shell by the operculum. Topshells are even less aggressive grazers than periwinkles and have minimal impact on seaweed growth.

Additional species of the middle shore

Seaweeds
Common Green Branch Weed *Cladophora rupestris* is a dark green alga of the middle and lower shore, both on rocks and in pools. It is a branched filamentous species giving a feathery appearance. Several dense layers of cellulose and a chitin-like material protect the alga from drying out. It is frequently found living under *Fucus* where it remains moist at low tide. A range of pigments absorb light in the shade of the *Fucus*. Between the filaments a small micro-community of animals exists.

Fig. 2.73
Sea Lettuce *Ulva lactuca* in a rockpool.

Sea Lettuce *Ulva lactuca*, up to 40cm in very sheltered pools although usually much smaller. Light green alga where the frond is a sheet of undifferentiated tissue, two cells thick. It can recover fast from desiccation to full metabolism. It may be very abundant under brown algae, especially if the nitrate level is high, e.g. fertilizer run-off from fields.

Ceramium species (1–30cm in length) is a red alga that often grows attached to other algae especially fringe weeds like *Corallina* in pools and on the rocky turf of Pepper Dulse. It is a fine, branched, filamentous alga with characteristically curled, forked tips giving it the common name of Pincer Weed. The filaments can be covered in diatoms and microscopic animals.

Rocky Shores

Fig. 2.74
Gem Anemones *Aulactinia (Bunodactis) verrucosa* in a rockpool crevice.

Fig. 2.75
Barnacle-encrusted Mussels *Mytilus edulis*.

Fig. 2.76
Dogwhelk *Nucella lapillus* feeding on barnacles with, inset, an enlarged specimen.

Sea anemones

With careful searching in rockpools the beautiful Gem or Wartlet Anemone *Aulactinia verrucosa* can be found from here down to the kelp zone. The transparent and mottled tentacles provide good disruptive patterning to camouflage into the background. If they retract when disturbed, a series of warty lines radiate down the column.

Molluscs

Common or Blue Mussel *Mytilus edulis*, 1–10cm, is a large bivalve mollusc. It attaches itself to the rock by tough protein threads secreted by the byssus gland, which is located on the foot. By breaking and producing new byssus threads minor movement of the body can be made on the rock. Two shells give protection and close at low tide to retain water. Under stress the metabolism and heart rate drop to conserve energy. They are filter feeders. The water is drawn in and out through siphons and those living higher up the shore will be smaller as the feeding time is less. The foot can be extended out of the shell, wiped over its outer surface where detritus settles, and be drawn in. Eaten by dogwhelks, starfish, oystercatchers and eider ducks it is an important food source. The planktonic larva settles out of water, triggered by a negative response to light. Roughness of the substrate will increase their settlement.

Dogwhelk *Nucella lapillus* 1–3cm: the shell is distinct with a groove across the shell lip. A carnivore, it eats barnacles, limpets and mussels using a radula modified for shell boring. Chemical secretion assists this action. The shell (siphonal) groove allows water in for gaseous exchange. Eggs are laid in capsules of 100s, most being infertile as food for the fertile ones to feed on. Only a few mini-adults emerge. The young migrate to the lower shore to feed, moving up as they mature. There is a wide variation in shell size, shape and thickness according to wave action. Able to withstand extreme wave action the body becomes broader with a wider aperture for a large muscular foot to emerge and hang on. A thicker shell gives protection from crabs on sheltered shores.

Towards the end of the twentieth century populations around the UK suffered a huge decline through the slow release of Tributyltin in anti-fouling paint. This is an example of imposex in species with the chemical simulating sex hormones and preventing reproduction. Recent recovery has been observed now that TBT has been banned from use in the UK and mutations have appeared in the population.

Fig. 2.77
Cladophora, filamentous green alga, magnified to show mucous home of the midge larva, *Clunio maritima*.

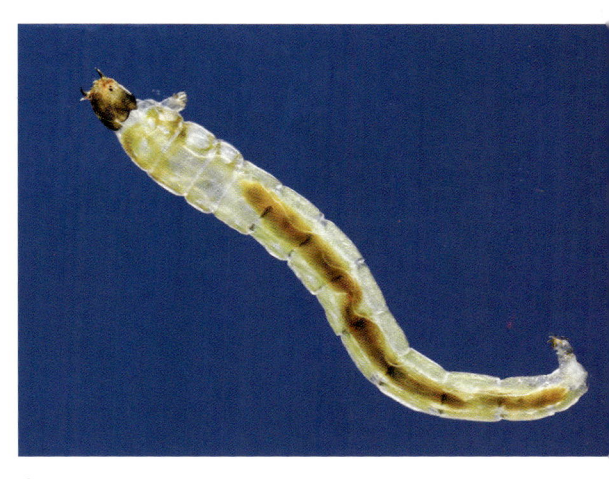

Fig. 2.78
Midge larva, *Clunio maritima*.

Fig. 2.79
Broad-clawed Porcelain Crab *Porcellana platycheles*.

Arthropods

Marine Non-biting Midge *Clunio maritima*, a type of chironomid fly. This marine insect is easily overlooked as it is just a few millimetres long and is abundant on most shores in all stages. As a larva it lives in a silk tube spun on weeds like *Cladophora* or *Corallina*. This traps silt and sand. The larva emerges regularly to feed on diatoms and biofilm growing on the weed. Emergence from the pupa happens on a summer spring tide with the male appearing first, swarming in large numbers over the barnacled rocks looking for a pupa with a female inside. He unwraps her and immediately attaches her to his body. She has legs but no wings and is completely dependent on the male. Sexual maturity must happen quickly as the entire reproductive process must be complete within the few hours of low tide. She lays a gelatinous mass of eggs soon after mating and dies. The male may mate with two or three females before the tide returns and he dies. This complex cycle requires two biological clock mechanisms: to be able to determine a day for spring tides and also time of day for emergence as this differs from shore to shore. Larval stages are important food sources for young crustaceans.

Broad-clawed Porcelain Crab *Porcellana platycheles*. Up to 2cm, it is flattened with sharp claws on the legs as it is found gripping the underside of stones and boulders in this and the lower shore. Often found in large groups, the pincers are very hairy to trap detritus on which they feed. The long, whip-like antennae show that this is not actually a crab but related to the lobsters. Long-clawed Porcelain Crab *Pisidia longicornis* is a similar but smaller crab found under stones, mainly in the lower shore.

Rocky Shores 53

Lower shore community

Fig. 2.80
Lower shore community.
LL = encrusting Red algae *Lithophyllum* and *Lithothamnion*.

Notes

- The community has a higher diversity than previously seen higher up the shore, especially in algae.
- Red and Brown algae are proliferating despite the low light; Serrated Wrack is the dominant brown alga and in more sheltered conditions will be covered in sessile animals such as *Spirorbis* worms.
- What little rock is free from algal colonization may have small encrusting animals attached, e.g. *Pomatoceros*. Bare or red algal encrusted rock occurs where whip-lash from wracks prevents animal settlement.
- Most species found only in the lower shore will have little resistance to desiccation.
- The *Laminaria* or Kelp is found just at the bottom of the Lower Shore and is unlikely to be seen if the tides are neap.

Serrated or Toothed Wrack *Fucus serratus*

- 50–80cm in length.
- Commonest species of the lower shore and partly uncovered at neap tides. Lives for three years; on slow draining shores it may occupy a third of the area of the entire littoral region.
- Intolerant of desiccation – cell wall thickness 0.42 microns.
- Fronds are flat and at low tide only the top surface frond dries.
- Growth, form and breeding is variable; related to climate and temperature, e.g. fronds are longer with fewer branching in Scotland, compared with shorter branched individuals in Devon.
- With an increase in latitude, it is found higher up the shore.
- After the tide returns, recovery to full metabolism is the slowest of the fucoid algae.

> **Aspects of living in the lower shore**
> - Relatively stable environment with a high productivity compared to higher zones. This leads to a greater biodiversity that creates high levels of competition for space, food, light, etc.
> - The light intensity is severely limited at high tide because of the depth of water.
> - Full photosynthesis can only occur when covered by water.
> - Cloudy (turbid) water will reduce the light levels further and restrict the number of species able to survive here.

- Like many algae of the lower shore it can adapt to the low light intensity by developing additional pigments for absorbing maximum light for photosynthesis.
- Fronds are often colonized by *Spirorbis*, small, filter feeding, polychaete worms which secrete a calcareous, spiralled tube (diameter 3mm).
- The flat fronds also prevent the area under the alga from drying out; numerous organisms will colonize this space.
- Intolerant of heavy wave action, at such times it is replaced by *Himanthalia elongata*.

Irish Moss *Chondrus crispus*
- Red alga with flat frond up to 15cm long; branched.
- Variable in shape (both broad and narrow) and size, usually exhibiting tips.
- Forms dense tufts around the base of the kelp, as like other red algae it is very shade tolerant.
- Often found in rock pools of the middle and lower shore as it is tolerant of grazing.
- Cell organelles contain accessory pigments called phycobilins that absorb light and pass the energy via a chain reaction to the chlorophyll for photosynthesis.

Dulse *Palmaria palmata* (see Fig. 2.116), *Lithophyllum* and *Lithothamnion* spp.
- Calcareous red algae encrusting on the rock.
- Rock-like algae, from deep red in the shade to pale pink in the open; often white at edge where bleached and dried.
- Resistant to grazing and tolerant of shade and wave action; often covers the base of rock pools.
- In the water-covered crevices, under the *Fucus*, they are well adapted to survive the very low light.
- The cell walls become calcified as a by-product of photosynthesis.

Coral Weed *Corallina officinalis*
- Calcareous red alga, 4–10cm.
- Chalky alga which covers a wide area of the shore but survives best lower down where it shows up darker red (see photo right); bleaches easily in the sun. Forms a dense turf under the dominant brown algae.
- Intolerant of desiccation; a dominant rockpool species.
- Tolerates wave action, and is shade-tolerant.

Sea Mat *Bryozoans*
- 1–2mm, but side by side forms extensive covering.
- Colonial animals forming mats of tiny individuals living side by side.
- The animals live in limey chambers and filter the seawater for food.
- Hermaphrodite; fertilization occurs within the colony before release. Asexual reproduction increases the area of colony across the substrate.

Orange Sponges and Bread-crumb Sponge *Halichondria panicea*
- Lies within the crevices to avoid desiccation.
- The holes on the surface (oscula) pass water and waste out; fresh seawater is absorbed through the surface.
- Orange encrusting sponge, *Hymeniacidon*, can be abundant, filling crevices.
- Purse Sponge *Grantia compressa* is a second common species of sponge, present here attached to the base of the *Corallina*; flattened with a single osculum at the apex.

Dogwhelk *Nucella lapillus*
- A common predator feeding on barnacles and limpets.

Fig. 2.81 Purse Sponge *Grantia compressa*.

Fig. 2.82
Serrated Wrack *Fucus serratus*.

Fig. 2.83
Serrated Wrack from a very sheltered shore with freshwater influence.

Fig. 2.84
Irish Moss *Chondrus crispus*.

Species of the lower shore

Brown algae

Serrated or Toothed Wrack *Fucus serratus*. A thick midrib is in the centre of a frond edged with serrations. However, it is softer than the other fucoids. The sexes are separate unlike the fucoids of the upper shore and the conceptacles are more streamlined at the tips. Like the Bladder Wrack, female gametes produce chemical attractants (pheromones) to attract the male, called fucoserratin.

Red algae

This zone has a layer of red algae producing a turf below the dominant brown algae. They are all typically shade-tolerant due to the low light levels and with accessory pigments called phycobilins. These pigments like phycoerythrin and phycocyanin enable the seaweeds to photosynthesize under very low light levels and restricted wavelengths. With blue light reflected away at the surface and red not penetrating to the lower zone it is the mid-wavelengths like green that are absorbed by the accessory pigments. It is noticeable how much darker the seaweeds are in this zone compared to higher areas of the shore. Plants transplanted lower down the shore increase the production of these accessory pigments and may develop other types. All pigments are prone to bleaching in high illumination, as can be seen with Pepper Dulse, which can be found in the middle shore. *Corallina* and *Lithothamnion* are two red seaweeds that have a high chalk content as a by-product of metabolism. This extra hardness makes them resistant to wave action as well as to grazing in this rich community. They are both common in rockpools.

Additional species of the lower shore

Seaweeds

Thongweed *Himanthalia elongata*, up to a metre in length. A narrow, strap-like brown alga. The first year of growth is just a small button, like a mushroom 2cm across. In the second year a branching frond grows from the centre. The reproductive conceptacles are based on this. It is characteristic of extreme wave action, where it replaces the Serrated Wrack in dominating this part of the shore. The two species compete for a similar niche but Thongweed has a wider stress tolerance. Theoretically this means Thongweed should be found on all shores with this wide tolerance; however, the Serrated Wrack grows quickly and if the buttons of

Fig. 2.85
Thongweed *Himanthalia elongata* including the first year buttons.

Fig. 2.86
Green Sponge Fingers *Codium fragile*.

Fig. 2.87
Orange Sponge *Hymeniacidon perleve*. Also Beadlet Anemone and red algae, e.g. *Ceramium*, attached to barnacles.

Thongweed are beneath they will be shaded out and killed. Therefore, where they compete the Wrack will win and only when the conditions become extreme can the Thongweed survive as the Wrack disappears. With such a wide tolerance (large potential niche) this means Thongweed can appear in other situations, like extreme shelter and rockpools, where competition is not so strong.

Green Sponge Fingers *Codium fragile* is a branched, spongy green alga growing up to 30cm. It may grow singly beneath brown algae and in pools. It has a high concentration of chlorophyll which gives a dark appearance as it is able to absorb much light with an action potential similar to kelp species. It is widely found but with a rather fragmented distribution.

See also *Chondrus, Mastocarpus, Cladophora, Ulva, Ceramium* which may also be found in the zone.

Encrusting sponges

The Bread-crumb Sponge is common under the humid fronds of the wrack, filling the crevices with its yellow or green asymmetrical mass. It is also found in deep clefts and overhangs of rock where water continues to drip at low tide. When under water they filter the water of plankton and detritus. It is very sensitive to desiccation. Oxygen is obtained by diffusion. Although hermaphrodite, the gonads ripen at different times ensuring cross fertilization. Also in damp crevices is the Orange Sponge *Hymeniacidon perleve* which may also grow on other substrates including seaweeds.

Fig. 2.88
Hydroid colony: *Obelia*. The main stem is coated with diatoms.

Hydroids

Several species of hydroid grow attached to the seaweeds or rock. A colony consists of a stalk from which project asexual polyps that are feeding stages going on to produce sexual forms called medusae. This dispersal stage produces gametes and after fertilization a larva hatches, settling on the shore. Guided by a positive response to light it moves about to eventually attach itself permanently and develop a new colony. Feeding is similar to that of the sea anemones and food is passed along the colony.

Marine worms – polychaetes

These are common and varied, from filter-feeding detritivores attached to a substrate, to errant carnivorous worms. Keeled Tube Worm *Pomatoceros triqueter* form calcareous white tubes, which are triangular in section, across hard substrates like rock and shells. These are around 2–6cm in length. At the open end of the tube a crown of tentacles appears at high water to filter water for food and to obtain oxygen. At low tide an operculum closes the hole to prevent desiccation. A common species that exists from the middle shore down is the Greenleaf Worm *Eulalia clavigera*, most easily seen crawling across rocks between barnacles and mussels. It is a scavenger on dead or damaged animals, particularly the latter. Although it is bright green and around 10cm long, it is narrow and may need some searching to find. Under stones at low tide may be scale worms, flattened polychaetes with dorsal scales. The number and position of these vary between species, which are carnivorous on small animals also living under stones. After the separate sexes mate the female retains the eggs and some days or weeks later release the larvae, normally into the plankton.

Sea slugs

This is a commonly used term for molluscs with no obvious shell as it may be internal. They are very diverse in shape, colour and size. Many are very small and only a small minority, the larger or more common, are mentioned here. The Sea Hare *Aplysia punctata* is perhaps

Fig. 2.89
Hydroid colony: *Clava* (left), *Dynamene* (right).

Fig. 2.90.1
Bryozoan or Sea Mat colony.

Fig. 2.91
Keeled Tube Worm, *Pomatoceros*.

Fig. 2.90.2
Bryozoans feeding.

Fig. 2.92
Green Leaf Worm *Eulalia clavigera*.

the largest, coming on to the shore to spawn like the majority of sea slugs. Extensions at the side of the body (parapods) act like wings and are used in vigorous swimming. Up to 20cm long with a small internal shell they are dark purple-brown in colour. This varies with the diet, which consists of different seaweeds. Often spawning can occur in mass numbers, filling rockpools in great chains. When disturbed they may eject a purple dye. A much smaller, similar species is *Elysia viridis* but this lacks the shell. It feeds on *Cladophora* and *Codium*, green seaweed, and during this can transpose intact chloroplasts to the surface of its own body. These react by photosynthesizing for the mollusc when it sunbathes. The largest group of sea slugs are the Nudibranchs possessing external gills and no shell. The Sea Lemon *Doris pseudoargus* is up to 7cm. The nine gills are arranged in a circle around the anus and it is usually found in summer when they spawn. Feeding on sponges, they have a warty surface caused by internal chalky deposits. The largest

Rocky Shores 59

Fig. 2.93
Spawning Sea Hares.

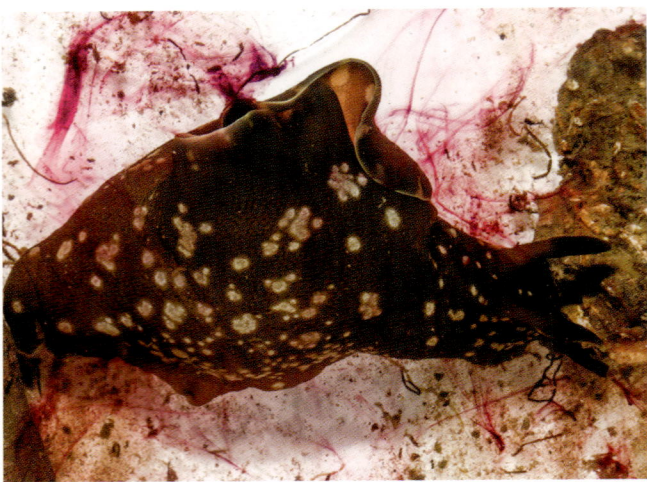

Fig. 2.94
Sea Hare *Aplysia punctata* with purple dye.

to be encountered will be the Grey Sea Slug *Aeolidia papillosa*, up to 10cm. Common under stones, it feeds on sea anemones whose sting cells are undigested and transported intact to the dorsal surface and used for defence (Fig. 1.30). They spawn in summer when long trailing ribbons of spawn containing over 400,000 eggs can be seen in pools.

Crustacea

A number of different crustacea hide under rocks and stones including crab species unable to cope with the problems higher up the shore. Velvet Swimming Crab *Necora puber* is a common species, brightly coloured with red eyes and bright blue patches on the joints. It is an aggressive crab, one that will turn and attack rather than hurry off. The hind legs are well adapted like paddles for swimming. Omnivorous, it will feed on kelp as well as crustaceans and molluscs. *Xantho hydrophilus* is a powerful-looking crab but is a herbivore, feeding on seaweed. Also under the stones and weed will be huge numbers of amphipods. These are different to the sand-hoppers, called gammarid shrimps; these will attempt to swim instead of hop as a form of escape. Isopods are also common, particularly *Idotea* species associated with seaweeds through all stages of development.

Fig. 2.95
Elysia viridis.

Fig. 2.96
Velvet Swimming Crab *Necora puber*.

Fig. 2.97
Idotea species, an isopod, on a bryozoan colony.

Fig. 2.98
Cushion Stars, *Asterina gibbosa* (left) and *A. phylactica* (pair, right).

Echinoderms

These are normally found very low down the shore but the Cushion Star *Asterina gibbosa* can exist in pools from the lower middle shore down into the sub-littoral. Up to 5cm across, these small, stubby starfish are common under stones feeding as a scavenger. They start life as a male and when they are about four years old they change to female. These can lay up to 1,000 eggs. By contrast the rare *A. phylactica* is only found in a few localities and occurs higher up the shore in rockpools. Upon laying eggs it will brood them for three weeks until the young starfish emerge.

Rocky Shores 61

Fig. 2.99
Blenny *Lipophrys pholis*.

Fig. 2.100
Tompot Blenny *Parablennius gattorugine*.

Fig. 2.101
Five-bearded Rockling *Ciliata mustela*.

Seashore fish

A number of fish have adapted to live permanently on the shore, even when the tide goes out. The Common Blenny or Shanny *Lipophrys pholis* is the commonest littoral fish with highly variable colour. These are the obvious, darting fish found in pools, on occasions even in the upper shore. Those will be smaller ones whilst the larger, 10cm individuals may be found out of water living under stones and seaweed in the lower shore. Unlike other fish the gill arches do not collapse out of water and so for short periods they can air breathe. The powerful jaws can crush barnacles, the main diet, as well as crabs and algae. The eggs are looked after by the male, continuing for some time after they hatch. The young move off-shore to feed and return as they mature. Rocklings, a similar size to the Blenny, are less well adapted but may remain on the lower shore when the tide recedes. One difference is that they have sensory barbels around the mouth to assist finding food in the low light. Shore Rockling *Gaidropsarus mediterraneus* has three barbels and the Five-bearded Rockling *Ciliata mustela*, five. The Butterfish *Pholis gunnellus* looks eel-like and is very slippery to pick up. Along the back are dark brown spots. Perhaps one of the most fascinating is the Clingfish *Lepadogaster purpurea* which is flattened, with two blue spots on the back and modified pelvic fins to form a strong sucker. This makes it almost impossible to remove from the rock and could be useful to avoid wave action and predators.

There are fish that visit the shore to feed at high tide, and some that may remain in deep rockpools like the wrasses. Corkwing Wrasse *Crenilabrus melops* is very colourful with a dark spot behind the eye. Ballan Wrasse *Labrus bergylta* is also brightly coloured and considerably larger than the former wrasse. Interestingly, they begin their life as a female but later change to a male.

Seashore birds

As the tide recedes and most marine predation stops, the shore, now under stress, has terrestrial, predatory visitors in the form of birds. These could be starlings and crows, especially in winter when food can be scarce on land. Several birds are resident feeders moving away just at high tide. The piping call of the Oystercatcher *Haematopus ostralegus* can be heard on most seashores. The black and white bird with its long red bill will feed on shellfish, especially mussels. The powerful, sensitive bill re-grows to allow for wear. The shape varies according to the diet: softer food allowing for quicker growth

Fig. 2.102
Cornish Sucker or Clingfish *Lepadogaster purpurea*.

Fig. 2.103 The sucker under the Clingfish.

Fig. 2.104 Ballan Wrasse female.

Fig. 2.105 Oystercatcher in flight over the seashore, winter plumage.

Fig. 2.106 Oystercatcher.

Fig. 2.107 Turnstone.

produces a slim bill, whilst hard food creates a 'hammer' bill. They nest on the shore, usually in the upper splash zone, when they are three years old. On hatching, the young move quickly into hiding to avoid gulls but will be fed for up to a year. Oystercatchers are adaptable to different types of shore and are good swimmers. Under some conditions, e.g. storms, they move inland and feed in fields and on lawns. Turnstone *Arenaria interpres* is a superbly camouflaged wader found feeding on invertebrates, flicking over seaweed and stones across the shore. It can be especially common on the rocky shore during the winter.

See also crabs, limpet, mussels, dogwhelk, anemones, periwinkles and topshells, redshank, curlew, heron, Candy-stripe Flatworm and animals of the Laminarian Zone.

Laminaria zone: the transition from littoral to sub-littoral

Aspects of the zone

- It is rarely uncovered except by an extreme low tide.
- The relatively constant environment favours a high diversity of life.
- High levels of inter-specific competition with less abiotic stress.
- Greatest depth of water and so light is at a minimum intensity.
- Highest productivity of any zone, partly due to its long immersion time, which offers ample opportunity to obtain nutrients for growth.

Notes

- Photographs were taken at one of the lowest tides of the year, near to Chart Datum.
- The close-up photo was taken by lifting up the kelp blades in front, so this is directly underneath.
- The *Laminaria*, erect in the water with red algae attached is *L. hyperborea* and *L. digitata* in the foreground lying flat.

Fig. 2.108
Laminarian zone.

General features of the Laminarians or kelp

- Kelp beds are like a marine forest, with layers of algae and animals.
- They tolerate less than 20 per cent desiccation.
- Growth is prolific: most of the productivity is from the continuously growing lamina which grows at the base and erodes at the tip, like a conveyor belt.
- Structurally the most advanced of the algae, the trumpet-shaped cells in the stipe are believed to have a transport function (moving materials through the stipe.
- They exhibit alternation of generations; the dominant phase (the kelp plant) is the sporophyte. This bears sporangia which release zoospores into the water, which germinate to produce a gameteophyte stage, of which little information is known.
- Sporangia develop on both sides of the lamina surface.
- A cross section through the stipe reveals annual growth rings; the average age is about five years.
- Kelps are harvested commercially for alginates (used in cosmetics, toothpaste and ice cream), potash, soda, iodine, and animal fodder.
- All adapt well to low light intensities.
- In very sheltered conditions the lower shore may be sand or mud. The deposition of material will allow the replacement of the kelps by Eel Grass *Zostera* species. If small stones are present, Boot-lace Weed *Chorda filum* grows.

Tangle or Oarweed *Laminaria digitata*

- About 1 metre in length, lamina is split into many 'digits'; splitting increases with the wave action.
- Holdfast is branched and broad, giving stronger attachment than *Saccharina latissima* to the rock.
- The stipe is flexible so at low tide the plant goes limp and lies flat, thus remaining in the shallow water and not drying out.
- The stipe is smooth and oval in section; its length varies with depth.
- These listed features enable it to survive a high degree of wave action. On very sheltered shores, it may grow as a single blade.

Fig. 2.109
Laminarian zone community.

Cuvie *Laminaria hyperborea*
- Grows to 1–3 metres.
- Lamina is split, which reduces the effects of wave action.
- Holdfast is huge and dome-shaped giving the best attachment in extremes of wave action.
- The stipe is inflexible, supporting the kelp upright, which would cause the alga to dry out. It survives, therefore, only in the sub-littoral zone where it will be unaffected by the tides. The spray from extreme wave action may push a small number onto the lower shore.
- The stipe surface is rough, enabling red algae to colonize it. *Palmaria palmata* is a common epiphyte here. The stipe is round in section.
- Typically found in deep water off shore and in areas of wave action.

The photographs were taken on a moderately sheltered shore and one kelp species is missing, found under more sheltered conditions:

Fig. 2.110
Sugar Kelp *Saccharina latissima*.

Sugar Kelp or Sea Belt *Saccharina latissima*
- Up to 2 metres.
- Unlike the other kelps the lamina is a continuous ribbon with a frilled edge; the central part is thickened.
- The holdfast is branched but very small in comparison with that of the other kelps.
- Unable to cope with intense wave action, it is limited to sheltered regions and deep rockpools.
- It is called the 'sugar kelp' because when it is dry a white sugary substance develops on the surface.
- The stipe is flexible so at low tide the plant goes limp and lies flat, thus remaining in the shallow water.

Fig. 2.111
Sugar Kelp at low spring tide in a sheltered bay.

Fig. 2.112
Laminaria hyperborea with rough, upright stalks, some colonized by red algae.

Species of the Laminaria zone

The kelp's name is given to the zone as they dominate this region of the sublittoral edge. *L. digitata* and *Saccharina latissima* live at the low water springs mark or higher if in a deep rockpool. The latter species is restricted to sheltered places but the former is widespread. In deep water it is restricted by competition with *L. hyperborea*. This species grows long rigid stipes in deep water and soon shades out the other kelps. Kelps growing in deeper water develop more pigment than those higher up to enable them to absorb what little light there is. Many organisms colonize the kelp both for space and food, e.g. sea mat grows on the lamina to gain access to circulating water containing their food. The Blue-rayed Limpet feeds on the kelp. The holdfast is a micro-habitat containing a micro-community. Based on plankton as the producer, the primary consumers are thousands of sedentary polychaete worms and other minute organisms which filter the water. Small brittle-stars also filter feed. Carnivorous polychaetes feed on the sedentary worms; the omnivore at the top of this food web is the Hairy Crab *Pilumnus hirtellus*, one or two may live under each holdfast.

Additional species of the Laminaria zone

Brown algae

Mermaid's Tresses or Boot-Lace Weed *Chorda filum*. The very long, unbranched, brown tubes can be many metres in length. The tiny holdfast allows it to grow only on very sheltered shores where it will attach to stones and shells in the sublittoral. It also occurs in areas of low salinity such as the lower parts of estuaries. The tubular nature causes it to inflate after photosynthesis and so floats near the surface. As it matures the tube becomes covered in tiny white hairs.

The annual plant Furbelows *Saccorhiza polyschides* is the largest European seaweed, up to 3 metres or more, and grows very fast. The broad, flat stipe is rigid with ruffles which help to dissipate wave energy, giving it an advantage in surviving the surf. The holdfast is bulbous, growing up to half a metre or more in diameter when fully grown. The rigid stipe does not enable it to avoid desiccation and it usually forms a community with *L. hyperborea* in deep water but often extends on to the lower shore if spray allows. It occurs near to sandy areas so the seaweed can get an occasional sand blasting of which it is more tolerant than other kelps. The short-lived holdfast is not colonized by a micro-community like the Laminarians.

Superficially Dabberlocks *Alaria esculenta* could be mistaken for Sugar Kelp but it is found in extreme wave-exposed conditions. Here it can entirely replace the kelp. From the holdfast there grows a stipe with a long and very tough mid-rib up to a metre or more. From this mid-rib grows a thin frond which is easily damaged by the waves and individuals will be found that have next

Fig. 2.113
Bootlace *Chorda filum*.

Fig. 2.114
Furbelows *Saccorhiza polyschides*.

Fig. 2.115
Dabberlocks *Alaria esculenta*.

to no frond at all. Around the base of the stipe will be found the pod-like, reproductive fronds, the sporophylls. These are around 20cm long and contain high levels of phenol compounds to make them unpalatable to eat, a feature found in some other algae.

Red algae

As depth increases so the red algae become more dominant. *Chondrus crispus* and *Mastocarpus stellatus* form dense tufts around the base of the kelp. *Palmaria palmata* often grows attached to the kelp as a way of reaching the light. All have accessory pigments contained in cell organelles called phycobilisomes. These pigments absorb light and pass the energy via a chain reaction to the chlorophyll for photosynthesis. The red algae are very shade-tolerant, living under the kelp, and require a fraction of the light used by land plants. In fact, if the light is too intense pigments soon become bleached; the tips of *Chondrus* are often white or yellow. *Chondrus* may dominate the smaller algae as few herbivores will graze upon it and it will out-compete wracks.

See also *Codium*, *Cladophora*, *Ulva*, *Corallina*.

Fig. 2.116
Red Algae: upper species is *Mastocarpus*; lower species is Dulse, *Palmaria palmata*.

A wide diversity of animals live in this zone because of the abundance of food and because it is a region of least abiotic stress in which to live. Few show adaptations to survive varying abiota unlike at the top of the shore. It is the competition for food and space which dominates life here and as a consequence there is no single dominant animal species. The commonly found animals are given here.

Fig. 2.117 Paddle worm *Phyllodoce lamelligera*.

Fig. 2.118 Scale worm.

Fig. 2.119 Grey Topshell *Gibbula cineraria*.

Fig. 2.120 Painted Topshell *Calliostoma zizyphinum*.

Marine worms – polychaetes

The wide diversity of worms found here include the Greenleaf Worm from the previous zone. A much larger species of paddleworm, *Phyllodoce lamelligera*, occurs around holdfasts and crevices. So too are a number of different scaleworms. These have scales (elytra) covering the back. Both of these groups are carnivores.

Molluscs

Two species of topshell are common in the lower shore feeding on biofilm and micro-algae. Grey Topshell *Gibbula cineraria* grows up to 1.25cm and lacks the purple banding of *G. umbilicalis* and the hole beneath the shell is small. Lacking the stress tolerance of other *Gibbula* species it is restricted to the lower shore. The Painted Topshell *Calliostoma zizyphinum* is taller at 2cm and is a beautiful cone-shaped shell, commonly found amongst the holdfasts on moderately sheltered shores. A pale form, almost pure white, occurs. The shiny surface is due to shell wiping, where the foot cleans the shell of detritus and a build-up of micro-algae. This contributes almost a quarter of its daily food. It is also thought to eat young cnidarians. Unlike other topshells the larval stage is absent with small adults hatching from eggs laid on the shore. The European Cowrie *Trivia monacha*, around 1cm, has a shiny shell and feeds on ascidians like *Botryllus*. The sea slugs (Nudibranchs) become more diverse in this zone.

The limpet *Patella vulgata* is still common across the lower shore but other species do occur. *P. intermedia* has a dark foot whilst that of *P. ulyssiponensis* is yellow orange. The latter can be double the size of the former – at 60cm it is the most abundant limpet in the lower shore of wave-exposed shores. Blue-rayed Limpet *Ansates* (*Patella*) *pellucida* is a 0.5–1.5cm translucent individual with blue lines radiating down the brown shell. Adult individuals are common on the blades of kelp where they rasp away depressions, feeding as they go. The young appear to be unable to eat kelp and start life on Serrated Wrack and *Chondrus*, moving to kelp as they mature. During their life they move extensively and may enter the holdfast and commence eating the base of the stipe from the inside, eventually weakening the structure. It could be that the ones entering the holdfast are a subspecies variant (var. *laevis*) and by being protected here will escape an early death when the kelps shed their fronds in autumn. Subsequently, though, weakened holdfasts will cause the entire kelp to be lost in storm conditions.

Fig. 2.121 European Cowrie *Trivia monacha*, feeding on Ascidian colony.

Fig. 2.122 *Limacia clavigera*.

Fig. 2.123 Sea Lemon *Doris pseudargus*.

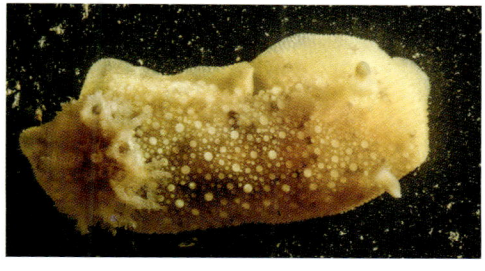

Fig. 2.124 Limpet *Patella ulyssiponensis* encrusted with red algae.

Fig. 2.125 Underside of two limpet species: (left) *P. intermedia* and (right) *P. ulyssiponensis* with distinct yellow-orange foot.

Fig. 2.126 Blue-rayed Limpet *Ansates pellucida* on kelp frond.

Fig. 2.127 Blue-rayed Limpets living under the stipe and within the holdfast of *L. digitata*.

Arthropods

Many of the species found in the lower shore community will be here like the *Xantho* and *Necora* crabs. A relative of *Xantho* is the Hairy Crab *Pilumnus hirtellus*. This small, omnivorous crab, 15mm long, is common inside the holdfast of the kelp and under stones. Sea spiders or Pycnogonids are found in holdfasts and associated with fringe weeds where they feed on sponges, hydroids and bryozoans. *Pycnogonum litorale* is one of the more visible species and feeds on anemones. They are related rather distantly to arachnids but do look a little spider-like (*Nymphon*, especially, being extremely narrow with long legs). They extend up into the middle shore in pools. Most sea spiders are easily overlooked as they are small, some just a few millimetres long. All move very slowly over the substrate.

Fig. 2.128 Hairy Crab *Pilumnus hirtellus*.

Fig. 2.129 Sea Spider *Anoplodactylus*.

Fig. 2.130 Sea Spider *Achelia*.

Fig. 2.131 Sea Spider *Pycnogonum litorale*.

Rocky Shores

Fig. 2.132
Edible Sea Urchin *Echinus esculentus*.

Fig. 2.133
Green Sea Urchin *Psammechinus miliaris*.

Fig. 2.134
Common Starfish *Asterias rubens* beginning to feed on a mussel.

Fig. 2.135
Bloody Henry *Henricia oculata*.

Echinoderms

Echinoderm species in general are found in this region as none can survive long out of water. The tube feet enable them to attach to the substrate in the surf. Edible Sea Urchin *Echinus esculentus*, 6–12cm diameter, is affected adversely by high temperatures and in southern regions of the British Isles is restricted to deep water. Due to its large size it represents the most important grazer since it can cause considerable damage to the kelp forest. Green Sea Urchin *Psammechinus miliaris* at 4cm (maximum diameter) is a more abundant urchin, found higher on the shore, particularly around *Corallina* where it feeds on both plant and animals. These include barnacles, mussels, sponges and hydroids.

Common Starfish *Asterias rubens*, 5–30cm is widely distributed and on occasions can reach almost plague proportions when severe damage to mussel beds can occur. The tube feet are used in feeding as well as for attachment to the rock and movement. It feeds by inverting the stomach onto food which consists of soft bodied animals, e.g. sponges, sea squirts, hydroids. Bivalves like mussels have the shells opened by the tube feet on the 'arms'. This results in digestion outside of the body. The sexes are separate with fertilization being external to produce plankton larvae. Other starfish that could be found here are several very similar species that are difficult to tell apart, sometimes referred to as Bloody Henry *Henricia* species. They vary in colour but can be intense blood-red through pinks and orange. They may be detrital feeders, collecting particles with mucus or feed by everting the stomach onto sponges and hydroids.

Fig. 2.136
Brittle Star *Ophiothrix fragilis*.

Fig. 2.137
Sea-gherkin *Pawsonia saxicola*.

Brittle stars resemble starfish but the arms break off if handled roughly. They filter water of plankton and detritus; larger ones feed on dead animals. Small individuals, less than a centimetre in diameter, can be extremely common although easily overlooked amongst fringe weeds and holdfasts.

Sea Cucumbers are strange organisms and the species Sea-gherkin *Pawsonia saxicola* may be encountered under stones in the lower shore. Usually small ones occur here, a few centimetres or so, but do grow up to 15cm in length. The smooth, white body has black tentacles. It is a suspension feeder.

Sea squirts
Also known as tunicates, these represent a large group of animals that are closely related to animals with backbones possessing some characters of the Chordata. Attached to a hard substrate, the body is essentially covered in a sac or test (the tunic) with two siphons to draw water in and out. *Ciona intestinalis* is a common solitary species whilst others like the Star Ascidian *Botryllus schlosseri* are found in colonies. The latter are coloured blue, yellow or brown and the tiny individuals (called zooids) are collectively held inside the test. The small colonies may spread over rocks and seaweeds. The Light Bulb Ascidian *Clavelina lepadiformis* is another solitary species and is transparent so the bright internal structures can be seen. Like so many organisms found lower down the shore, they feed on material suspended in the water by filter feeding.

See also sea anemones, hydroids, sea slugs, bryozoans, mussels, crabs and polychaete worms.

Fig. 2.138
Star Ascidian *Botryllus schlosseri*.

Fig. 2.139
Light Bulb Ascidian *Clavelina lepadiformis*.

Rocky Shores

Part 2: Ecology of the shore

ZONATION OF BROWN SEAWEEDS ON A SHELTERED ROCKY SHORE.

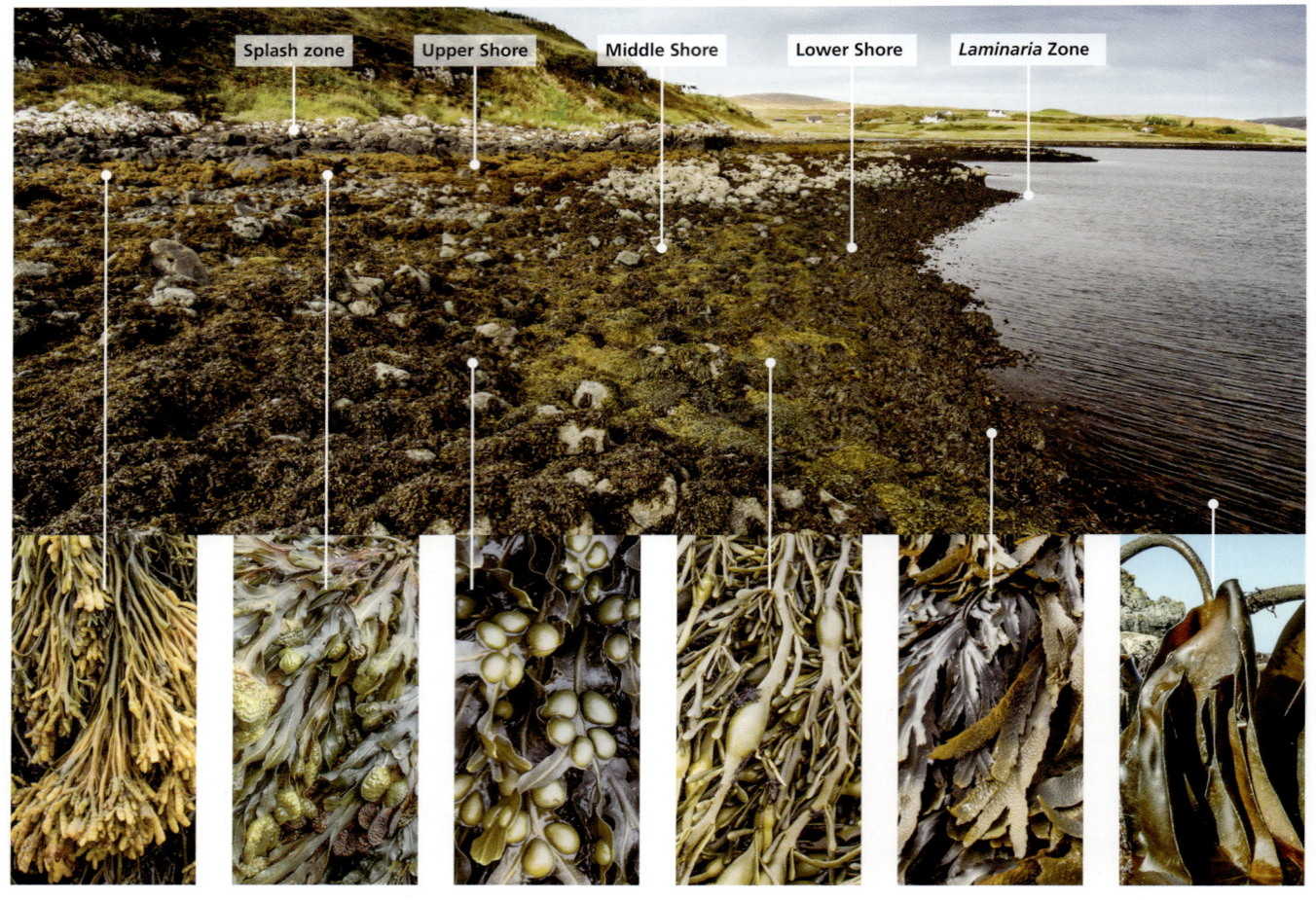

Splash zone — Upper Shore — Middle Shore — Lower Shore — *Laminaria* Zone

Fig. 2.140.1 Channel Wrack
Fig. 2.140.2 Spiral Wrack
Fig. 2.140.3 Bladder Wrack
Fig. 2.140.4 Knotted Wrack
Fig. 2.140.5 Serrated Wrack
Fig. 2.140.6 *Laminaria*

	Channel Wrack	Spiral Wrack	Knotted Wrack	Bladder Wrack	Serrated Wrack	Kelp
Cell wall thickness/μm	1.2	1.47	1.02	0.69	0.42	–
Metabolism recovery after reimmersion	95%	49%	35%	20%	0	0
Wavelength of light for full photosynthesis	–	–	–	600	500	150
Reproduction	Hermaphrodite	Hermaphrodite	Separate sexes	Separate sexes	Separate sexes	Separate sexes

Zonation of the rocky shore

General features

No other environment on earth has such a huge cross-section of variety from all the kingdoms of life as the rocky seashore. From the simplest ancient organisms of bacteria and cyanobacteria, through complex algae to rooted plants in the splash zone; even fungi are there symbiotically as lichens. There are representatives of almost all animal groups, whether single-celled protists, simple multi-celled sponges or chordates with back bones. It is an exciting place to study ecology as this biodiversity forms into clear and varied communities. Even from a distance of a kilometre some of these can be observed at low tide in the form of bands in the cliff of exposed shores. These are biological zones, in particular the dark tar lichens of the splash zone, the grey barnacles down the middle of the shore and the dark brown kelps at the base. On sheltered shores this may not be so obvious, with seaweeds covering the entire littoral region, but a close examination will reveal the communities that have made up the chapter so far: splash zone, upper, middle and lower shore. This banding of communities is zonation and is due to the environmental

ZONATION OF PERIWINKLES AND TOPSHELLS

Fig. 2.141.1 Small Periwinkle
Fig. 2.141.2 Rough Periwinkle 
Fig. 2.141.3 Edible Periwinkle 
Fig. 2.141.4 Purple Topshell 
Fig. 2.141.5 Flat Periwinkle 
Fig. 2.141.6 Painted Topshell 

	Small Periwinkle	Rough Periwinkle	Edible Periwinkle Purple Topshell	Flat Periwinkle	Painted Topshell
Nitrogenous excretory product	uric acid	uric acid	ammonia	ammonia	ammonia
Main diet	lichens	lichens/micro-algae	micro/macro-algae	*Fucus* spp.	red/green algae, some animal
Lethal temp limit °C	46.3	45	Winkle: 46 Topshell: 42	44	34.5
Water loss/day as % of body weight	3.7%	5.6%	5.35%	8.35%	–

Fig. 2.142
A moderately sheltered shore with large numbers of wracks, small splash zone and a pale, barnacle-encrusted area. The latter shows that some wave action occurs and this variation leads to the highest biodiversity compared to exposed or very sheltered shores.

gradient which occurs up and down the shore. No one reason accounts for the zonation patterns: they are the result of interactions between a number of physical, chemical and biotic factors.

In addition to community zonation down the shore, other changes occur. For example, productivity (biomass) is low on the upper shore but increases towards the lower shore. Descending the shore there is an increase in species diversity and community complexity which in turn increases the competition towards the lower shore. This is the result of the abiotic factors becoming less stressful in the lower regions for marine organisms along with a relative constancy of the environment there. Compared to air, water reduces sudden fluctuations such as in temperature. This gradation of conditions will mean the shore is more terrestrial at the top and more marine towards the bottom: adaptations of the organisms will reflect this accordingly.

Fig. 2.143
Temperatures are most variable in the upper shore, often freezing in winter and hot in the summer.

Fig. 2.144
Green areas of *Ulva* on the shore survive where freshwater streams run across the rock.

Limiting factors affecting zonation

Desiccation as a result of exposure at low tide will have a profound effect on the upper limit of a marine species' vertical range. The lower limits of a species' range are more likely to be due to biotic reasons such as competition.

Wave action increases the humidity of the atmosphere and increases the upper limit of species. The middle shore tends to have the highest degree of wave action on the shore (the damage caused by the punch of a wave). Wave action in the lower shore is more surging.

Light is needed for photosynthesis. All seaweeds need to be in water for this to occur. The water will alter the wavelengths of light and reduce the intensity. Smaller algae, for example, the red algae, will photosynthesize with 10 per cent of the light required by the brown algae. The compensation point for *Laminaria* is only 320 lux of light, whilst a typical land plant is nearer 1,800 lux.

Temperature: immersion in water buffers against temperature change so upper shore species will have to tolerate the greatest variation. It will also affect the rate of metabolism. Bladder Wrack can just respire at −17°C, *Ulva* at −22°C with 17°C optimum. High temperatures will increase drying out and increase salinity in pools due to water evaporation.

Aspect is the direction the shore faces. A southern aspect has more illumination and warmth but dries faster; a northern aspect is cooler and darker. Thus on a north-facing slope, community bands will be higher up. Some species like the red alga *Catenella* can survive high on a northern aspect shore.

Slope: a flatter shore will expose a greater area of substrate for colonizing and will not drain as quickly as a steeper one.

Turbidity is the cloudiness of the water. Large amounts of plankton can increase the turbidity, as will detritus and sewage pollution. This restricts the intensity of light reaching the algae on the rocks but increases food for suspension feeders.

Substrate: the hardness and particle size of rock will influence the ability of an organism to attach itself. Soft rocks will be suitable for burrowers, e.g. piddocks. Large boulders and rocks give greater shelter for animals and the angle of the rock strata may produce more crevices and pools.

Fresh water: seepage of water from the cliff can dilute the seawater. Few of the organisms on the shore can tolerate salinity changes. *Ulva* is so tolerant it is a good indicator of fresh water on rocky shores. The Common Shore Crab can tolerate changes in salinity for short periods. Upper shore rockpools are particularly vulnerable to salinity variation.

Biotic factors: these are the biological factors influencing the community. Grazing is perhaps the most important to consider, where herbivores will often determine the presence or absence of the dominant seaweeds, e.g. a high density of limpets will limit the capacity of wracks to become established. Algal turf, like *Osmundia* and *Chondrus*, will slow down the drainage on the shore and reduce desiccation. The fucoids have a 'whiplash' effect, which is where water movement causes a sweeping action of the algae across the substrate and prevents the attachment of spores and larvae. Competition is an important biotic factor and is discussed below.

Interspecific competition

This is competition between different species. Better feeding efficiency and reproductive rates in certain conditions will help the winner. But if conditions were to vary, hitherto successful specializations become a hindrance. *F. spiralis* will shade *Pelvetia* on the upper shore, *Ascophyllum* shades out *F. vesiculosus* in the middle and Laminarians with a flexible stipe outcompete those with the rigid variety. The whiplash from the fucoids prevents barnacles from growing around their base. (If barnacles do develop, their calcareous plates can grow across the rock and cut the seaweed's holdfast, causing it to detach.) Two species of barnacle, *Chthamalus* and *Semibalanus*, compete for space in the upper and middle shores. The former is more tolerant of drying as it has a non-porous shell, an operculum, high temperature tolerance and larvae settle out of the plankton on just a film of water. Hence, it is found on the highest part of the beach. As it merges with the *Semibalanus* population

Fig. 2.145
Spiral Wrack competing in a rockpool to reach the light.

Fig. 2.146
Beadlet Anemones on an overhang of rock evenly spaced.

it begins to lose the battle because all those specializations are at the expense of growing slowly. The shell of *Semibalanus* is porous but quick to grow and soon displaces the competitor. *Semibalanus* is restricted by dogwhelk predation. Competition in overlapping niches has led to zonation of the barnacles.

Intraspecific competition

Competition is greatest amongst members of the same species as their resource requirements are most similar. Older seaweeds will shade out younger ones which try to develop below their fronds. Only on the death of the older plant will spores have a chance to grow. Animals usually have the ability to move away from a competitor and in this instance we see territorial behaviour. Beadlet Anemones are aggressive to each other and have been shown to butt each other over a period of time, with the weaker individual moving away. Anemones on an overhang of rock may be seen to have a regular distribution pattern – all a similar distance apart.

Rocky Shores

Vertical range and adaptations of organisms

Organisms are rarely able to live in a variety of environmental conditions, having adapted to a narrow range of conditions by natural selection so that each has its own specific niche. Spores and larvae may be deposited on any part of the seashore but they will only develop if the environmental conditions are favourable enough to let them. For example, Laminarian spores do settle on the upper shore whilst *Pelvetia* spores settle on the lower. Survival is unlikely for any length of time because *Laminaria* cannot survive drying and *Pelvetia* could not cope with the competition; where one species performs well another will find conditions lethal. In this way organisms become partitioned into zones where they do best. There will be some overlap and where this occurs each organism is at the edge of its niche, that is at the limit of the conditions which it can tolerate. In this situation the specimens we find may not be typical of their type but poorly developed variations. For example, mussels on the upper shore are small as they do not obtain enough food; Bladder Wrack exposed to strong wave action may not have any bladders.

Sessile or sedentary organisms tend to be more highly specialized than mobile ones. Barnacles are the only species that can maintain life at 50°C. Mobile animals can move away from stressful situations; fish move with the tide and crabs will shelter under rocks. Zonation in animals is best seen in static species, which, like the algae, are anchored to the rock and must tolerate the local micro-climate. Animals that do move have the problem of possibly straying from their niche.

Supply-side ecology: the species living on the shore and the zonation that occurs is, principally, down to whether young stages, e.g. spores or larvae, are available to colonize. The longevity of a larva living in the plankton is limited and if these stages do not arrive in time then the species will not occur. This is why there are remote areas of the world missing key species. An extreme example may be the Galapagos Islands, a thousand kilometres away from other land in the Pacific; the larvae of many molluscs, particularly limpets, die before reaching the isles. In the absence of these molluscs there is an available niche. The iguanas that did reach the islands have evolved a unique marine form and they graze on algae, something not found anywhere else on the planet. The study of life cycles, dispersal and the recruitment of new individuals to a population is termed 'supply-side ecology'.

In many cases these young stages can be initially distributed by the tide throughout the habitat. Additionally some will be chemically attracted to existing populations, e.g. barnacles; others will settle wherever they find space. It will then be down to local conditions whether they survive or not. If there is insufficient water (too high on the shore) they die. If there is inadequate light for an algal spore (too low on the shore) they die. If an alga begins to grow where there are high densities of limpets, it will die by being grazed unless it happens to land on the shell. Then it might survive if the limpet is in a pool that provides water to the young seaweed. Some settling larvae, e.g. Edible Periwinkle, have the capacity to move to find better conditions. Abiotic and biotic factors determine whether the young stage will grow and fit within the zonation patterns that we observe. The exceptions help to prove the rule and individuals will be found outside of what we might consider their zone due to localized variations in the conditions, for example in pools or crevices.

Maintenance of zonation position is crucial. Animal movements are controlled by taxes (responses to light, gravity and humidity) which change, often with the state of the tide. This helps to keep the organism in the conditions which suit it best. Edible Periwinkles constantly stray from their niche but reactions to light and gravity stimulate it back to its optimum position. Resources in an ecosystem, e.g. space, light and food, are limited, and organisms compete for these resources. Specializations like a faster growth rate will help the competitor to win and dominate over its rival in a constant environment.

Features of the wave-exposed rocky shore

Although reference has been made to wave action in this chapter the communities that have been considered so far represent the most typical from moderately sheltered and exposed shores. 'Fetch' is a term referring to the distance of open water with no barriers. Seashores facing the Atlantic, such as those on the west coast of the British Isles, can expect severe exposure to wave action as the fetch over which the wind can pick up energy is many thousands of kilometres. Headlands and wave-cut platforms will show signs of the extreme action of the waves. The main elements to observe are:

Fig. 2.147 Marine Iguana in the Galapagos Islands, feeding on seaweed.

Fig. 2.148
Wave action eliminates species, typically predators, unable to cope with the wave force, reducing diversity. This leaves grazers and suspension feeders, e.g. limpets and barnacles, to dominate; intense grazing removes macro-algae. In sheltered conditions, macro-algae do not have to contend with these forces and grow well; predators, e.g. crabs, thrive feeding on the grazers. Compare Figures 2.142 and 2.150.

Fig. 2.149
Zonation on a wave-exposed headland with no obvious wracks and dominated by barnacles and lichens. Note the very extensive splash zone; this photo was taken on a calm day.

- *Verrucaria* and Rough Periwinkle zone is very extensive.
- There is poor growth of seaweed and therefore low productivity.
- Biodiversity is generally lower than sheltered shores as it is a difficult place to live favouring attached rather than mobile organisms.
- There is an absence of fucoid algae (wracks), these being replaced by a barnacle zone.
- The lower limit of the barnacles may be determined by over-predation by Dogwhelks.
- Mussels and occasionally Beadlet Anemones are in crevices.
- The tough, red, calcareous coralline weeds form the dominant algae of the shore.
- The limpet *Patella ulyssiponensis* (which has a thicker shell than *P. vulgata*) is able to withstand a greater force and feed on the red coralline seaweeds.
- Attached *Laminaria*, with their large holdfasts, and encroaching replacement by Dabberlocks *Alaria esculenta*, which has a very strong midrib.
- On a more gradual slope Thongweed *Himanthalia elongata* will form a zone near the red algal zone.

Fig. 2.149
Close-up of a wave-exposed shore. There is some wrack on the upper shore.

Rocky Shores

Fig. 2.151
Close-up of a wave-exposed shore. There is some wrack in the upper shore.

THE EFFECT OF WAVE ACTION ON ZONATION

Sheltered conditions | Exposed conditions | Wave action

Fig. 2.151.2
Larger splash zone. Channel Wrack and a small amount of Spiral surviving in the upper shore but no other wracks; instead dominated by Limpets and Barnacles. Where freshwater stream runs down the shore grow Green *Ulva* and the Horned Wrack *F. ceranoides*.

Fig. 2.151.3
Large splash zone and no wracks. Only strongly-attached animals are present, e.g. Barnacles.

Fig. 2.151.1
Small splash zone and most of the tidal rock area covered with wracks.

The effect of wave action on zonation

The increased or decreased action of waves will have a modifying effect on the communities we have seen so far, changing the species such that they may be unrecognizable. Some of the differences are covered here.

Zonation under these conditions will be very clear due to the reduction in species but what is not immediately obvious is that the position of the zones will be displaced up the shore relative to chart datum. Spray from the waves will increase the humidity on the shore so that desiccation is less of a problem and algae and animals survive further up the beach. The easiest to see will be an extension of the splash zone. Spray helps the lichens, especially the tar lichen, to grow higher and more expansively on the cliff, which in turn gives a greater area for the Rough Periwinkle to feed. The surging of water can even permit barnacles to live above the normal tidal limit. The *Laminaria* will be clearly visible at low tide unlike on sheltered shores where the desiccation risk keeps them submerged.

The difficulty in holding onto the rocks under these conditions may change a species dominance in the community by removal of competitor species. For example, a large surface area is a disadvantage with wave action and Serrated Wrack becomes rarer until it disappears, fa-

Rocky Shores

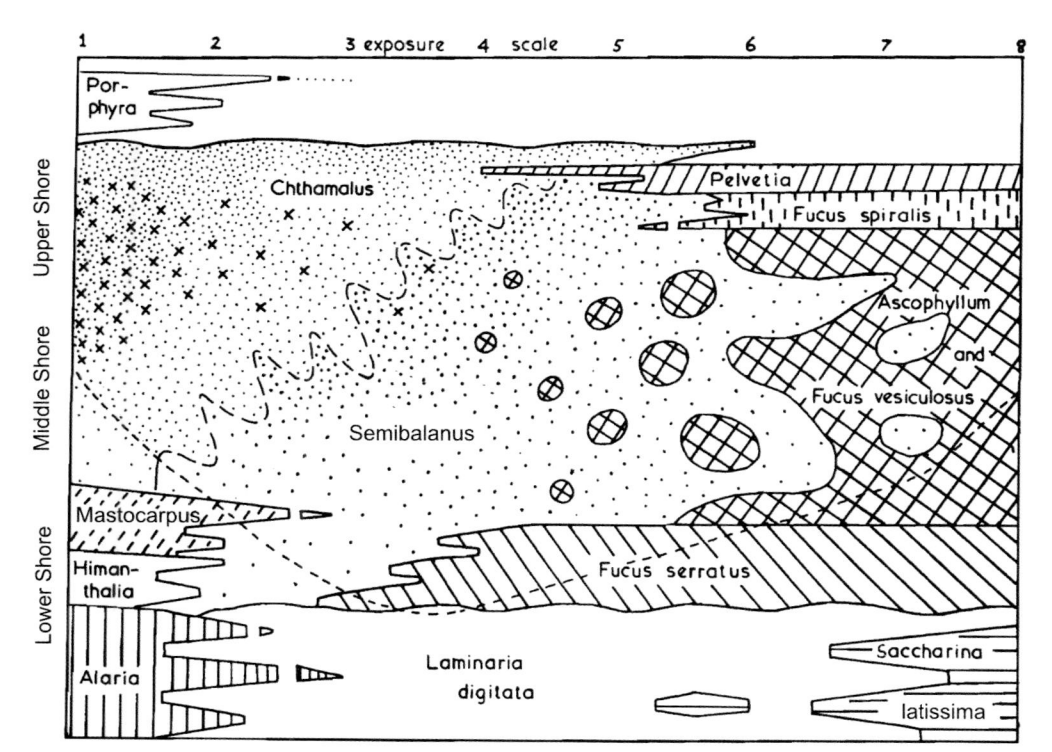

Fig. 2.152
Ballantine's Exposure Scale.
(Reproduced by permission of the Field Studies Council)

vouring the more strap-like Thongweed. Knotted Wrack cannot survive strong wave action and the bladderless form of Bladder Wrack takes over. Even the tough kelps may be replaced by Dabberlocks in extremes.

Limpets' shells are sensitive to wave action and their longevity is reduced by high environmental stress. This can increase metabolism and affect feeding behaviour resulting in death after four to five years (compared to seventeen years in sheltered conditions). *Patella ulyssiponensis* is the limpet best able to survive here with the strongest attachment, although its presence is also down to the ability to feed on the coralline weeds that can dominate the rock here. Biofilm will be present but will be severely reduced by the waves. Biofilm production is at its height in very sheltered shores. Waves batter the softer, large seaweeds and they may be unable to remain attached. This is why the tougher, mainly calcareous, small and slow-growing seaweeds survive. The firmly attached barnacles and mussels will increase in density as they can hold on and have more space available with less weed growth.

With the conditions favouring those species that are well attached it may seem strange that dogwhelks, which need to move over the surface to feed on barnacles and mussels, are present. They show a distinct change in the shape of the shell and they adapt musculature to provide strength up to five times that of dogwhelks in low-energy areas. On sheltered shores they become longer, have a narrower operculum and the edge of the shell can be thick to protect against predation by crabs. Mobile creatures like crabs cannot survive wave action on exposed shores and this latter adaptation is unnecessary in the dogwhelks. Needing to hold tight, they have a much wider opening or operculum so that increased muscle in the foot can emerge through the broad shell to grip the substrate. The shell is not as long, since the tip tends to become eroded.

Unlike the tides, there is no simple method of predicting or measuring the level of wave action on a shore. However, the biologist Bill Ballantine developed a scale based on the organisms that are permanent residents, that is, having to tolerate the conditions from one year to the next. This is an example of using indicator species to signify the environmental conditions. Ballantine Exposure Scale (BES) goes from 1 to 8, extreme wave action to extreme shelter, respectively. Finding a rocky shore representing BES 8 can be difficult as with increasing shelter sediments become deposited and often the lower shore is very sandy. However, they are present on the edge of sea lochs and fjords where the steepness of the slope prevents the build up of sediment. These shores will be covered with wrack seaweed and have a very narrow lichen band and splash zone. By contrast the extreme conditions of a BES 1 has no sign of seaweed except for the spring low tide mark where Dabberlocks grow. Barnacles dominate the shore. Compare the examples of shores shown here with the diagram of the exposure scale, Fig. 2.152.

Fig. 2.153 Tidal rapids, flowing for a mile from an enclosed sea loch.

Fig. 2.154 Wide tidal rapids at low tide.

Fig. 2.155 The underside of a rock from the centre of a tidal rapid showing a wide diversity of encrusting organisms.

Tidal rapids

Tidal rapids occur wherever a body of seawater, such as a marine lake, is contained by a narrow exit point constricting the flow of tidal water to the sea. The speed of flow will depend on the state of the tide. Neap tides will have reduced flow compared to spring tides. On a high spring tide the lake becomes full. As the sea level outside the lake drops water flows through the constriction becoming ever faster the further the outside level drops. As the height difference between the outer and inner areas reaches maximum the speed can be very rapid, only easing to a stop as the sea level outside rises once more to equalize the levels.

Unlike with normal wave action, with tidal rapids there are no sudden 'punches' of energy. As long as the organisms can resist or tolerate the drag of the current by hanging on during the worst of the flow there are many benefits. The flow produces a continuous supply of nutrient-rich water for algae. Suspension feeding animals that filter the water of plankton and detritus will likewise have a plentiful food supply. Mobile creatures like echinoderms will be able to feed during quieter periods and can hold on with tube feet as they would in the surge of the lower shore. Crabs and molluscs hide during the very rapid periods and emerge to feed when it lessens.

Tidal rapids are a remarkable and diverse rocky shore habitat and tend to be found in the western coasts of Europe. The most famous example is Lough Hyne which was designated as Ireland's first Marine Nature Reserve in 1981 in the south-west of the country. The Hebrides of Scotland have a number of good examples, and like Lough Hyne can be 20–30 metres in length, or more. Examining the rocks in the lower shore of tidal rapids can be very rewarding as they are encrusted with huge numbers of hydroids, sponges and tunicates, which attract a suitably large collection of predators. However, care should be taken as the speed of flow can increase while you are engrossed.

Rockpools

When the tide goes out it will leave pockets of water trapped in hollows and depressions to produce distinct rockpool communities. For some species this will enable them to survive further up the shore. For example, in spring it is possible to find kelp growing in the middle and upper shore, but high temperatures in summer will kill it. Serrated Wrack can invariably be found in rockpools of the middle shore. At low tide many organisms will use the pool for shelter as well as to combat desiccation. Purple Topshells can feed out on the rocks at low tide but during this time they will lose water and their temperature will rise. They may have a quick dip in a pool to refresh – but with care as pools will host predatory crabs and fish.

As well as biotic issues there will be added abiotic ones. Not all the species discussed previously will be found in the pools as these pockets of still water can exclude them. It may be that they are already specialized for their niche, and life in the rockpool will require additional adaptations for survival. The limiting factors operating in a zone will not necessarily apply to the rockpools there and the difference in conditions may modify the community composition.

Conversely there will be species more likely to occur in the pools. Coralline seaweeds form a fringe of weed

Fig. 2.156
Small pool from the middle shore. It is surrounded by barnacles but they are absent in the pool which is dominated by encrusting red algae. Limpets graze all other algae away so that the only other growth is on their shells where they cannot reach.ç

Fig. 2.157
Upper shore pools are dominated by *Ulva intestinalis* which are tolerant of fresh water entering the pool. Low salinity prevents grazers like limpets from surviving and it is the lack of grazing that allows the *Ulva* to grow unhindered.

Fig. 2.158
With sufficient depth fringe weeds border the pool, here the graze-tolerant *Corallina* red alga. With reduced numbers of limpets Sea Lettuce grows well. Note the difference between the organisms within and outside the pool.

Fig. 2.159
Shallow pool with large numbers of Edible Periwinkles which selectively feed on Sea Lettuce. Some Irish Moss is present; otherwise it is dominated by graze-resistant seaweeds. The encrusting red is bleached a pale pink as it is exposed to full sunlight.

Fig. 2.160
Deep pools from middle to lower shore may be dominated by Sea Oak *Halidrys siliquosa*, shading out the pool, but there may be large numbers of small algae and animals attached. Thongweed is growing (top right) and in the sheltered conditions loses the strap nature seen elsewhere.

Fig. 2.161
Snakeslock Anemone *Anemonia viridis* (grey form) clones itself to cover large areas of pools.

Fig. 2.162
Snakeslock Anemone (green form). Here *Zooxanthellae* algae live in the tissue carrying out photosynthesis as it basks in the sun.

around the perimeter as they are resistant to grazing. With them being permanently under water they become coated in diatoms and biofilm which encourages a micro-fauna over the surface. These dense stands of seaweed will be good hiding places for small spider crabs and other crustaceans. Deep rockpools will have their own vertical zonation of algae. The size of pool will have an effect, which may be increasing diversity with increase in size. Most of the limiting factors relating to rockpools will be strongly influenced by the length of time it is standing before the tide returns and by the ambient shore climate.

Rocky Shores

Fig. 2.163
Young chiton *Acanthochitona crinatus* in a rockpool during mid-winter instead of out on the rocks where it would have less chance of surviving in the low air temperature.

Fig. 2.164
Prawn *Palaemon*.

Limiting factors operating in rockpools

Temperature: high air temperatures in summer heat the water, affecting the dissolving of gases in water as well as increasing evaporation. In winter, upper shore rock pools may freeze especially where they contain freshwater runoff.

Salinity: increased evaporation will cause the salinity to rise whilst rainwater dilutes the seawater. Either will cause an osmotic stress for the organisms because few seashore creatures have the ability to regulate the body fluid concentration. The Common Shore Crab *Carcinus* is one of the exceptions as it has an organ at the base of the antennae which removes excess water. Many marine worms can tolerate the changes until the sea returns. Upper shore pools are more likely to have dilute seawater (brackish water) because of water running off the land.

Oxygen and pH levels: the amount of dissolved oxygen varies with temperature and the degree of photosynthesis. In sunlight it is easy to see bubbles of oxygen on the fringe weeds. By late afternoon this slows, stopping completely at night. The balance between respiration and photosynthesis also affects the carbon dioxide content. Carbon dioxide produces an acid in water and its addition and subtraction from the water changes the pH. Too much dissolved oxygen will slow down photosynthesis (called the Warburg effect) and seaweeds high up will reach their peak rate by mid-morning. A decline in photosynthesis then occurs.

Organic matter: rockpools will trap dead and decaying organisms, and seaweeds washed in from the lower shore often become caught, particularly after a storm. This attracts scavenging animals. Prawns are typically found here as well as most of the detritus-eating Crustacea. Prolonged periods of decay in upper shore pools may eradicate oxygen completely, rendering them anoxic and therefore free of all but the most highly specialized organisms.

Organisms of the rockpools

Upper shore: these pools will be dominated by *Ulva* species as they are most tolerant of temperature extremes as well as ionic changes due to the lower salinity. Channel Wrack is notably absent. In fact a pool dominant in *Ulva* may substantially alter the chemical composition so much that it will exclude wracks and *Chondrus*. Both *Carcinus* and the prawns, *Palaemon*, can osmoregulate and may survive here.

Middle Shore: Serrated Wrack may grow well but few other lower shore species do. The encrusting red corallines and *Corallina* both grow, particularly if shaded.

Fig. 2.165
Hermit Crab: common in rockpools they often have a covering on the shell, here a sponge *Suberites*.

Fig. 2.166
Hermit Crab: shell is covered in a hydroid colony of *Hydractinia*. Beneficial to both animals, the host has increased crypsis and the sessile animal on the shell is moved ensuring fresh supplies of enriched water for filter feeding.

They may dominate on more exposed shores and give their name to the type of pool. Many small, delicate species perform well in these pools, e.g. *Ceramium*, *Chondrus*, *Nemalion*, *Scytosiphon*. The sides of the pools will have the most abundant growth, of fringe weeds, in some cases as limpet grazing may be restricted. The floor will be grazed clear except for encrusting red algae. Small weeds will grow on the shells of the limpets – the only place they will not be consumed. Shallow pools will be colonized by the Snakeslock Anemone. The green form contains symbiotic algae living in the tentacles. In bright sunshine the plant will be able to produce food for both. Barnacles are absent from rockpools, producing a clear dividing line near the edge. This may be due to problems with larval settlement or competition with the sheltered rockpool species.

Lower shore: with the displacement of organisms up the shore in these desiccation-free pools sub-littoral species will colonize the lower shore. 'Copses' of kelp live in the deeper ones with the much branched Sea Oak *Halidrys siliquosa*. These pools may have echinoderms and octopus more typical of offshore habitats. Fish will include a variety of pipe fish and hermit crabs. Smaller individuals of the latter will occur in pools higher up the shore.

Feeding mechanisms of animals

Summary of methods

Plankton and detritus feeders: these animals can be called both suspension or filter feeders as they collect what is suspended in the water and invariably require some form of filtration method. Many are selective over what is consumed and this may depend on particle size. Species in this category include mussels, using their gills; barnacles by combing the water with their hairy limbs; porcelain crabs trap debris in the hairs on the pincers; sponges absorb water through the surface and waste is sent out through common pores called osculae; sedentary polychaete worms have long tentacles covered with mucus which is moved by beating cilia towards the mouth; sea squirts with a perforated pharynx; brittle stars using cilia on their arms.

Debris feeders: these are primarily large scavengers such as crabs that use complex cutting mouthparts and pincers. Prawns, like *Palaemon elegans*, are a more delicate scavenger in rockpools with smaller pincers.

Biofilm grazers: primarily the molluscs with varying types of radula or tongue.

Seaweed grazers: these are in the minority with Flat Periwinkles being the principal species using a radula with teeth for rasping.

Predators: this diverse category includes many crabs. Others are sea anemones and hydroids, which paralyse prey with nematocysts before ingestion; dogwhelk are shell borers with a radula and chemicals; starfish can open shell with their tube feet and digest the food with an inverted gut; cuttlefish and octopus capture prey with suckers on the tentacles and then bite with a beak in the mouth; blenny uses teeth on powerful jaw; cormorant and gulls catch prey in the beak and swallow whole.

Fig. 2.167
The parasite *Sacculina*, a small, yellow sac under the abdomen of a Shore Crab.

Fig. 2.168
Knotted Wrack floating at mid-tide on a sheltered shore.

Effect of predation and grazing on community diversity

The species richness within a habitat will depend on food preferences, and the intensity of grazing and predation. Where a limited number of grazers and predators exist then richness will be poor. If an area of shore has a range of different grazers and predators it can lead to a high richness of species. However, there is a threshold beyond which over grazing and predation will cause a rapid decline in richness. For example, over grazing prevents young algal stages reaching maturity.

Edible periwinkles are selective feeders on young seaweed with a preference for *Ulva*. This weed can dominate pools and areas of the shore. Removal of *Ulva* by grazing permits other species to colonize the rocks. The presence of Bladder Wrack in a pool will often be down to the presence of the periwinkle grazing out *Ulva*. When populations of dogwhelks declined in the 1970s and 1980s, so did the variety of species on the shore – as a result, mussels frequently dominated.

Epi-fauna and parasitism

Considering close relationships between species we have already come across symbiosis in lichens and anemones. Here it has been a harmonious association with both partners benefiting. Looking at *Corallina* fronds under the microscope reveals a complex world of epi-fauna, that is a micro-community of animals living on the surface such as attached tube worms and bryozoans. These are using the seaweed as a substrate on which to grow with the algae benefiting little. Bryozoans are a frequently found on seaweeds and some other animals and by being away from the rock surface they are more likely to receive a flow of particle-laden water on which they can feed. Seaweeds attach to other plants as a way of reaching the light and reducing competition.

Feeding relationships are inevitably one-sided; the dogwhelk kills the barnacle and consumes it in one go, then moves on to another one. It therefore lives on 'capital'. Parasitism is a nutritional method whereby the organism does not kill the prey but lives upon it, thereby living on a 'steady income'. Parasites are very specialized for this existence and invariably modify the host. Parasitism is commonplace on the shore. Some copepods are adapted as external parasites only on the surface of fish. The flukes found in the digestive gland of periwinkles are internal forms, using the mollusc as a secondary host. One extreme parasite is found on the common shore crab, *Carcinus*, and is visible externally although it derives its nutrition internally. These crabs are affected by a species of barnacle-type parasite, *Sacculina*. The name is derived from the adult female, which is a yellow sac attached to the underside of the crab's abdomen. It looks nothing like a barnacle. This sac is to help the tiny male parasite find her, penetrate the wall and then become a parasite within her body as a testis to provide sperm. Large numbers of extensions from the sac thread through the crab body for food. The release of hormones by the parasite makes physiological and behavioural changes to the crab, e.g. delaying ecdysis and stimulating them to move into deeper water.

Chapter 3
PLANKTON

Fig. 3.01
Compass Jellyfish *Chrysaora hysoscella* caught in a rockpool.

Fig. 3.02
Sea Gooseberry or Comb Jelly. Note the columns of cilia, just visible. (Photo: MC)

Introduction

Plankton are defined as aquatic creatures that cannot determine where they go but drift and are at the mercy of the water movements. Fish can generally decide where they will swim, e.g. to hunt for food, and are called nekton. A jellyfish is an example of a planktonic organism which, although capable of making pulsing movements that propel it through the water, cannot control its direction independently of the water currents. This is why mass strandings of jellyfish on a beach can occur as a strong on-shore current brings them to the edge where the tide leaves them stranded. Whilst some are large and visible, most plankton are small and microscopic. There are strong similarities between freshwater and seawater plankton but it is the latter that has the greatest variety. They can be divided into two main groups based on nutrition. The algal types, called phytoplankton, are single cells carrying out photosynthesis; the animals are called zooplankton. In addition, but outside the scope of this book, two further groups are present: the bacterioplankton (prokaryotes) and viroplankton (viruses). Plankton are a huge and important topic and a discussion of the seashore is impossible without a brief mention of the subject here in this short chapter.

Phytoplankton

It is this sector of the plankton group that is so important for photosynthesis and primary production in the oceans of the world. The principal constituent is made up of diatoms, a large algal group. Although we may see them in chains and clusters they are single-celled organisms which may remain attached when they divide through asexual means to produce two or more cells. These clusters may create the most beautiful structures like stars (e.g. *Asteroplanus*) or necklaces (e.g. *Thalassiosira*). The cell has a transparent wall called a test or frustule around it. Most importantly this is made of silica, with the cell using silicic acid to secrete the wall around it. As the name diatom might suggest, this frustule is made of two halves; one is smaller than

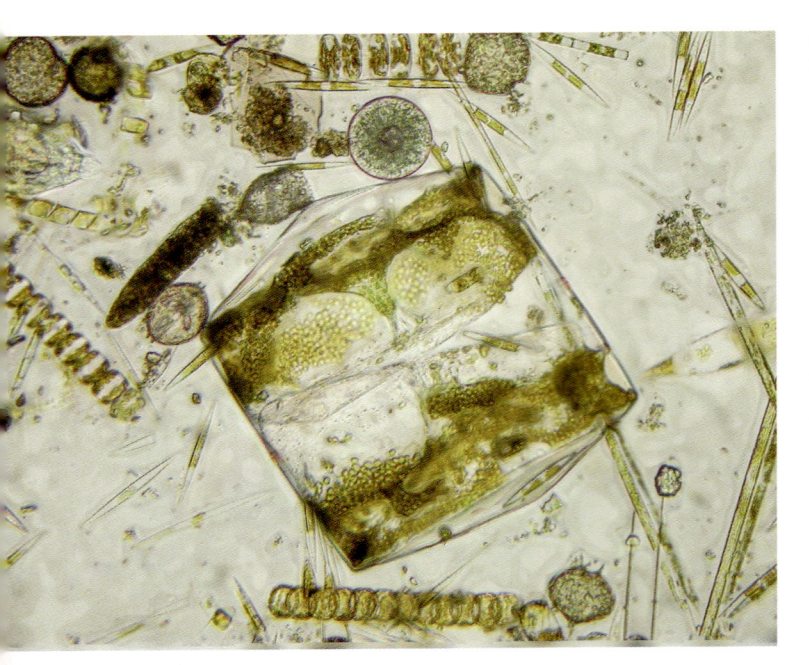

Fig. 3.03
Sample of diatoms at a magnification of more than ×100.

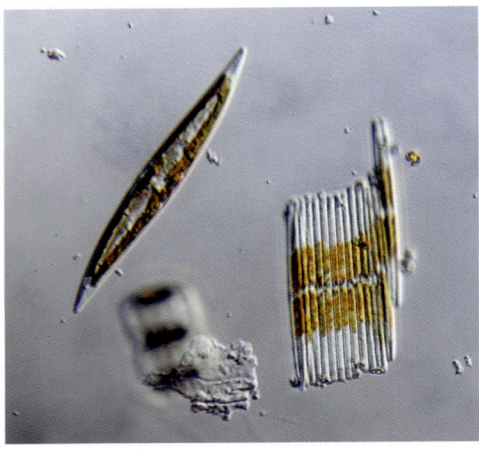

Fig. 3.05 Diatoms: Carpenter's Rule *Bacillaria paxillifer*, a diatom colony that can move. (Photo: MC)

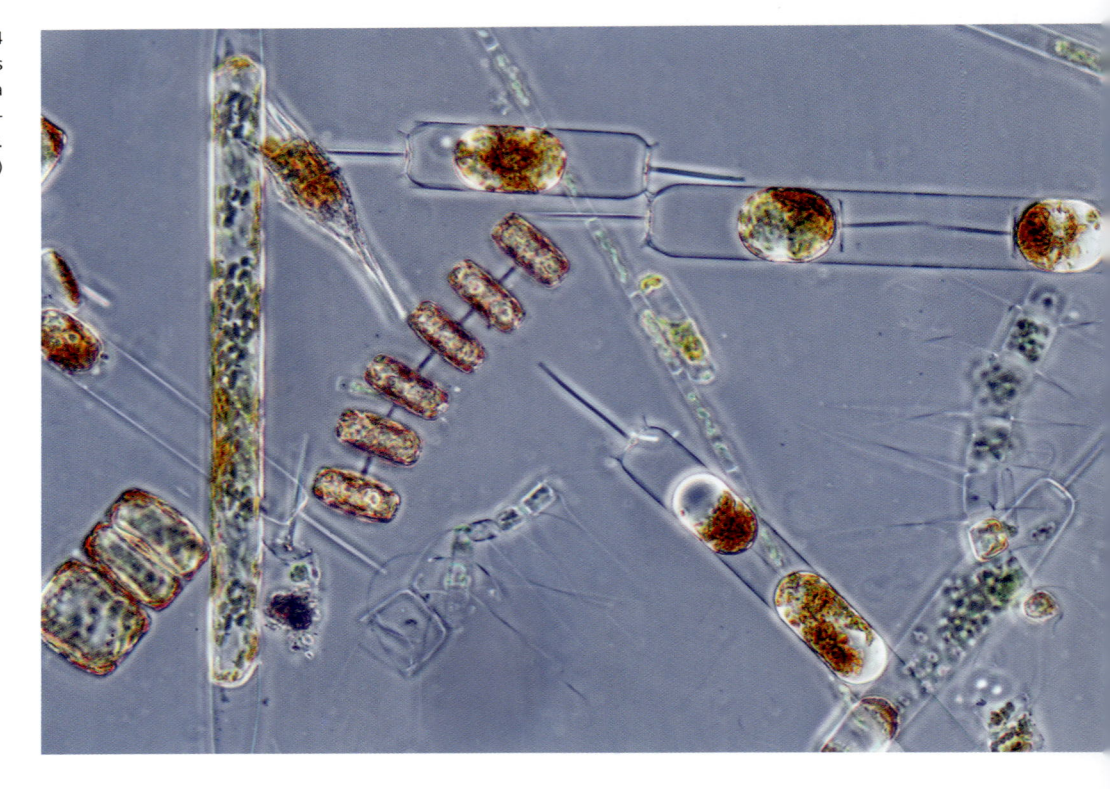

Fig. 3.04
Diatoms: the small chain is *Thalassiosira* and above this a species of *Ditylum*. Note the glass-like quality of the silica body. (Photo: MC)

the other so fits inside (this construction is often compared to a petri dish). These two halves are called valves. When a diatom divides to make two new diatoms, one valve goes to each daughter cell which then produces a new, second valve to fit inside. As it always goes inside the original, parental valve each new generation is slightly smaller. In time this results in very small diatoms. At this point it produces an auxospore by a form of sexual reproduction that restores the diatom to the original size.

Within this transparent silica wall the diatom uses chloroplasts to carry out photosynthesis. Rather than ecologists counting the density of diatoms in the water column they look at the concentration of chlorophyll. Recently, scientists have identified diatoms having the urea cycle taking place as part of its metabolism. This is very similar to animals that convert dangerous ammonia, the result of removing surplus amino acids which cannot be stored, into urea. Diatoms are variable in shape and size, and generally divided into two forms: centric diatoms which are radially symmetrical, and pennate ones, which have bilateral symmetry. The round forms are the most widely known and typical of the plankton and include some of the largest diatoms. Many forms are benthic, that is found attached to substrates like seaweeds and rock where they can develop stalks. Benthic varieties in estuarine mud exude carbohydrates that glue them together, forming dark, dense mats over

86 Plankton

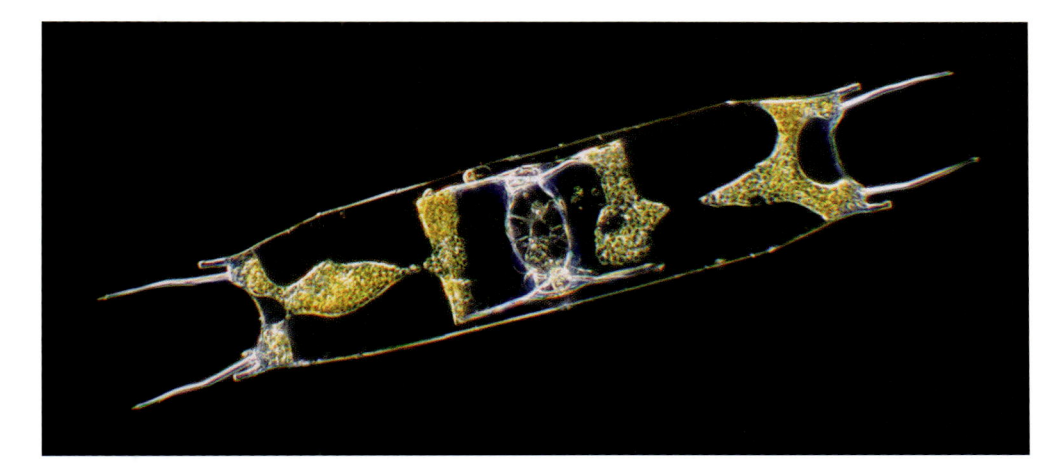

Fig. 3.06
The diatom *Odontella* splitting to form two cells. (Photo: MC)

Fig. 3.7
Dinoflagellate *Ceratium*.

Fig. 3.8
Spume covered rocks caused by a storm at sea during a bloom of plankton.

Fig. 3.9
Red Tide in a brackish lagoon caused by a bloom of dinoflagellates.

the surface (see Figs 5.16–5.18). These diatoms are very active, often moving in and out of the mats creating a dynamic structure. Perhaps one of the most exciting pennate diatoms to find in a plankton sample is a sliding diatom, *Bacillaria paxillifer*. A single cell is very slender and usually seen side by side, each sliding up and down one another, not necessarily in the same direction. This has led to the name 'carpenter's rule' diatom as they extend the colony back and forth until they are touching only by the tips. This amazing movement is thought to be found on diatoms possessing a raphe – a groove or slit in the wall. Mucilage secreted in pores along the grooves absorbs water to cause the expansion. Pennate forms show the greatest diversity of shape and form.

Dinoflagellata represent the second largest primary producer in the sea. These single celled protists not only photosynthesize but can be predatory and parasitic. They may be mixotrophic, i.e. ingesting other organisms while carrying out photosynthesis. Some can be symbiotic, living inside animals like the sea anemones. The single cell has two whip-like flagellae, one attached around the girdle and one at the end, that generate a screw action through the water. They are smaller than diatoms and can be very abundant. Toxin forms can be dangerous to animal life and in huge blooms dinoflagellates create what is known as a 'red tide'.

Plankton   87

Fig. 3.10
A tintinnid, *Ptychocyclis* species from the marine ciliates. (Photo: MC)

Fig. 3.11
Tomopteris, a planktonic polychaete worm.

The phytoplankton around the oceans of the world are the most productive of life on the planet and vitally important in the absorption of climate-changing gases like carbon dioxide (carbon sinks). When looking at production on land it is measured as a standing crop due to the long growth period of land plants. In the sea a standing crop appears to be quite small compared to the animal life, being almost unsustainable in energy terms. However, what makes the phytoplankton so unique is their speed of reproduction. Through simple binary fission the diatoms and dinoflagellates can rapidly double their biomass. It is because of their diversity and importance to life on earth that diatom communities, in all aquatic systems, are used as a diagnostic tool to monitor environmental conditions. This has been used for many years. It was Sir Alistair Hardy who first devised a plankton net that could be towed behind ships plying across oceans so that there was constant monitoring of plankton.

Zooplankton

Phytoplankton are the base of the food web in the oceans. Zooplankton feed on the phytoplankton or each other and hence are both herbivorous and carnivorous. Zooplankton may be either temporary or permanent planktonic creatures. The latter, the holoplankton species, have adapted to have their complete life cycle within the plankton. Copepods are the best example, having the largest number of species of any crustacean group and being the most abundant organism in the seas. Here they may be parasitic as well as free living with some growing up to 5mm in length. A single, central eye is a basic sensory organ in the middle of the head. Two pairs of antennae protrude; the first pair may be very long, aiding buoyancy in the water, while the second pair enables swimming. This is typical of the Callanoids, the biggest group of copepods. These can be trapped in small rockpools and seen as small, mobile dots in the water. The marine species carry one egg sac attached to the end of the body. Callanoids are the most important herbivore of the plankton, consuming up to several hundred thousand diatoms a day. The larger species may also eat other zooplankton. They are an essential prey item for nektonic organisms and Callanoids are known to feed at night in order to avoid fish and other predators; they migrate vertically nearer the surface at that time, drifting down through the water column by day.

Arrow worms are a phylum group, the Chaetognatha, and (with a few exceptions) are all holoplankton. They are important prey for fish and can constitute around 6 per cent of all the plankton. However, this density varies between regions and seasons. Far from being a docile worm-type organism, they are actually voracious carnivores, feeding on animals equivalent or smaller than themselves. They ambush prey, grabbing it with teeth and spines, usually swallowing it whole and digesting it very quickly. They grow up to 4cm long but are usually much smaller.

The most diverse portion of the zooplankton is without doubt the temporary plankton (meroplankton) where the planktonic stage is only one phase in the life of the marine organism. Many shore organisms seen in previous and subsequent chapters have external fertilization, releasing their gametes into the seawater for the egg to become fertilized. The egg then hatches into a larval

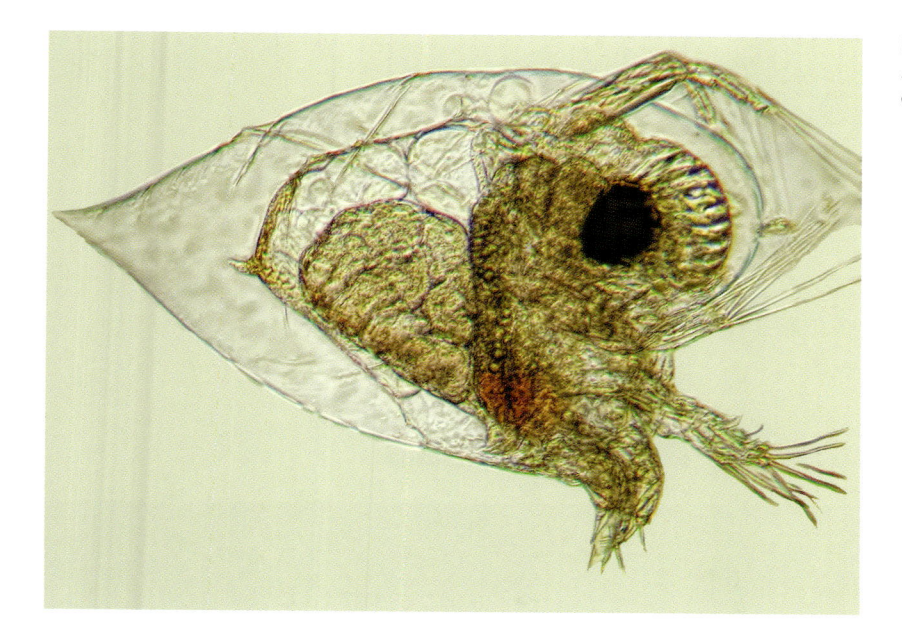

Fig. 3.12
Evadne, a marine cladoceran crustacean.

Fig. 3.14
Copepod, top view. (Photo: MC)

Fig. 3.13
Copepod *Calanus* carrying eggs. Side view. (Photo: MC)

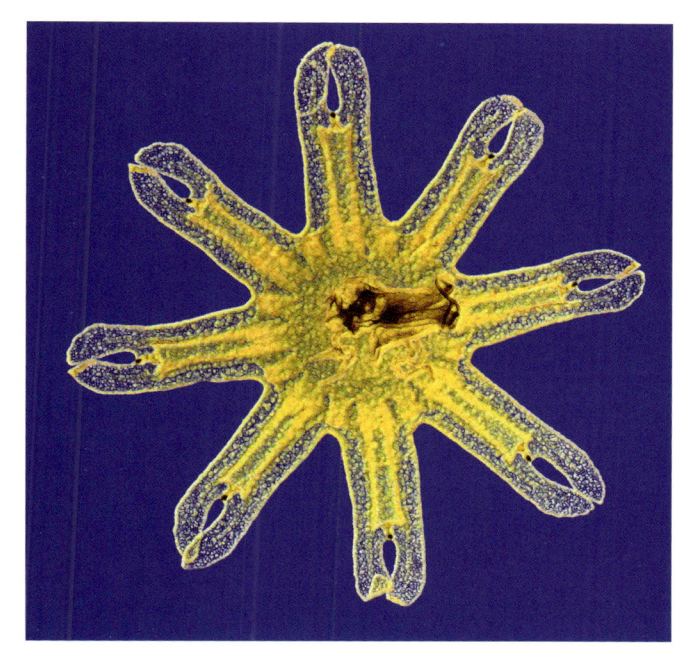

Fig. 3.15
Ephyra stage in the life cycle of an *Aurelia* jellyfish. (Photo: MC)

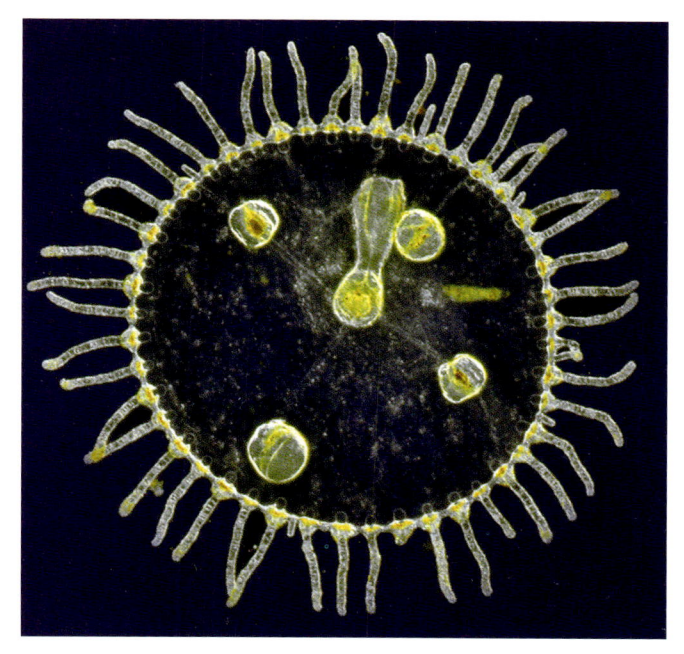

Fig. 3.16
Medusa phase in the life cycle of *Obelia* hydroid. Note the small gonads present (adult stage Fig. 2.88). (Photo: MC)

Plankton 89

Fig. 3.17
Young planktonic worm *Polydora*.

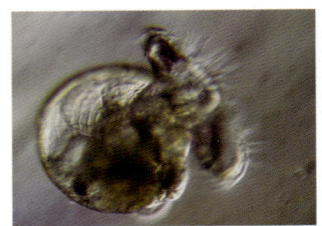

Fig. 3.19
Veliger larva, possibly of an edible Periwinkle.

Fig. 3.18
Second planktonic larval phase, called an aulophora II, of Sand Mason worm.

stage that lives in the plankton for a period before settling back on the shore once more. Even some internally fertilized individuals can have a planktonic larva.

Life in the plankton is tenuous with survival rates being extremely low. This is why a parent creating offspring for the planktonic way of life will produce huge numbers. A common shore crab typically has 800,000 eggs at a time. A planktonic stage in an organism's life cycle can have great advantages: there is plenty of food available, and ocean currents are important for dispersal and for providing a different environment from that of the adult, reducing competition. Different species will have differing longevity before the larva must find a suitable habitat or die; often this is just a matter of weeks.

The barnacle *Semibalanus* on the rocky shore mate during the autumn but retain the larval stage inside until the spring when they are released at a time of the maximum phytoplankton bloom, between March and May. One barnacle is thought to be able to produce as many as 8,000 larvae. The larva, called a nauplius, goes through six instar stages, growing and feeding on diatoms over several weeks. This metamorphosis then goes into a final phase called a cypris larva, which settles onto a hard substrate and sheds its skin to become an adult. The nauplius stage becomes more complex with each instar and accumulates fat droplets, visible inside the triangular shaped body. The cyprid stage is a very different, non-feeding phase living off fat. After a few days it drops out of the plankton and can move around to select a suitable settlement point, attracted chemically by the presence of adult barnacles. It can delay the settlement until satisfied and then uses a pair of glands to secrete a superglue to attach it permanently to the substrate. Copepods also have nauplii larvae.

Plankton

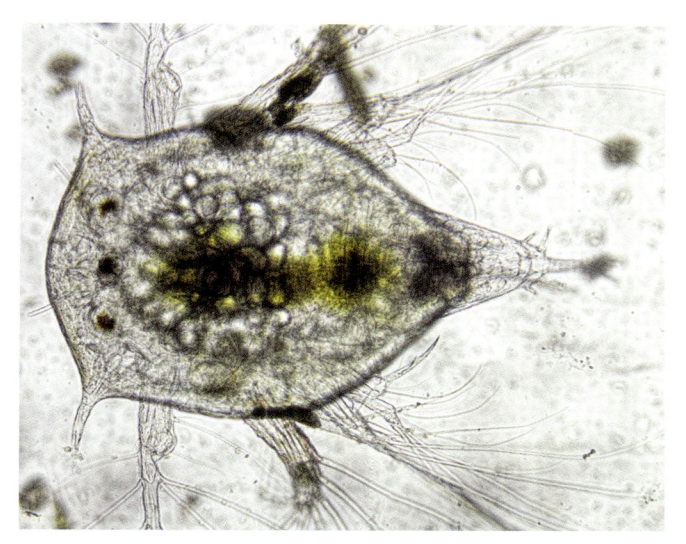

Fig. 3.20
Late stage nauplius larva. Note the fat droplets stored inside the body.

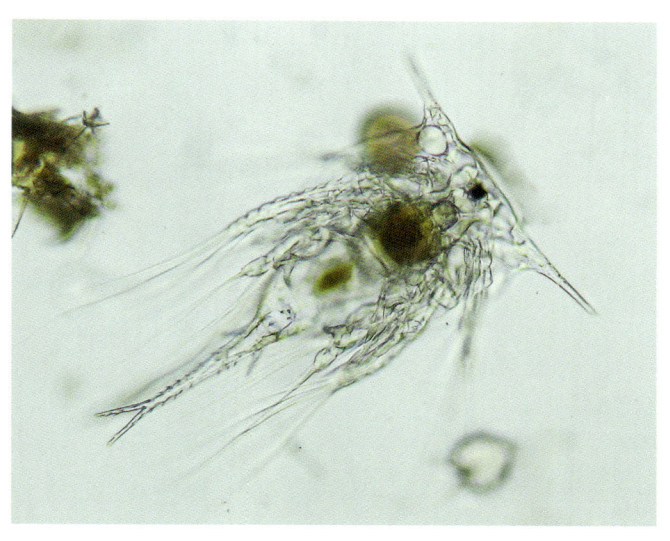

Fig. 3.21
Early stage nauplius larva. (Photo: MC)

Fig. 3.22
Zoea larva of a crab. (Photo: MC)

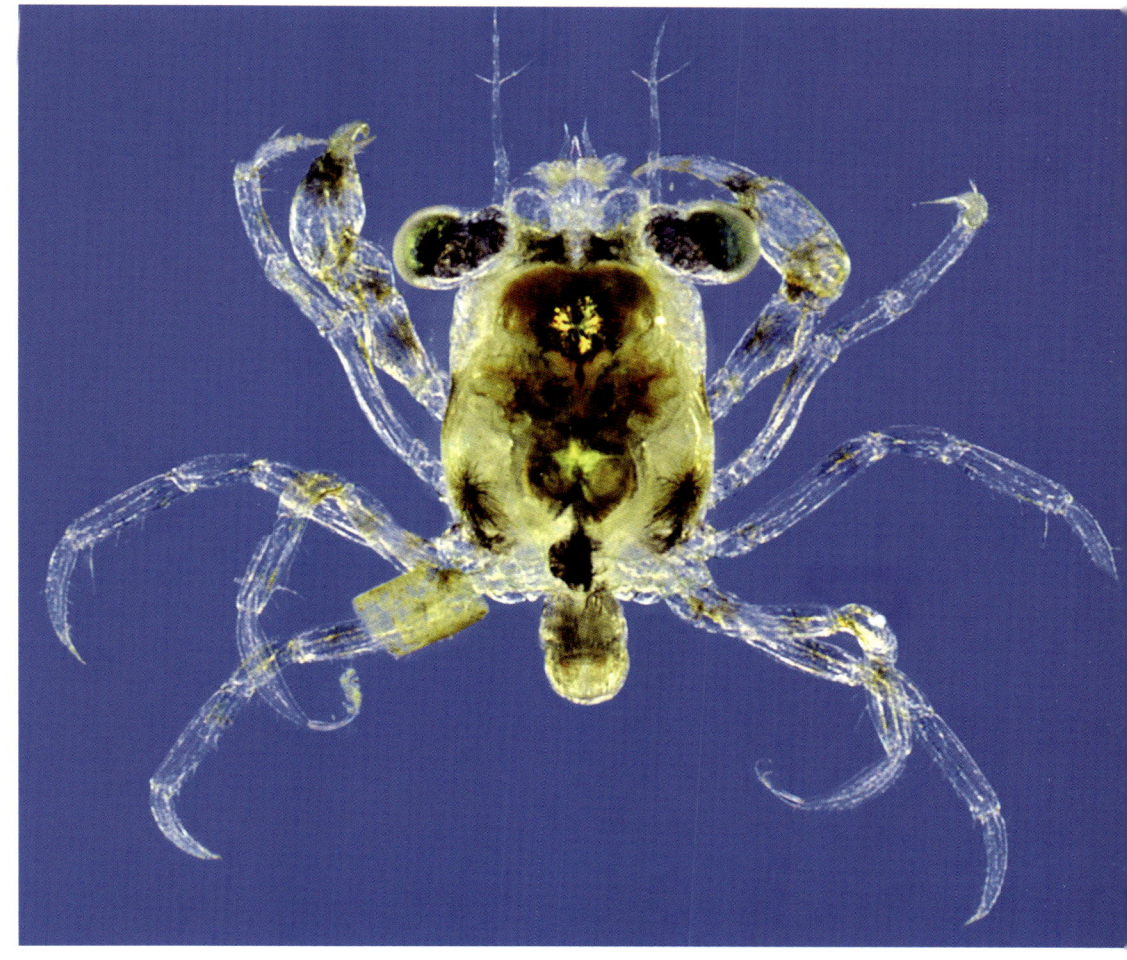

Fig. 3.23
Megalopa stage larva of a crab. (Photo: MC)

Decapoda, which includes crabs, either have a rapid nauplius stage inside the egg or none at all. The hatching larva is an advantaged individual, called a zoea stage. They vary between the species and the carapace (over the head and thorax) has distinctive long spines, both out of the back and forward between the predatory compound eyes. Porcelain Crabs have very long spines with the front one projecting more than the length of the body beyond the head. With a development of stalked eyes eventually the zoea metamorphose into a megalopa larva, visible to the naked eye, and it is this that settles and develops into a tiny adult on the shore.

Plankton 91

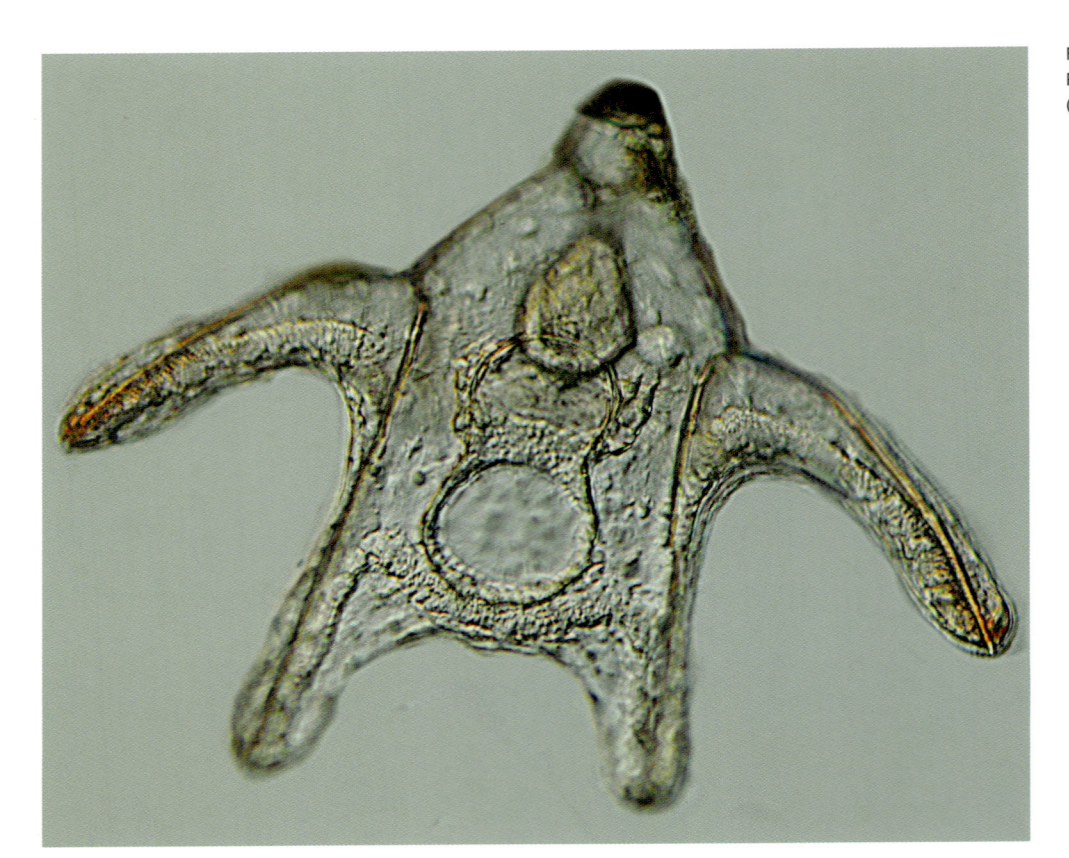

Fig. 3.24
Pluteus larva of an echinoderm.
(Photo: MC)

Many gastropod molluscs, e.g. Edible Periwinkles, produce a planktonic larva beginning with the basic trochophore stage, usually in the egg or soon afterwards. The main stage is the veliger larva which lives in the plankton. They show a great diversity of form and develop a shell with a muscular foot covered in cilia. They are distinctive under the microscope: they look like a bag with two ciliated ears protruding.

The marine worms, Polychaetes, have some beautiful and diverse examples living in both holo- and meroplankton. An example of the former has to be *Tomopteris helgolandica* which can be abundant near the water surface in their younger stage when they may be 1–3cm long. Females reach three times this size as they mature. They are predators in the plankton. The family of worms called Syllids are fascinating as they live as adults on the bottom, feeding on hydroids. Syllids have an interesting sexual reproduction called epitoky whereby the sexes grow an extension at the end of the body (the stolon) which breaks off. This swims up into the plankton where it grows antennae and general accoutrements of an adult including gonads – but no gut as they do not feed. After a nuptial dance the two sexes mate and the female then broods the eggs in a pouch. Worms that live on sediment shores use the plankton as an important dispersal medium and there are some larvae that when encountered have exceptionally high densities, particularly the Spionids, e.g. *Polydora*. The larvae are like small teddy bears hurtling around under the microscope. In such high densities they may be just visible to the naked eye.

Plankton blooms

Plankton communities vary seasonally and diurnally. As diatoms photosynthesize so oxygen can build up inside the frustule making it more buoyant and causing it to move up towards the light. As the light compensation point is reached at the end of the day the oxygen is used in respiration and the more soluble carbon dioxide is released instead. The diatom begins to sink until the sun appears and it starts to rise again. If by dawn it has sunk too far it will be out of the lit zone, where there is insufficient light for photosynthesis, and it enters the dark zone. Unable to produce food, it dies and sinks to the bottom where it contributes to the build-up of dead and accumulated silt. Over the millennia, accretion of diatoms has led to the formation of diatomaceous rock. Ultimately most nutrients sink out of the water column and if a bloom is to occur again nutrients need to move off the bottom and back to the lit zone. This includes nitrates, phosphates and especially silica for the frustule formation.

Fig. 3.25
Epitokous planktonic phase of the polychaete *Myrianda*. A female brooding eggs. (Photo: MC)

This nutrient redistribution is associated with spring and autumn for several reasons. A common occurrence at this time is the appearance of storms with prevailing wind action. This disturbance causes a drawing of nutrients off the bottom. Most important is the breakup of the thermocline. Temperature will change with depth but when the sea is relatively calm in winter or summer the surface will be at a very different temperature to deep water. Instead of seeing a gradual reduction in temperature with depth, an area occurs where there is a sudden drop in temperature with depth before it becomes relatively constant. This region of dramatic temperature change is the thermocline. Arrival of waves and a change in temperature causes the thermocline to break up and that produces a mixing of the water which includes a movement of nutrients. As well as silica and other materials, spores of the phytoplankton appear in the lit zone. With the necessary nutrients and conditions photosynthesis takes place and the single-celled creatures divide and multiply to cause a plankton bloom. Animal species use these blooms as a source of food for the larval stages, and the shore organisms reproduce accordingly. There are two peak blooming periods, the spring being the main one followed by a usually lesser one in the autumn. The peak nauplii development is in the spring and in autumn limpets reproduce.

Chapter 4
SEDIMENT SHORES

Fig. 4.1
Open coast sandy shore with some wave action and limited biodiversity in the clean sand.

Part 1: The communities

Introduction

Compared to the rocky shore, sediment shores can look barren and devoid of life. At high tide, when water movement is low, finely suspended particles rain down onto the shore. These depositing shores are moulded by different degrees of shelter to produce a range of sand types, from clean and coarse (with few organisms) to muddy, bacteria-rich ones (with many organisms). In all cases shelter will cause the material to settle and any movement, including water currents, will disturb the surface, leaving ripples. Typically, the substrate is unstable. Any disturbance of the surface by water currents or occasional storms will affect the substrate and therefore the communities. Due to the very nature of their formation, depositing shores have gentle slopes, hence the term mudflat. In comparison to the hard, rocky shore these can be referred to as soft, low energy shores. Estuaries are typically sheltered shores where the velocity of the seawater slows allowing considerable deposition to occur, especially at high tide. Current speed can be quite variable and the resulting substrates will be a mix of gravels, sands and fine silty mud. Estuaries occur

Fig. 4.2
Sheltered sandy shore with high organic matter and organism densities. Large numbers of feeding birds occur.

where fresh water runs into the sea and may display a change (zonation) along the length from pure fresh water to fully marine conditions. Fresh water is less dense, floating on the salty water. With changing tides, mixing gradually occurs so that salinity will vary along the estuary length.

Fig. 4.3
Estuaries are often near urban areas, or pass through them. There are mud-banks at the side and variable salinity.

Fig. 4.4A, B, C
Sediment under the microscope, all magnified ×50.

A: Open coast (Fig. 4.1), large sand particles from various rocks, no organic matter or organisms visible.

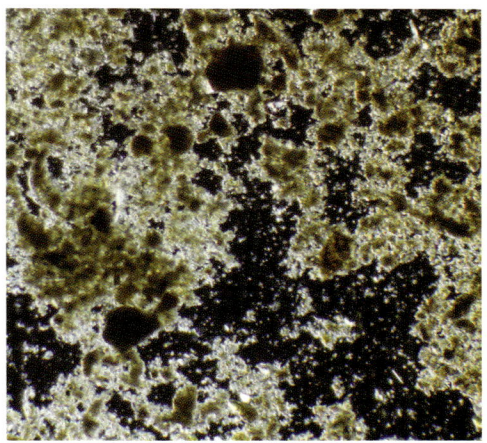

B: Mudflats, small silt particles, high in organic matter, diatoms, bacteria and micro-fauna.

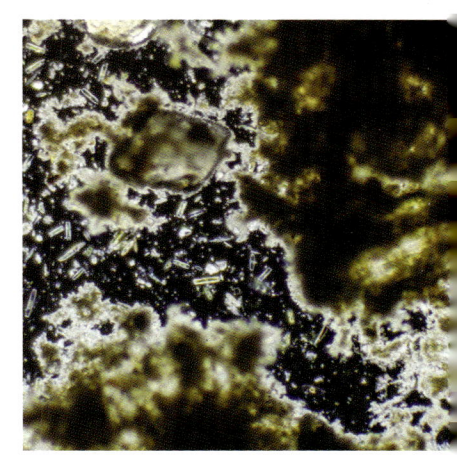

C: Estuary (Fig. 4.3), mixed particle sizes, high in organic matter, diatoms, bacteria and micro-fauna.

The substrate

The particles may be of quartz, feldspar or shell fragments. They will be of an irregular shape and viewed under a microscope will have pits and crevices. This gives a large surface area for the attachment of bacteria and microscopic algae, particularly diatoms. Between the particles, the interstitial space is a micro-community called the meio-fauna, based on bacteria and diatoms. Mud particles are much smaller than those of sand. This yields a particularly large surface area with small interstitial spaces. The combination of both gives a richer community and a greater productivity. The smaller interstitial spaces in mud means that water does not drain away and at low tide the surface of mudflats remains wet. Consequently, communities living in the mud will not suffer from desiccation. Sandy shores, which have a steeper slope compared to mud, do drain quickly so that upper shores suffer from desiccation, and fewer species can survive.

Water turbulence grades and sorts the particles so that many shores will show a transition from high water mark to low water. This could be shingle through sand to mud in the lower shore. The slope of the shore may reflect this with steeper shingle, gently sloping sand and mudflat.

Sediment Shores

Fig. 4.5
Mixed sheltered and open coast with a wide variation in particle size, producing a range of habitats including salt-marsh (foreground) mudflats, sand banks, estuarine conditions near freshwater outlets and sand dunes (background).

Problems and features of living here

Sediment shores are clearly very different from the rocky variety but this makes them no less exciting to explore: they just require a little more effort. There is no fixed substrate for attachment, except for the occasional stone which may be present, and on the surface organisms will be very vulnerable. Instead, the species are burrowers, requiring very distinct adaptations to live under the surface. For many animals their need for oxygen and food will mean some form of link to the surface. Few producers are visible and the water is turbid – that is, cloudy with silt and organic matter. Turbidity reduces the ability for photosynthesis and primary production; consequently there will be a mixture of chemosynthesis and photosynthesis to produce energy by micro-flora in the form of bacteria and diatoms.

Depositing shores are typical of estuaries and here salinity changes daily, even hourly. These brackish conditions will impose osmotic problems on the organisms, severely reducing the diversity of species able to survive leaving a limited number that have adapted; these will have populations reaching high densities. Habitats such as this have become essential feeding stations for wading birds. For migrating birds, they have often been termed nature's hotels where flocks of many thousands stop off in the spring and autumn. Most waders have adapted to particular prey items, shown by the shape and length of the bill.

In very sheltered areas, often protected from the open sea by shingle ridges and sand bars or along the edge of estuaries, salt-marsh may develop. Here the sediments have been colonized by rooted plants called halophytes that are adapted to the saline conditions (Chapter 5).

Precautions in fieldwork

Soft mud can be very dangerous and the probability of sinking through the sediment increases towards the lower shore. This is especially so on large estuaries like the Solent. Sediment shores can be a vast expanse with some famous ones like Morecombe Bay running to many square miles of sand. With such gentle slopes an incoming tide moves at a speed that is impossible to out-run. Always check tide times and return to the upper shore before the tide is due. Look out for and check local warning signs that may be displayed in car parks or on footpaths. Sediment shores can look idyllic but are potentially dangerous places.

Sediment Shores

Upper and middle sandy shore communities

Fig. 4.6
Sandy shore at low tide. Note the wet areas that have not drained in the lower shore and can sustain life, whilst the upper and middle are dry. Wind drying the upper shore sand creates the dunes behind.

Fig. 4.7
A landscape of Lugworm burrows in the middle shore.

Fig. 4.8
Curlew feeding on Lugworm.

The main substrate is sand with a minimum of fresh water and moderate amounts of organic matter trapped in the sediment. On open coasts where the sand is a little unstable and is cleaner (less organic matter) there will be fewer burrowing animals.

Problems of living here

- The surface dries at low tide and drainage occurs through sand, making the upper shore difficult to colonize.
- The substrate is unstable.
- No substrate for attachment.
- No shelter, hence burrowing existence.
- No seaweeds present for food or shelter.

Sediment Shores

Fig. 4.9
Dwarf Eel Grass *Zostera noltii*, an important food plant for migrating geese and ducks.

Fig. 4.10
Lugworm *Arenicola marina*.

Fig. 4.11
Lugworm burrow: cast and nearby depression, marking where the burrows are located.

Fig. 4.12
A terebellid worm showing the tentacles and the red gills.

Upper and middle sandy shore species

Flowering plants
A close examination of the surface in the middle shore may reveal Dwarf Eel Grass *Zostera noltii* growing leaves up to 20cm across the surface of sand and mud. They are barely a millimetre wide. *Zostera marina* is found in the lower shore and sublittoral.

Polychaete worms
The middle of a sandy shore may be dominated by the hillocks and pits of the Lugworm *Arenicola marina*. Permanently burrowed beneath the sand, they grow to 20cm in length. They live at the bottom of a mucus lined, U-shaped burrow and consume sediment in front of the body. Organic matter is digested from the sand along with micro-organisms. Clean, coarse sand will not support lugworms. Above the position of the head, where sand is being engulfed, a depression occurs at the surface. A cast on the surface marks the tail end. This is where sand is defecated at the surface, on average every 45 minutes. Defecation brings the lugworm into the wading birds' feeding zone but at its normal depth Lugworm can only be reached by long-billed birds like curlews and often only the abdomen is taken – which the worm may well survive. The tube is irrigated by body movements to oxygenate the thirteen pairs of red gills. This irrigation may also help in the growth of the micro-organisms on the sand. At low tide atmospheric gaseous exchange takes place but Lugworm can survive anaerobically for nine days. Lugworm can tolerate quite low salinity and may occur in estuaries. Small worms are common highest up the shore, migrating down with maturity. Worms mature after two years and spawn typically in late autumn, to coincide with neap tides. Triggered at this time by low temperature, synchronized spawning on those tides ensures that the sperm and eggs remain in pools on the surface for fertilization. The larvae produced will be swept up the shore by the incoming tide, increasing the chance of survival. Densities can be high: up to 150 per square metre.

The Terebellid Worm, *Neoamphitrite figulus*, is a sedentary worm up to 25cm in length. These worms prefer muddy sand with high levels of organic matter. This might include estuaries and sheltered bays. This species may occur on rocky shores amongst holdfasts and in sediments trapped under large stones. The worm has a tapering body and at the top are three pairs of long, strand-like, red gills. The numerous tentacles lie on the sand surface collecting detritus which rains down at high water.

Sediment Shores

Fig. 4.13
Tellin shells in the typical 'butterfly' shape.

Fig. 4.14
Tellin with siphons extended.

Fig. 4.15
Common Cockle Shell *Cerastoderma edule* with short siphons. Because of these, in comparison to the Tellin, the animal needs to be near the surface.

Fig. 4.16
Spiny Cockle *Acanthocardia echinata*.

Bivalve molluscs

Whilst the edible Periwinkle may be found at the surface, feeding on micro-organisms, the typical molluscs in the middle shore will be bivalves that can burrow. The Tellin Shell *Tellina tenuis* is 2cm across the shell and is found on fine, clean sand, especially on beaches open to the coast. On shores where the sand becomes muddier with more organic matter, including in estuaries, *T. tenuis* is replaced by the Baltic Tellin *Macoma balthica*. Tellins have a flat, pink or white, glossy shell. Normally lying on the sand, it can come to the surface or be disturbed by waves. A large foot provides for rapid burrowing as the tide goes out. It has two separate, long siphons. When burrowed, one siphon draws in food like a vacuum cleaner from the surface; the other moves fluids in the other direction getting rid of waste. Water brings in detritus and oxygen. The gills then filter the detritus which is passed to the mouth for consumption. The density of tellins is high in an area of sand, and surface contact with the siphons may be the way in which they can space themselves to prevent intraspecific competition. A number of bivalves have the ability to regenerate siphons quickly if they are eaten by predators like flatfish, for which they are a good source of food at the surface. Competition with a close relative, *T. fabula* is avoided by *T. tenuis* living at higher level on the beach and the former in the lower shore and sub-littoral. Empty tellin shells are common, lying like butterflies on the sand, often with a small hole near the top of one shell. This is where it has been drilled by a Moon or Necklace Shell *Polinices* so that the muscle that holds the two shells closed can be cut and the animal eaten.

The Common Cockle Shell *Cerastoderma edule* has a thick rounded shell, 3–5cm, with distinct ribs and growth rings. They can be very common in sand and muddy sand, and even in fine gravels. The two siphons are very short and so they are restricted to living at the surface where they are susceptible to temperature variation and predation, particularly by oystercatchers. They filter the water of suspended detritus and micro-organisms with the outlet siphon being narrow to produce more pressure than the inlet one, thus ensuring that waste is ejected away from the inlet water. Cockles spawn between March and August, the larva lives in the plankton for about three weeks and is often accidently consumed by parents. It is tolerant of low salinity. They can live for up to nine years, but half that is more typical. A similar species, Spiny Cockle *Acanthocardia echinata* is found at the very lowest part of the shore. They can be quite spectacular with their hooked spines and red muscular foot but also for the fact that they can 'jump' into the water column by a rapid expulsion of water if predators such as starfish come near.

Sediment Shores

Crustacea

The Common Sand-hopper *Talitrus saltator*, up to 1.5cm in length, is similar to *Orchestia gammerellus* which is found in shingle and rocky shore strandlines (Fig. 2.34). In both cases the first pair of antennae is short with the second pair being long, distinguishing them from similar amphipods found further down the shore. They can be very abundant in the strandline amongst flotsam. They burrow in the sand on the upper shore, leaving the tell-tale signs of many small holes in the surface. They emerge at night to feed on organic debris and are occasional predators. The 'hopping' is achieved by releasing the flexed abdomen very rapidly. They have cyclical migrations from the strandline to ensure feeding and immersion in water using a body clock and navigation by the sun and possibly moon. Sand-hoppers are globally important to the tourist industry. Attempts to clear up sandy beaches by removal of the strandline and sand-hoppers has resulted in the disappearance of the sand. When they eat the organic matter they produce faecal pellets high in a mucus, probably from the seaweed. This helps to bind sand grains together and maintain the sandy beach for tourists to enjoy.

Eurydice pulchra is an isopod crustacean, less than 1cm in length, with very long antennae and an oval body. It is covered in black, star-like chromatophores which can darken and lighten the body. It is similar to *Lekanesphaera* (see Fig. 5.32). It burrows temporarily in sand at low tide but swims vigorously with a rising tide to migrate back and forth across the shore. It is at this time that it feeds as a highly predaceous carnivore, with tearing mouthparts. Digestion within a distensible hind gut may take up to three weeks. The sexes are separate and mating takes place while swimming. The eggs are retained in a brood pouch.

Common Shrimp *Crangon crangon*, around 5cm long, is very abundant in the middle shore and below. It burrows quickly into sand by clearing it with the legs. The peppered colouring is due to chromatophores which give good camouflage. It is an important carnivore, preying on worms, crustaceans, molluscs and very young fish and is itself eaten by large fish. Shrimps will also be found in the lower reaches of an estuary.

Fig. 4.17
Common Shrimp *Crangon crangon*. Note the eyes on top of the head so they can protrude through the sand when burrowed.

Fig. 4.18
Common Shrimp trying to burrow.

Lower sandy shore communities

Fig. 4.19
There is little sign of life except for the tube of the Sand Mason worm.

Problems of living here

- No substrate for attachment or shelter.
- Burrowing existence necessary.
- The turbulent surf creates instability on the sand surface.
- No seaweeds are present for food.

The main substrate is sand with moderate amounts of organic matter trapped in the sediment. On open coasts where the sand is a little unstable and is cleaner (less organic matter) there will be fewer burrowing animals.

Fig. 4.20
On sheltered sand with ripples Edible Periwinkles may venture out at low tide to feed in hollows.

Sediment Shores

Fig. 4.21
Daisy Anemone *Cereus pedunculatus*, top view.

Fig. 4.22
Daisy Anemone, side view.

Fig. 4.23
Sand Mason *Lanice conchilega*, a close-up of the tube surface.

Fig. 4.24
Redthreads *Audouinia*.

Lower sandy shore species

Sea anemones

Daisy Anemone *Cereus pedunculatus* is 3cm, pale grey-buff coloured, with a trumpet-shaped column. It has up to 700 tentacles. Buried in muddy sand, only the tentacles show at the surface. Usually anchored below to a shell or stone, it consumes depositing organic matter as well as crustaceans. It is adaptable; found near the entrance to estuaries and in rockpools. *Peachia hastata* is a worm-like anemone with twelve tentacles. It is capable of true burrowing as it does not attach to hard substrate. It has parasitic larvae, on the sea gooseberry.

Polychaete worms

There are several sedentary worms occurring in the lower region of sandy shores and the most prominent is the Sand Mason *Lanice conchilega*, 20cm in length. The animal itself is not obvious as it lives in a 35cm tube, with the distinctive 4cm top showing above the sand, made from sand and shell fragments glued together with mucus. The worm's fine pink extensible tentacles collect food deposited by the tide. *Owenia* is a worm producing a similar type of tube, which is smaller and finer. *Owenia* can carry its tube around unlike the Sand Mason. Redthreads *Audouinia* (around 7–15cm in length) lives permanently buried within a mucus-lined tube. The thin worm is covered in long, coiled red threads, which are the gills, emanating from most body segments. It is a deposit feeder like the others here, meaning it feeds on the organic particles that become deposited on the sand surface.

There are predatory worms that move through the substrate searching for prey, like the Cat Worm *Nephtys hombergii* (8–15cm in length). The white, flattened muscular body has a dark line along the back and a single thread at the tail end. It has no permanent burrow and is an active swimmer. Carnivorous worms like the Cat and Ragworm use an eversible proboscis or pharynx to feed, essentially turning the front part of the gut, which has backward facing spiny teeth, inside out. This projects forward out of the mouth and now has the teeth pointing forward for grasping prey. By taking it back inside the body the food is dragged into the gut. The Cat Worm also uses this mechanism in burrowing. It has some tolerance to low salinity and may exist in estuaries.

Fig. 4.25
Cat Worm *Nephtys hombergii*.

Fig. 4.27 Common Razor Shell *Ensis ensis* showing the powerful foot used for rapid burrowing.

Fig. 4.28
Banded Wedge Shell *Donax vittatus*.

Fig. 4.26.1, 4.26.2, 4.26.3 Cat Worm extending the pharynx, used in feeding and burrowing.

Fig. 4.29
Haustorius arenarius, an amphipod living in the sand.

Bivalve molluscs

As in the middle shore it is the burrowing bivalves that do well here. Both tellin species can occur, along with the Common Razor Shell *Ensis ensis* (up to 13cm). There are several different species but this one occurs on most sandy beaches at the very lowest part of the shore and into the sub-littoral. It is a long, narrow shellfish. The siphons are short and so it lives near the surface. The outlet siphon forces water out quickly to ensure that waste is blown clear of the inlet. They are sensitive of surface vibration and can burrow very fast using the large muscular foot which can push as well as pull the body down through the sand. The presence of razor shells can be noted by a small keyhole in the sand produced by the siphons; when it burrows, water shoots up from the hole. Living in the surf region is hazardous as water movement can uncover the creatures and so speedy re-burrowing is crucial. Water is forced out of the mantle to soften the sand and the streamlined form allows for rapid burrowing. The Banded Wedge Shell *Donax vittatus* (3–4cm) is another surf dweller with a powerful muscular foot. The shell is a variable colour, from white through brown to purple and with a toothed edge to the shell. A very active burrower, it survives on exposed sandy beaches where it moves with the waves.

Sediment Shores

Fig. 4.30
Masked Crab *Corystes cassivelaunus*.

Crustacea

Small crustaceans find living in the surf difficult, with regular disturbance from the sand. One species of amphipod, *Haustorius arenarius* (1cm long) is well adapted with good swimming and burrowing ability. In fact it is thought to mate when disturbed and swimming, possibly because at such times it is able to find a partner. Little is known about its biology. The wedge-shaped body, with larger segments at the rear, assists in burrowing. It is nocturnal with very small eyes and filter feeds. Although *Carcinus* can burrow for short periods there is only one true burrowing crab species. The Masked Crab *Corystes cassivelaunus*, around 4cm in length, has long and very hairy antennae that link together to form a tube. This is comparable with the siphons of bivalves so that whilst buried in the sand it can connect to the surface. Water is drawn down the tube and under the carapace by the head. This is the reverse of the flow found in other crabs. It will forage for food at night on bivalves, worms and amphipods. After storms large numbers of dead Masked Crabs can be found washed up on the shore.

Echinoderms

The Sea Potato or Heart Urchin *Echinocardium cordatum* is typically around 5cm across but can grow significantly larger and is thought to be a species complex, as it is quite variable. They lie in a deep (15–30cm) burrow and so avoid the main effect of the turbulent surf at the surface. Behind the mouth are spade-like spines modified for digging, along with the tube feet. The burrow is lined with mucus to give it some stability and it acts as a respiratory channel to connect it with the surface. The water current is maintained by cilia. It deposit feeds by using large tube feet which collect sand grains and pass them to the mouth to consume organic matter. The anus is at the top of the back so that faeces are carried out of the burrow by water currents. It is continually moving around and feeding. This urchin is quite distinct from the rocky shore (radially symmetrical) types as it is bilaterally symmetrical with no suckers on the tube feet.

Fig. 4.31
Sea Potato *Echinocardium cordatum*.

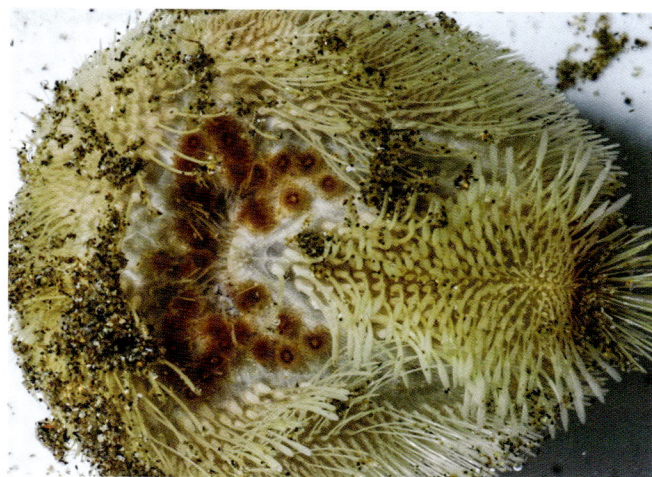

Fig. 4.32
Sea Potato underneath showing digging spines, right, and large, red tube feet.

Fig. 4.33
Sand Star *Astropecten irregularis* burrowing.

Fig. 4.34
A polychaete worm *Acholoë squamosa* on a Sand Star.

Fig. 4.35
Burrowing Brittle-star *Acrocnida brachiata*.

A burrowing starfish found at a very low spring tide is the Sand Star *Astropecten irregularis*. It is a pale, rigid-bodied starfish that remains burrowed just beneath the surface unless disturbed by the surf when it quickly reburrows. A carnivore, it feeds on bivalves, small crustacea and worms by pushing them into the mouth with the tube feet. A polychaete worm *Acholoë squamosa* can occasionally be found living under the arms of the starfish in a groove. This is not a parasitic but a commensal relationship, i.e. they have a close bond but are not so dependent as a symbiotic relationship. The Burrowing Brittle-star *Acrocnida brachiata* has a central disc of 1cm diameter with very long arms (around 16cm) attached. These arms are held near the surface for suspension feeding on debris and can raise and lower the body, especially when spawning.

Sediment Shores 105

Estuarine and muddy shore communities

Human debris, e.g. wrecks, colonized by seaweeds and animals.

Middle shore of sand and mud. Stones colonized by Horned Wrack.

Lower shore consists of fine mud and covered in *Ulva*.

Upper shore of Common Reed with Sea Club-rush; dead seaweeds become trapped within the stems.

Pools form in hollows, ideal for *Hydrobia* and *Corophium*. Larger ones will have trapped fish, e.g. gobies.

Fig. 4.36 Estuary and muddy shore community.

Fig. 4.37 Aerial view of the Clyde Estuary showing the extensive mud-banks on either side. Buoys mark the channel for shipping which requires regular dredging to keep the waterway open.

Muddy shores form where conditions are very sheltered and the finest material settles out of the water column. This may mix with sand to fill interstitial spaces. These shores will have high levels of detritus incorporated into the sediment. Mud is typical of estuaries but mudflats do form away from freshwater influx and these can hold the highest biodiversity. All macro-organisms will require adaptations to survive and where the conditions are most difficult a few species dominate and can be found in huge densities.

The sediment types may vary between shores depending on local conditions and could be a mix of all of those listed below.

Gravels
- Give stability to the estuary edge, further supported by a small, developing salt-marsh.
- Larger pebbles are used by Fucoid algae for attachment.
- Only burrowers with thickened shells could live here, e.g. cockle.

Sand
- Sand fills the spaces between the gravels and is home to a fauna of small worms and nematodes.

Mud
- Very soft mudflats dominate the shore.
- The surface does not dry as drainage is poor; zonation across the shore is unlikely due to a lack of abiota gradient.

> **Problems of living here**
> - Minimal movement of water results in a de-oxygenation of the substrate.
> - The abundance of bacteria and organic matter with low oxygen content results in a sulphide layer, i.e. a blackened mud, high in hydrogen sulphide.
> - Mud is easier to burrow in than sand but is also more likely to collapse.
> - Variable salinity in estuaries, changing during the course of the tides, causes osmotic problems for the organisms.

Estuarine and muddy shore species

Macro-algae

Where gravels and stones are present, algae will have a hard substrate for attachment. Depending upon the position of the shore, both Spiral and Bladder Wracks can survive lower salinities but often hybridize with each other developing a thinner and curly form. However, there is the Horned Wrack *Fucus ceranoides* that is adapted and is characteristic of variable salinity. In fact it can be known as the Estuary Wrack but does occur on rocky shores where there is a constant supply of fresh water running over the surface. It grows up to 70cm long and has distinct forked tips on the frond. Any air bladders will be along the length of the frond and it has a distinct midrib. All the wracks produce good cover and shelter for animals like periwinkles, amphipods and crabs. Green alga of the genus *Ulva* may form a spring carpet of green over the surface of estuarine mud. It is a typical alga of a shore with variable salinities but creates these thick green carpets because of high concentrations of nitrate, run-off from farms up river.

Micro-algae and micro-fauna

Diatoms are an easily overlooked microscopic component of estuarine mud. These are benthic (bottom dwelling) species. *Pleurosigma* is a common diatom here and secretes a mucus coat to resist desiccation. It can even undergo a daily migration to the surface of the mud, in bright sunlight, a distance of about 3mm, returning at night. The distribution of diatoms in the estuary is determined by the salinity as well as light reaching the mud if it is turbid. Also, if the sulphide layer is too near the surface the diatom density is reduced. The peak diatom bloom in the estuary is during the summer. Flagellate protists, like *Euglena*, are common in the mud, developing distinct green patches on the surface, moving up in bright sunlight. This rhythm is linked with tidal movement. Other protists include the ciliates, both free living ones and stalked forms. Tiny shells (less than 1mm) are actually foraminiferan protists. The shell is of calcium carbonate and chitin. They are like amoebae in a shell, moving and feeding by the pseudopodia. They consume diatoms and bacteria. All these microscopic forms live in the spaces between the particles of mud and sand.

Roaming through these interstitial spaces are nematodes reaching densities of 28,000 per 100cm^2 of mud. They are just visible to the naked eye and show up as tiny white worms. Living in the top few centimetres of mud, they emerge at night, when environmental stress is minimal, to feed on bacteria and deposits. Harpacticoid copepods may be found here but using their thoracic appendages for swimming, more typically they will be

Fig. 4.38
Horned Wrack *Fucus ceranoides*.

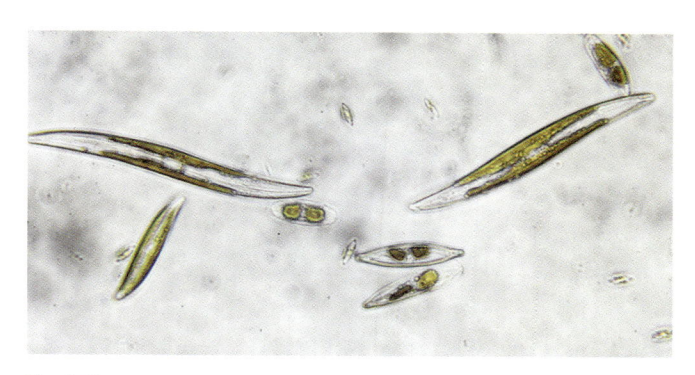

Fig. 4.39
Pleurosigma, an estuarine diatom.

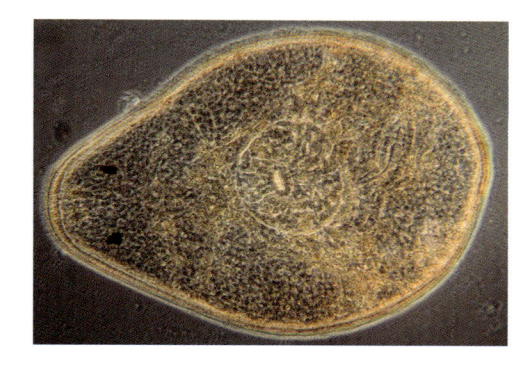

Fig. 4.40
An estuarine microscopic flatworm living in the mud, ×100.

Fig. 4.41
Candy-stripe Flatworm *Prostheceraeus vittatus*.

Fig. 4.42
Ragworm *Hediste diversicolor*.

Fig. 4.43
Peacock Worm *Sabella pavonina*.

in the estuarine plankton and different from the species found in the open sea. Mud-dwelling species are smaller and elongated. They browse on algae and detritus.

Copepods show a zonation up the estuary relating to salinity. There are a number of strange creatures living in the estuarine mud – not least *Lineus ruber*, a nemertine worm. This elongated, flattened animal is not a true worm and can be found on other shore types but here burrows into the mud to emerge at night to feed on the nematodes, capturing them with an eversible pharynx. They tolerate salinities down to 0.8 per cent by covering their body in slime so the water cannot penetrate. There are several types of flatworms found on seashores. Microscopic varieties, impossible to identify, can be found in the interstitial spaces. There are larger species visible and the most beautiful is the Candy-stripe Flatworm *Prostheceraeus vittatus* found under stones, usually on mud. This species cannot tolerate reduced salinity unlike *Procerodes littoralis*, which extends up the estuary.

Polychaete worms

Ragworm *Hediste (Nereis) diversicolor* grows to 6–9cm; it is abundant in mud and characteristic of estuaries where it is tolerant of very low salinity. They are greenish in colour with a red line (a blood vessel) running the length of the worm. It lives in a burrow and secretes mucus around it. An omnivore, it will feed on most suitably sized prey including other worms. Mucus is secreted around the burrow to trap organic matter and plankton, which it consumes. Spawning normally takes place in the spring with the male bringing the sperm near to a female burrow. She collects it and fertilizes the eggs which develop into larvae within the adult's burrow. The larva therefore avoids the plankton and remains on the shore. Dispersal occurs later when they are more able to control their movement. In more saline areas and also on sand as well as mud the Ragworm is replaced by the King Ragworm *Neathes virens*, a large (up to 40cm long) iridescent green animal. It scavenges and predates on other worms. All ragworms are an important prey item for wading birds. Dug for use as fishing bait, commercial digging has decimated areas around the UK. The King Ragworm is now cultivated for bait.

The Peacock Worm *Sabella pavonina* is found on the lower part of muddy shores. The worm lives in a tube which protrudes by up to 10cm clear of the surface. To feed when covered by the tide it extends an array of tentacles called radioles, which collect suspended matter from the water. Cilia sort the particles by size with small ones going to the mouth for food; large particles are rejected and others are added to the tube with mucus.

Fig. 4.44
Peppery Furrow Shell *Scrobicularia plana* showing the foot as it burrows.

Fig. 4.45
Peppery Furrow Shell siphons above the mud. The inhalent siphon is the longer one.

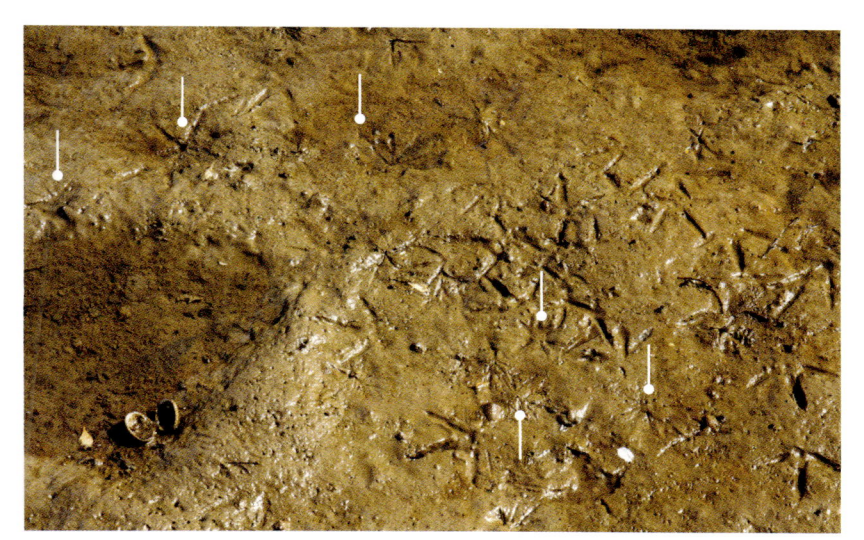

Fig. 4.46
Marks left on the mud surface at low tide by the siphons of Peppery Furrow Shell (arrowed) with footprints of feeding birds.

Fig. 4.47
Sand Gaper *Mya arenaria*.

Molluscs

The main bivalve in areas of low salinity is the Peppery Furrow Shell *Scrobicularia plana* (6cm). It has a thin shell that copes well with the soft mud and tends to be grey-black where it is stained by the sulphide in the mud. It produces very long, separate siphons for sucking up organic matter like a vacuum cleaner (deposit feeder). The length of the siphons means that individuals can live deep in the mud as they are very susceptible to frost (the surface of estuaries can freeze with the presence of fresh water). This has a very similar niche to the Baltic Tellin and where they overlap much competition occurs. Contrary to the name, Sand Gaper *Mya arenaria* lives mainly in mud. This is a large bivalve, 15cm long with a thin, soft shell for mud burrowing, stained black by the sulphide layer. This is a permanently burrowed species, never surfacing. The adult foot is greatly reduced and so the animal cannot reburrow if it is dug up. As it grows the bivalve moves deeper into the mud, the siphons increasing in length to reach the surface. They are so long they cannot be withdrawn into the shell. Up to 0.5 metres long the siphons are joined along the length and used to suspension feed.

A gastropod mollusc that is very abundant in estuarine mud is the tiny Laver Spire Shell *Hydobia ulvae* (0.3–0.6cm). Although small it may dominate the mud by its numbers and between 10,000 and 20,000 can exist in 1m² of mud. As a group the hydrobids have a number of species and telling them apart in the field is difficult. Unlike most organisms living on the shore, which have evolved from marine forms, these originate

Sediment Shores

Fig. 4.48 Large numbers of *Hydrobia* snails washed into the strandline.

Fig. 4.49 *Hydrobia* in the faecal soup.

Fig. 4.50 Slipper Limpet *Crepidula fornicata* colony.

from fresh water and are very tolerant of low salinity. They secrete mucus rafts which will carry them afloat on the water surface. This aids dispersal by the tide across the mud, usually with its egg capsules. Food varies from diatoms and detritus to bacteria and fungi on bare mud. They are the principal food of the Shelduck. The Slipper Limpet *Crepidula fornicata* (4cm) is not a true limpet, living on most substrates, and was introduced from America with oysters. The base needs to be attached to stone or shell, from which it generates colonies, by them attaching to each other. They change sex with age, small individuals being male, the female larger. It is a filter feeder and chief competitor with the oyster for food. Hence, it is considered by some to be a serious pest and is spreading along the coastline.

Fig. 4.51 *Corophium* in burrow.

Fig. 4.52 *Corophium*.

Fig. 4.53 Opossum or Mysid Shrimp *Neomysis*, closeup showing the brood chamber with eggs.

Fig. 4.54 Common Shore Crab *Carcinus maenas*.

Crustacea

There are several species of crustacea that are important as a food source, particularly the amphipod *Corophium volutator*. At 0.5–0.9cm in length they can be seen at low tide crawling over the surface of mud. The forelimbs are used to filter mud for detritus whilst the very large, second pair of antennae is used in locomotion. The animal lives in a U-shaped burrow just beneath the surface and the fifth pair of legs anchors it to the side. Vast numbers are found on the mud (around 12,000 per m^2) and they can tolerate very low salinities. With no other animal adapted to the niche, like *Hydrobia*, there is little interspecific competition and numbers are high. *Corophium* show a tidal rhythm, rising to the surface with an incoming tide, which moves them up the shore, then swimming down on a receding tide. This helps to keep them on the shore in a favourable environment. Males crawl over the mud looking for the burrows of females and after mating she retains the young brood pouch for two weeks. To tell amphipods and isopods apart, the former are normally flattened from side to side and the latter, top to bottom. *Corophium* is flattened like an isopod but is actually an amphipod. They are a prime food source for the Redshank.

Gammarid amphipods are common under stones and weed but can live out of water for short periods of time. The position of the species in the estuary depends on its ability to osmoregulate and they show pronounced zonation (see Fig. 4.64). They are all detrital feeders. The sex of the offspring is determined by temperature: for example in *G. duebeni* below 5°C they are male; above this they are female.

Lekanesphaera rugicauda is an isopod around 1cm or less in length and is common in estuaries and salt pans on the salt-marsh (see Fig. 5.32). Opossum Shrimps *Neomysis* are very different to the common shrimps and produce large numbers actively swimming in the estuary. Measuring 1–2cm in length they are especially abundant at the water's edge on an incoming tide, penetrating high up the estuary to feed on organic debris, bacteria and diatoms. They fall prey to fish, especially flounder. As the Common Shore Crab *Carcinus maenas* is the one species of crab able to osmoregulate effectively it can cope with the low salinities of the estuary. It osmoregulates with the antennal glands, small bladder-like organs at the base of the antennae. This allows the crab to penetrate far up the estuary, living in concentrations of only 0.6 per cent salinity. *Carcinus* shows seasonal movement: in summer it is common high on the shore moving seawards to survive the cold winters. Females carrying eggs move to the estuarine entrance. Hatching larvae are released into seawater with a higher chance of reaching the plankton of the open sea. It is both a carnivore and scavenger.

Fig. 4.55
Common Goby *Pomatoschistus microps*.

Fig. 4.56
Flounder *Platichthys flesus*.

Fig. 4.57
Flounder *Platichthys flesus* with copepod parasites on the back.

Fish

There is a wide cross-section of fish types living in estuaries and on mud. There are three key aspects of their biology which relate to the ecology: the ability to osmoregulate, feeding, and their reproductive habits. Just a few fish examples are given here to illustrate some of these points. The flounder *Platichthys flesus* is the commonest estuarine flatfish, tolerant of very low salinity and able to survive in rivers. However, they breed at sea with the young forms, sized around 1cm, entering the estuary to feed on small invertebrates of the mud such as crustaceans, bivalves and ragworm. This happens in spring so the warm period of the year is spent in the estuary. They then return to the sea (when they are closer to 9cm), where they carry on growing and eventually breed. They develop impermeable scales to stop water entering the body.

A permanent and most characteristic brackish water fish is the Goby. Of the several that live in estuaries probably the Common Goby *Pomatoschistus microps* (7cm long) is the most important, with the ability to live in almost any part of the shore. It can enter fresh water and compete with minnows feeding on chironomid larvae. It is at home in creeks and deep pans on saltmarsh where it feeds on copepods and small crustacea. It spends the winter in deeper water, moving up the estuary to breed in the spring. Three-spined Stickleback *Gasterosteus aculeatus*, is at 6cm one of the smallest fish in the estuary and it is the most common of the sticklebacks. A freshwater fish that has adapted to salt water, the estuarine variety has twenty to thirty bony plates on the body flanks as an adaptation to the salt, whilst the freshwater form has only four to five plates. It feeds on small crustaceans.

Sediment Shores

Fig. 4.58
Male Shelduck, behind, courts the female as she feeds by sucking mud through the front of the bill and then squirting it out the side to filter animals.

Birds

Shelduck *Tadorna tadorna* are small colourful ducks (around 60cm) with a distinct red bill, green head and brown band on the shoulders. The bill has a fine filter along the edge. Mud is sucked in the front and squeezed out of the sides through the filter, retaining any organisms in the mouth. The main diet is *Hydrobia*. Each duck may eat many thousands of these tiny snails per day. They nest on sand dunes in old rabbit burrows and rarely form large groups, with a few pairs moving across the mud together. Little Egret *Egretta garzetta* is a small white heron with white plumes, black legs and bill, and yellow feet. It is another example of a species moving north and west in Europe possibly with climate change. It bred for the first time in the UK in 1996, after numerous winter visits since the 1980s. Almost 800 pairs now nest in the UK with many more arriving in winter to feed in estuaries and other wetland. They eat small fish and crustaceans.

Wading bird species are adapted for life on sediment shores and a few are mentioned here. The Redshank is very common in estuaries and around the coast. Legs and bill are of medium length for a wide range of prey whilst the larger species such as Curlew and the godwits have longer bills for penetrating deeper into the sediment. The former is one of the few to be able to reach lugworm. The Ringed Plover, a small wader, has a short bill and feeds on surface dwellers like *Hydrobia*. Waders are discussed in the next section.

See also *Littorhina littorea*, Oystercatcher, Mussel (discussed in Chapter 2).

Part 2: Ecology of sediment shores

Fig. 4.59
Estuary at high tide showing the turbid, murky water.

General features

- Sediment necessitates burrowing which requires many adaptations to obtain nutrients and oxygen from the outside.
- Primary productivity on the shore is poor. Many of the nutrients and much of the organic matter originates in other habitats, e.g. salt-marsh, up river, nearby shores.
- Bacteria are important producers here; large plants are absent.
- The communities are dominated by animals.
- Three types of community are identified:
  a) micro-flora; b) micro-fauna; c) macro-fauna.
- Zonation of communities down the shore is not so marked as in rocky shores.
- Zonation of organisms does occur along an estuary.
- There is a great deal of overlap between the types of sediment shore: stones, sand and mud.

Turbulence sorts the particles so that the greater the wave action the coarser the material deposited on the beach. Sand is more unstable than mud. Waves tend to scour the sand clean of organic matter. Severe gales may remove sand and in calmer months redeposit.

Slope: the gradient is proportional to the particle size; shingle creates steep banks and silt forms mudflats. Water content, too, is affected by size of particles. Mud draws water up by capillarity at low tide. Coarse sands have large air spaces and so drainage is rapid.

Aspect: south-facing shores are most likely to dry out; any shade will slow this down as well as giving protection from a drying wind.

Fig. 4.60
Sediment surfaces are likely to freeze in winter especially where fresh water raises the freezing point.

Summary of the limiting factors affecting organisms			
Shore type	Very coarse sandy shore	Fine sandy shore	Muddy shore
Turbulence	High	Average – low	V. slight – negligible
Particle size	> 2mm	0.2 – 0.002mm	< 0.002mm
Slope (typical)	Steep	Gradual	Flat
Water content	Low	Variable	High
Drying out	Rapid	Slow	Negligible
Oxygen level	High	Low	De-oxygenated
Sulphide layer	Absent	Slight	Present
Organic detritus	Slight	Variable	High: dark colour
Number of macro-organisms	Low – absent	Variable	High
Meio-fauna in the interstitial space	Low	Medium	High

Oxygen and sulphide layer: oxygen diffuses into the substrate from the water and air; bacteria feed on organic matter and release hydrogen sulphide. Without oxygen this produces ferrous sulphide, giving black sand. With oxygen, an oxide, similar in colour to clean sand, develops. This is the pale, oxidizing layer at the surface.

Temperature: high air temperatures will increase drying and kill micro-fauna at the surface of mud – these micro-fauna are usually unaffected by desiccation. In winter interstitial water may freeze, causing a high mortality rate, e.g. in razor shells. This is especially so in estuaries where the salinity is lower and the freezing point not so depressed. However, some organisms are quick to recolonize, particularly polychaetes; bivalves are much slower. Temperature becomes more constant with depth. To avoid extremes of temperature, micro-fauna can migrate away from the surface.

Salinity: rain on the shore can affect the micro-fauna in the interstitial spaces by diluting the seawater. Macro-fauna will burrow deeper. Salinity is more variable on these types of shore than others and animals either conform, regulate or move away. Avoidance of fresh water is the common feature: *Inachus*, a spider crab, moves into deeper water; Ragworm burrows and tolerates the absorption of water by its tissues. *Carcinus* and other kinds of crustacean can osmoregulate.

Zonation on sediment shores

Three forms of zonation can be distinguished: horizontal down the shore, a vertical pattern down through the sediment, and a variation along estuaries from fresh water to the open sea.

Horizontal zonation

Although poorly defined, zonation does occur here. Digging and sieving sand at several points down a sandy shore will give a horizontal distribution of species from the strandline to the sub-littoral. The gradual slope ensures that the community boundaries are not obvious as the transition between limiting factors is less marked. Also, the ability to burrow helps to avoid changes on the surface. Where the substrate shows a change from gravels near the top, through sand to mud further

Fig. 4.61
Ripples sort the particles to create a mini-zonation of organisms.

Fig. 4.62
Zonation occurs along this small estuary, both in salinity and sediments including the off-shore sandbar. Salt-marsh plants exist along the edge.

Fig. 4.63
Large estuary. The prevailing wind is from the left leaving a sheltered sediment in the foreground, colonized to form a salt-marsh. The shore top right will have grades of shingle, gravel and silt.

down, a more noticeable fluctuation in communities will be seen. For example, the thick and tougher shells of bivalves, e.g. Venus Shell, are needed for burrowing in coarse material; the Sand Gaper and tellins have thinner shells and will be limited to finer substrates.

Mud does not drain at low tide, the fine material holding the water by capillarity. Desiccation, one of the major limiting factors in causing zonation on seashores, does not apply here and as a consequence zonation is almost imperceptible. The upper region of sandy shores does drain, however, as the particles, and therefore their spaces, are larger than mud. There are few species here. Sand-hoppers live most of the day burrowed in the sand near the strandline and emerge at night to feed on organic matter washed in by the sea. The density of Ragworm peaks in the upper shore where freshwater runoff reduces the salinity. The Lugworm is the dominant animal in stable sand but almost non-existent on muddy shores where burrows will collapse. There is a marked difference in Lugworm age range across the middle shore, with those near the top of the shore being the youngest. A comparison between sand and rocky shores is fascinating as it introduces both similar and quite dissimilar limiting factors as well as analogies between niches.

Vertical zonation

Macro-fauna: the larger organisms burrow within the sediment giving a vertical zonation (see Fig. 4.68). All are dependent upon the surface for their oxygen, food and possible gamete dispersal. Differences in vertical distribution reduces competition, both intra- and inter-specific, for space. Younger individuals are often nearer the surface; for example, the Sand Gaper moves deeper with age and if dug up it cannot reburrow.

Micro-fauna and micro-flora: on a sandy beach ripples form and this represents a microscopic sorting of the sediment particles. This will affect the micro-fauna. Many congregate in the trough between the ripple ridges, where the finest particles are present and water will collect. The top of the trough is coarse material which dries out. The depth to which animals will survive depends on the depth of the oxidizing layer, that is, the depth of oxygen. Only anaerobic organisms will enter the sulphide layer. The surface is alkaline, changing with depth to become acidic. Environmental stress does not develop gradually with depth from the surface but suddenly. The micro-fauna (for example, copepods) are limited to a range of a few centimetres changing diurnally as they migrate. Most interstitial animals live close to their lethal limit.

Fig. 4.64 Distribution of animals along an estuary with salinity.

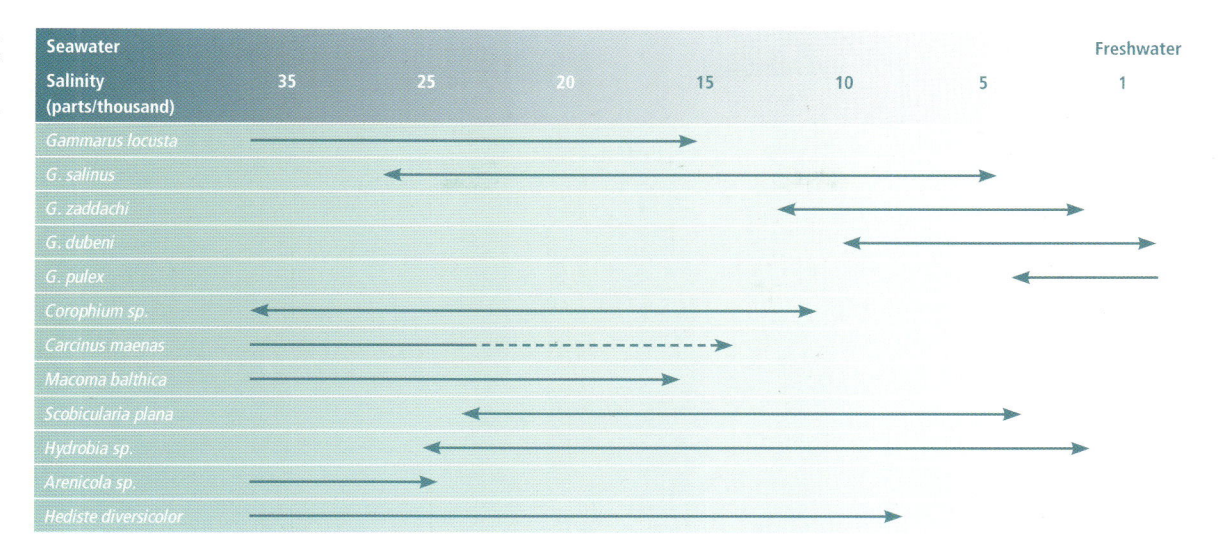

Seawater							Freshwater
Salinity (parts/thousand)	35	25	20	15	10	5	1
Gammarus locusta	←――――――――――→						
G. salinus		←―――――――――→					
G. zaddachi					←――――――→		
G. dubeni						←―――→	
G. pulex							←→
Corophium sp.	←――――→						
Carcinus maenas		←―――― - - - - ――→					
Macoma balthica	←―――――→						
Scobicularia plana			←―――――――→				
Hydrobia sp.		←――――――――――→					
Arenicola sp.	←――→						
Hediste diversicolor	←――――――――→						

Fig. 4.65 An estuarine gammarid crustacean.

Meio-fauna: this term largely reflects the intermediate sizes of animals between the macro-fauna, clearly visible to the naked eye, and micro-fauna, which are microscopic. Although its use in science is variable it is generally defined as animals between 0.5mm and 1mm and living in the interstitial spaces. Different species of copepod may be classified in the meio- or micro-fauna as their size varies so much.

Estuarine zonation

Estuaries are regions of semi-enclosed water where rivers enter the sea. As the tide flows inland the denser seawater creeps along the bottom with the fresh water flowing over the top and gradual mixing occurs. This is affected by the width and depth of the estuary such that a strong pressure of river water may cause dilution and so reduce the salinity considerably. The usual result is a gradation of salinity along the length of the estuary. This may influence the distribution of some estuarine organisms, especially crustaceans – although food competition, problems of silt and predation also play a part. Zonation invariably occurs along the estuary. Wind action at the surface increases the water turbulence which will then affect the deposition of sediment. The sheltered side of the estuary may develop a salt-marsh whilst the more exposed bank could be an assortment of mud, sand and gravel. The scale of this depends on the size of the estuary. Small estuaries will have meanders and show properties of rivers with deposition on the inside bend and the presence of a salt-marsh will be represented by just a few characteristic species growing at the edge. Large estuaries, a mile or so across, could have extensive communities of salt-marsh on the sheltered side with mudflats and shingle beaches.

Fig. 4.66
Tellin shell burrowing.

Fig. 4.67
Siphons of a burrowed bivalve, *Macoma*.

The burrowing niche

Two challenges face animals when burrowing: entering the surface, and digging within the substrate. Both will be influenced by the grain size. Soft mud is easy to displace but the walls of the burrow will just as easily collapse. Ragworm line the walls of burrows with mucus to strengthen them whilst Lugworm restrict their habitat to sand, making burrows permanent. Bivalves require harder and thicker shells the harder the substrate. Cockles have thick shells and are found amongst gravel and coarse sand whilst Peppery Furrow Shells with their thin shells are restricted to mud. Bivalves begin to dig by probing forward with the muscular foot. The shell muscles contract quickly, forcing water onto the substrate like a water pistol to blow the sand away and soften it. Blood is forced into the tip of the foot, causing it to widen like an anchor. Muscles then contract to bring the body down, as it rocks from side to side. Worms are similar, but instead of blowing water they tap the substrate which draws water to the surface and softens it. Penetration is by the eversible pharynx. Some animals like the Sand Gaper and Lugworm remain burrowed all their lives and avoid much of the environmental stress found at the surface. This in itself can be problematic, however.

Living in a burrow
The chief problems are those of communication with the surface for oxygen, food and a mate. Living not too far from the surface, oxygenated water can be drawn down by a channel in the sediment by legs in *Corophium* or body movement in Ragworm. Bivalves use siphons with cilia on the gills to move a respiratory current of water through them. Food is considered in the next section. Male Ragworm search out female burrows and deposit sperm in the entrance. Many animals, however, shed gametes into the burrow and use water currents to carry them outside. This requires synchronization so that all the animals spawn together. A sudden lowering of temperature can stimulate worms whilst high temperatures affect the Sand Gaper. The state of the tide is important, to prevent the gametes or young being washed away.

Survival in the sediment

It would be easy to think that all the macro-fauna is beautifully in position, each in their own burrow and distance below the surface, minimizing competition. Whilst this is the ideal, in reality life in the sediment is quickly disturbed. It is well known that bait digging by people seeking worms for fishing lines will destroy this balance. However, a similar but natural disruptive process regularly occurs in the upper sediment. Small crabs, shrimps and fish the size of gobies feed on the more sedentary creatures. Their movement through the upper few centimetres of the surface, digging for prey and uncovering burrowed organisms, can produce a huge disturbance called bioturbation. Dislodged species not consumed may take a while to re-burrow and then fall prey to other predators. Bioturbation is patchy across a large area of mudflat and sediment, varying with the state of the tide and presence of the predators. Small fish like the gobies will be particularly significant in this process, bioturbating 1 per cent of the available surface. Even mass movement of Cockles, Lugworm or Ragworm influence the presence of smaller creatures like the Polydorid worms. *Corophium* is known to migrate out of an area after cockle disturbance.

Whilst sediment shores occur in sheltered areas, occasional storms can be devastating, whipping up the surface and dislodging populations. Piles of Sand Mason tubes can appear in the strandline or the broken tests of the Sea Potato scattered over the shore. Severe gales may remove bivalves, like cockles, and sweep them into piles for gulls and crows to consume.

Salt depresses the freezing point but just a small encroachment of fresh water onto sediment could cause it to ice over. In the winter burrowed populations can be susceptible to frost on a low spring tide. This is especially so for those near the surface of the lower shore like Razor Shells which could be wiped out on a very cold night peaking at the lowest tide. It is interesting that recruitment from the plankton enables a recovery of the population in the following year. When looking at suspension and deposit feeding bivalves and other organisms the age of the individuals within the population can be remarkably similar, rather than having a diverse age range. During feeding they may deliberately consume the larval stage preventing new individuals from settling. Only when a population has a crash, such as the freezing period, will the larvae be able to become established.

Feeding relationships on sediment shores

The apparently barren nature of these shores suggests that the source of energy is like few other ecosystems. Organic matter, washed in by the tide and down through rivers, accumulates amongst the sediment. Bacteria may live on this but they also represent a vital food producer along with benthic diatoms by using chemosynthesis and photosynthesis, respectively. These form two types of autotrophic nutrition. Chemoautotrophic is found in the ancient order of sulphur bacteria. Found in the sulphide layer, they can oxidize hydrogen sulphide to produce a source of hydrogen to attach to carbon dioxide and release energy. This does not use light and produces waste in the form of sulphides that can be toxic. These chemotrophs are anaerobic and so are found where there is no oxygen. Photoautotrophic bacteria and diatoms are in close proximity to the surface where light is available. They use water in photosynthesis as a hydrogen donor to combine with carbon dioxide to create carbohydrates. With an unsurpassed reproductive rate, bacteria productivity can be very high on muddy shores.

The food sources available to animals in the sediment ecosystem will be bacteria; micro-algae and protists like diatoms and flagellates (see algal mats, Figs 5.16–5.18); plankton; macro-algae, fucoids and *Ulva;* organic matter and detritus, including the strandline. The salt-marsh is an important source of organic matter (see Chapter 5).

Faecal soup

Surface bacteria in mud is consumed by a high proportion of animals. Most ingest large quantities of sediment and organic matter which is stripped of the micro-organisms and defecated back onto the surface. This becomes recolonized by the micro-organisms and the recycling continues. The surface is therefore like a soup of faeces in which the micro-organisms breed. Recycling takes about three days. *Hydrobia*, a tiny snail found in densities of many millions, avoids reconsuming their faeces for up to twelve days, which allows the perfect broth to develop! Some faeces is nutritionally ideal immediately: for example oyster faeces, eaten directly by King Ragworm and *Corophium*.

Methods of feeding

The snails like *Hydrobia* plough through the upper few millimetres, consuming as they go. *Corophium* uses its appendages to create a water current bringing the fine matter into the burrow, filtering the water of suitable food. This is suspension feeding and is a common method used in bivalves like the Cockle and Sand Gaper. With two siphon tubes one brings a water current in; the other is for waste. Those with two long, separate siphons, like Tellins, vacuum up material on the surface and are called deposit feeders. There are times when these organisms have been known to switch between suspension and deposit feeding, depending on the season. The Peacock Fan Worm places its tentacles high above the surface to feed on suspended matter. Where burrowed animals need that link with the surface in the form of siphons and tentacles they are in danger of having these remote structures eaten by fish and birds. Lugworm have to back up their burrows to defecate at the surface and can have the end of the abdomen nipped off. Whilst all these body parts can be regrown the process will take nutrients that would have been destined for other things and so will impede the population.

Fig. 4.68
Comparison of bill lengths with buried prey items.

Fig. 4.69
Redshank.

Fig. 4.70
Dunlin.

Fig. 4.72
Godwit.

Fig. 4.71
Ringed Plover.

Competition

Living on sediment shores is highly specialized and the diversity of species is less than the rocky shore. Those animals that have adapted to live amongst sediment have relatively few competitors. On the rocky shore a host of gastropod molluscs like periwinkles, top shells and limpets compete with each other. Here, *Hydrobia* is the dominant gastropod. Interspecific competition is therefore limited whilst intraspecific competition is a more important biotic factor. Densities of sediment invertebrates can be staggering. *Hydrobia* has been found at 300,000 per m² and *Corophium* at 12,000 per m².

Shore-birds of sediment shores

Waders are the birds most associated with these shores and their numbers can reach huge figures. In the Ribble, Morecombe and Dee estuaries, over a million waders a year are accommodated. Estuaries are essential feeding

120   Sediment Shores

Fig. 4.73
Heron is found feeding on most seashores. It can be territorial along estuaries, each with its own area for feeding, much like anglers.

Fig. 4.74
Little Egret is a small heron species with an ever-increasing distribution range.

grounds for these birds on their winter migrations. With these top carnivores visiting in such numbers it would be easy to make the assumption that predation has a significant effect on the invertebrate populations. However, this does not seem to be the case. Redshank feed primarily on *Corophium* whilst the Shelduck, *Hydrobia*. These birds are enormous in comparison to the prey size (an estimate of 100,000 times the weight of the prey item has been suggested). This necessitates a massive consumption of individuals. Typically, a Redshank needs to pick up a *Corophium* every half a second as it can only feed for around five hours when the tide is out. To quickly find a buried *Corophium* in the mud, they and all the other shore-birds go for optimal foraging, picking only the large adults and in the highest density patches. So even if 40,000 *Corophium* are consumed a day by the Redshank, the predator only takes a small portion of the population leaving younger ones to mature and avoiding low densities of prey.

As well as birds varying their diet according to abundance and size of the prey, there may be other factors. Redshank selection depends on temperature: it switches from *Corophium* to Macoma and Ragworm below 5°C. The end of the winter is when prey is at its least dense but at its maximum size. Waders feed throughout the year, at night as well as by day, their feeding rhythm being governed by the tides. Night feeding uses tactile senses. The bill is very sensitive and those which are very long, e.g. the Curlew's, have a prehensile tip that opens under the mud.

Interspecific competition between birds can be reduced in two ways: waders with different bill lengths go for prey at different depths; secondly, competition for the same prey may be avoided by age selection, e.g. Oystercatchers take three-year-old mussels whilst Eider Duck take only young ones. Intraspecific competition is avoided by territorial spacing in birds like the Heron and Little Egret hunting for fish and crabs. The latter has become common in the UK within the last twenty years as the bird has extended its range north and west.

Sediment Shores

Chapter 5
SALT-MARSH

Fig. 5.1
Aerial view of a salt-marsh developing along the side of an estuary. Protected from the open sea by several shingle spits (top right) an attempt has been made to build an earth embankment to reclaim the land but creeks have broken through flooding the lower area. (Photo: JA-T)

Part 1: The communities

Introduction
Sediment shores and salt-marsh are inextricably linked, with considerable overlap. Salt-marsh occurs in the very upper regions of the shore below which may be an extensive mudflat. Plants will grow along the margins of sediment shores and it is fairly certain that they will be salt-marsh inhabitants. There will also be a connection with some dune systems where the tide flows in behind the sand dunes to create patches of salt-marsh.

Salt-marsh formation
Along sheltered coastal areas where there is no wave action, sediment will settle out of the water and accumulate, a process called accretion. Flowering plants may colonize this mud, showing successive stages to produce a mature marsh of specialized plants. Due to the salt laid down with every tide, plant species will be adapted to survive this condition. So specialized is this that the few species able to cope with salt are called halophytes (salt-tolerant). This salt-marsh development typically occurs behind shingle spits and bars that offer protection from the open sea. The extensive salt-marsh at Blakeney in Norfolk, UK, is a good example. Scolt Head, also in

Fig. 5.2 Profile of a salt-marsh.

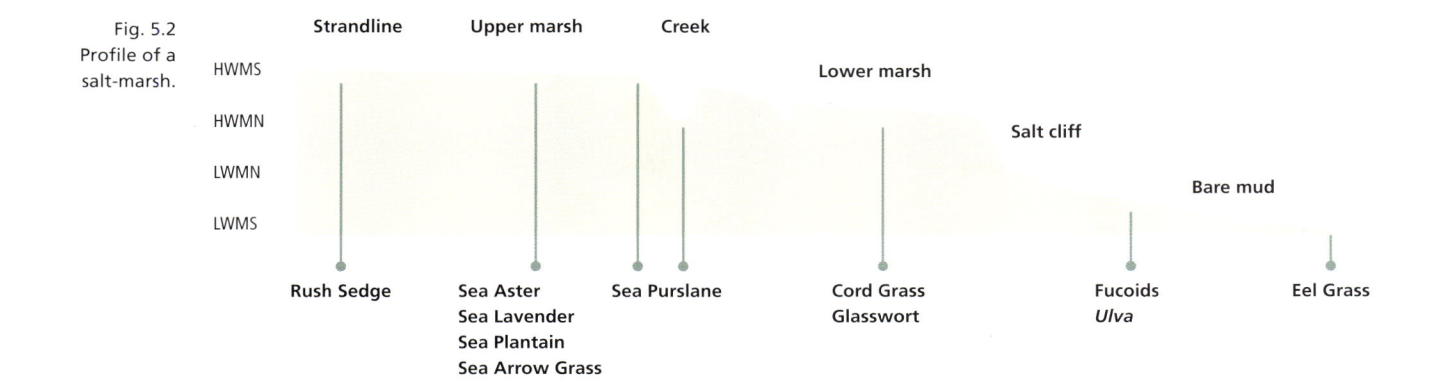

Zone	Vegetation
Strandline (HWMS)	Rush Sedge
Upper marsh (HWMN)	Sea Aster, Sea Lavender, Sea Plantain, Sea Arrow Grass
Creek	Sea Purslane
Lower marsh (LWMN)	Cord Grass, Glasswort
Salt cliff	Fucoids, *Ulva*
Bare mud (LWMS)	Eel Grass

Norfolk, is an example of a barrier island lying just off shore creating a vast salt-marsh. This vegetation will also occur along the banks of estuaries where there is maximum shelter. Initially, vegetation avoids strong currents although unstable mud is quickly colonized. Over time the build-up of plants increases stability and reduces water movement, further increasing the accretion rate. Vegetation will stabilize the substrate as their roots trap and hold sediment. Colonization and growth mainly occurs above the mean high-water mark (MHWM) with the salt-marsh developing to cover the upper shore. Below the marsh a small cliff may occur due to the erosion by tidal currents. Its existence and height will vary according to local conditions. The soil that develops below the marsh is a gley type, that is, based on alluvial material. Salt-marsh development encourages animal species to colonize and over time typical communities form.

Salt-marshes are high in nutrients as organic matter accumulates with the saline sediments. As a consequence much of this land has been reclaimed and cultivated by humans. To prevent the daily waterlogging by tides, sea walls and dykes are built to keep the water at bay.

Salt-marsh formation that is dominated by grasses is a feature of high latitudes where winter temperatures are low. In hotter conditions where temperatures do not drop below 20°C at any time of the year specialized salt-tolerant trees can grow. Instead of salt-marsh a mangrove ecosystem develops, a feature that occurs along the equator. These are highly biodiverse compared to salt-marshes with many species. Moving away from the equator this biodiversity diminishes: only one mangrove species, *Avicennia*, survives as far south as North Island, New Zealand; three bushy species as far north as Florida and Louisiana, USA. Other than temperature, the abiotic features of mangrove and salt-marsh are the same.

Fig. 5.3
Singaporean mangrove, a community with similar conditions to temperate salt-marsh but dominated by trees instead of grasses. The Red Mangle has prop roots to keep the tree upright in soft sediment and to 'breathe' oxygen.

Problems and features

The marsh is flooded and waterlogged by the tides, primarily spring tides as the marsh is at the top of the shore. The relative flatness means that drainage is slow after tidal flooding. Weak areas of sediment are more likely to erode with this drainage, forming twisting channels called creeks that dissect the marsh. Sometimes creeks can be deep and extensive with steep and unstable edges.

Fig. 5.4
Salt-marsh creek, bordered by Sea Purslane, and upper marsh communities.

creates a dark anoxic layer beneath the surface. With a build-up of anaerobic bacteria and sulphides, the soil is positively toxic as well as lacking oxygen for the root systems. Plants must obtain oxygen from the air above and transport it in special tissue (aerenchyma) from the leaves to the roots. Salt-marshes are characterized by a poor diversity of fauna due to the almost inedible leaves which can be tough and high in salt. Many animals are terrestrial species from land such as insects that have adapted to live here.

Special points of interest and caution

The soil of salt-marshes could be compared to a desert in that they are saline and fresh water is very difficult to obtain. The plants display strong structural and physiological adaptations to these inhospitable abiotic conditions. For example, plants develop salt glands to excrete salt and may have a different metabolic pathway for photosynthesis showing similarities to more tropical species. The dynamic zonation of communities is the result of colonization and succession of species over time. Macro-algae are low in variety due to attachment problems but some can exist in non-attached forms – these are called ecads. Micro-algae occur in the form of diatoms in the surface of the sediment. The highly specialized fauna that have adapted to live here do not feed on the plant tissue until it is dead and decaying.

Salt-marshes can be very safe as the vegetation provides good stability. It is stepping off the marsh into a creek that produces problems for people trying to walk from one side to the other. The lack of vegetation and very soft, often steep sides create a sinking hazard. Large-scale creeks should be avoided completely and local information obtained. Salt-marsh vegetation can be very tough, but in early spring when many young seedlings are trying to become established, such as the glassworts, walking across these places can be damaging to the community. Please treat them with care.

The soil or sediment has a high salt content which decreases towards the upper shore –although not in a linear fashion. (Local conditions may cause this disparity, particularly variations in drainage.) With so much salt in the soil, obtaining water will be almost impossible for vascular plants. Algae absorb water through their entire surface whereas vascular plants obtain it through the roots. If salt is more concentrated in the soil than in the plant, water will pass from the root to the mud, dehydrating the plant. Halophytes are plants highly specialized to tolerate the salt and ensure a suitable concentration gradient between soil and plant tissue. Salt may accumulate in the sediment to such an extent as to produce bare patches on the marsh, completely devoid of any plants. These areas are called salt pans where salt levels are so high no plants can tolerate the salinity. Generally there will be a gradation of soil salt on the marsh from high concentrations to low, from middle shore to strandline. With the halophytic plants adapting differently to salt, a zonation of plant communities will occur up and down the salt-marsh. The oxygenation of the muddy soil is very low to non-existent. Waterlogging

Lower salt-marsh – pioneer zone

Fig. 5.5
Lower salt-marsh community.

Problems of living here

- The bare sediment is unstable.
- A high concentration of salt in the sediment means that obtaining water is difficult for plants.
- Up to 50 per cent of the day may be covered by the tide, waterlogging the soil.
- Only the surface of the sediment is aerated; just below is de-oxygenated and toxic sulphides are present.

Cord or Rice Grass *Spartina* species

- Grows up to 1m.
- One of the first colonizers of bare mud.
- To avoid the anaerobic conditions it grows two types of root: (a) roots in the aerated surface; (b) roots in the deeper mud which have two thirds of the tissue as aerenchyma (air tissue – a tissue with large air spaces) which draws air down from the stem's aerial parts. Air passes out of the roots into the soil and aerates it.
- Investigation of the root area reveals an orange mud around the roots, an oxidized ferric compound that means it is aerobic.
- Growth of a fine root mass in the top of the mud begins to stabilize the surface.
- The deep roots are much larger and anchor the plant against possible wave action or turbulence.
- Rhizomes just below the surface are an important asexual method of reproduction; shoots grow off at intervals producing a new plant which allows rapid colonization.
- The biomass of roots is over two and a half times that of the aerial tissue.
- Salt glands are present on the leaves to excrete excess salt.
- If the concentration of salt is too great the plant sheds leaves with the salt.
- Thick cuticle on the leaves, and stomata sunk into deep grooves, slows down transpiration.

Fig. 5.6
Spartineum, an extensive area dominated by Cord Grass *Spartina*.

Fig. 5.7
During neap tides the secreted salt crystallizes and remains on the *Spartina* leaf surface near the salt glands.

Fig. 5.8
Cut stem of *Spartina* showing the extensive air tissue inside.

- It photosynthesizes along the C4 metabolic path unlike temperate land plants (i.e. it is based on a 4-carbon material being produced rather than the typical 3-carbon one of temperate regions. The former is more normally found in tropical plants). This is more water-efficient, reducing the usage by up to 50 per cent.
- It is susceptible to shading and is usually found on its own, sometimes forming large monoculture stands called a Spartineum.
- As a high-growing plant it is affected by drag from water currents and tidal movement; however, this reduces wave action and encourages the deposition of more sediment.
- An extensive root system discourages permanent deep burrowing animals.
- It is intolerant of intense grazing and is replaced by the common salt-marsh grass in this instance.

- It is affected by the amount of nitrogen content in soil: plants from lower marsh will be taller than those higher up where there is a greater degree of competition.
- By increasing the stability of the mud it can cause extreme stagnation and totally anaerobic conditions; this weakens the plants and may cause 'die-back', i.e. bare patches in the marsh (either in pan form or channels), or stunted growth.
- It represents one of the most important producers of detritus in the salt-marsh; it decays very slowly and is inedible when alive.
- The seeds are dispersed by the tide.
- Seeds need low salinity to germinate and do so in spring when fresh water/rain is present.

Glasswort or Marsh Samphire *Salicornia europaea*
- Grows up to 30cm tall.
- One of the first colonizers of bare mud, along with *Spartina* although the latter is best suited for very soft mud.
- It has fleshy succulent stems (leaves are reduced to scales which helps water conservation). Succulence allows plenty of water to dilute the high salt content (comparable with cacti).
- There are no salt glands present.
- Photosynthesis takes place in the stem, which is covered in a waxy cuticle to prevent water loss.
- It tolerates grazing.
- It is shallow rooted, avoiding the sulphide layer that adversely affects it.
- 20 per cent of the root volume is taken up by aerenchyma (air tissue), bringing air from the stem to the root; this is less than *Spartina* but roots are mainly in the upper aerated area.

Fig. 5.9
Common Salt-marsh Grass *Puccinellia maritima*.

Fig. 5.10
Glasswort *Salicornia europaea*. Note the burrows of *Bledius* beetles in the sediment.

- It cannot tolerate mud in regions with strong tidal currents because it is shallow-rooted with sediment accumulating around it.
- The cylindrical shape reduces drag by the water.

Common Salt-marsh Grass *Puccinellia maritima*

- A narrow-leaved, sprawling grass species spreading over the surface.
- An early colonist that can rapidly cover the surface of the sediment.
- Not as tolerant of salt as *Spartina* and *Salicornia* but in some areas may be dominant, forming hummocks.
- A variable species that merges in with upper marsh species.
- A shallow-rooted plant which may colonize bare mud and produces long stolons which trap sediment, speeding up stabilization.
- Fungi on the roots develop mycorrhiza, assisting the plant in obtaining sufficient nutrients in a well-drained soil.
- It produces fine tussocks, which can be colonized by invertebrates; spiders and mites are especially abundant.
- Leaves may roll to cover the stomata, slowing transpiration, conserving water.
- Produces a canopy of leaves early in the spring and will shade out other species such as *Spartina*.

Plants of the lower salt-marsh – pioneer zone

Cord Grass *Spartina* is one of the most important species of the salt-marsh vegetation by starting the colonization and the development. It exists in several forms and it is unclear as to whether this is due to genetic or environmental reasons. Competition for nitrogen with other species will limit growth, which may result in stunted *Spartina*.

S. anglica is the most abundant with a hybrid *S. townsendii* a close second. This former species is an example of a polyploid. It originated from a hybridization between a European species, *S. marina* (a diploid chromosome number of 56) and *S. alterniflora* (a diploid number of 70), an American species which was introduced in about 1870, appearing in Southampton Water and gradually spreading along the coast. The hybrid has a chromosome number of 126, although great variation in this number can occur. Originally the hybrid was sterile and reproduction was limited to asexual propagation by the rhizomes. The appearance of a sexual form has allowed considerable dispersal to occur around the British Isles and across the Channel to France. This genetic form grows more vigorously than either of the original parents. *Spartina* is very susceptible to pollution from industries found in estuaries and at one time it was believed that this led to the die-back on many marshes. It is responsible for recycling elements within the ecosystem: iron, zinc, copper, manganese, mercury and especially phosphorus. Whilst alive *Spartina* has limited protein value and it plays its highest nutritional

Fig. 5.11
Spartina colonizes sediment where Eel Grass is growing.

Fig. 5.12
Spartina, close-up of flower.

role when virtually decomposed. The litter of decaying leaves and stems collects in autumn and becomes colonized by a bacterial flora which break it down into a rich detrital soup, spilling out with the tide and enriching the estuary. This attracts many animals to come in and feed.

The second most important colonizer of the bare mud is the Glasswort *Salicornia*. The *Salicornia* genus has several species, all quite difficult to tell apart. *S. europaea* is the most widespread and common species and is an annual plant, germinating in April when rain dilutes the salinity of the mud; with the algae helping to provide stability the tiny seeds grow into small green balls. By expending energy it can draw salt up into the tissues which brings water. Salt is toxic in large quantities and to aid survival the Glasswort is succulent, storing the water to reduce the salinity. After only a few months it produces many tiny flowers on the surface which create minute seeds and then the plant dies, usually from the base of the stem up as salt is concentrated there.

The third colonizer is a grass like *Spartina* but significantly smaller – the Common Salt-marsh Grass *Puccinellia maritima* has finer leaves and creeps over the surface. Although it has the potential to grow up to 80cm tall it is usually found sprawling across mud, sending out horizontal stems, called stolons. Typically, they weave amongst the other plants but can become dominant when competition is low, where there is waterlogging and low salinity, the opposite of *Salicornia*. There are a number of different species but *P. maritima* is the most common and widespread species on salty sand and mud. *Puccinellia* has a wide range on the salt-marsh, is very variable and can be found almost anywhere around the other vegetation. Part of this success is due to its reliance on vegetative propagation to spread with minimal sexual reproduction. As a consequence it is often difficult to find a flower. As well as the stolons for asexual reproduction it is an apomictic plant (where the eggs are not fertilized but still develop, a type of cloning process). If a salt-marsh becomes grazed, usually by sheep, this grass becomes the most dominant species across the marsh with the sheep helping the spread by accidentally dropping pieces of grass and treading them in so they grow.

All three plants help in the accretion process, trapping sediment with each tide. The small *Salicornia* has an accretion rate of up to 3cm/year whilst *Spartina* is 5–10cm/year. The sandy silt collected by *Puccinellia* can reach 10cm/year. It is interesting to compare this with the mangrove, the salt-marsh equivalent in the tropics where accretion is much lower at around 0.2mm/year due to the pioneer vegetation being trees.

Fig. 5.13
Base of a *Spartina* leaf showing the ligule.

Fig. 5.14
Glasswort in flower on the stem.

Fig. 5.15
Ligule and leaf base of *Puccinellia*.

Additional plant species of the lower salt-marsh

Algae

Ulva and other algae tolerant of variable salinity grow across the mud surface and often under *Spartina* which provides them with some stability. Numerous diatoms and blue-green algae live in the surface sediment, secreting mucilage to anchor themselves and reduce water loss. These algal mats increase the stability of the surface and encourage further deposition to occur, in particularly, enabling plants like the glasswort to become established. Larger, brown algae may grow in forms called ecads amongst the lower salt-marsh vegetation.

Ecads are macro-algae deformed by environmental stress not normally encountered, e.g. sheltered areas where fresh water sustains a low salinity. They may at first appear to be broken fronds washed up and trapped by the marsh. *Pelvetia* is found in bare patches on the middle marsh. *Ascophyllum* produces a distinct form known as ecad *mackaii*. Only the air bladders are like

Fig. 5.16
Dark areas of sediment around the salt-marsh are mats of diatoms and bacteria.

Fig. 5.17
Underwater view of the diatom mats photosynthesizing and releasing bubbles of oxygen.

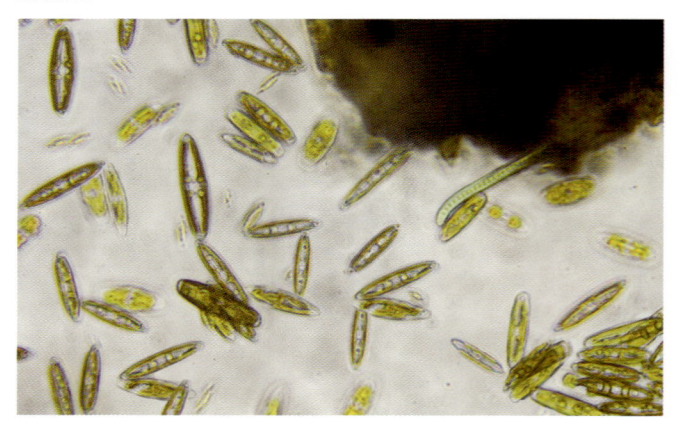

Fig. 5.18
Diatom mat sample under a microscope, magnified ×100, showing the diatoms and a strand of cyanobacteria.

Fig. 5.19
Ecad of Knotted Wrack, usual form on the right.

Fig. 5.20 Annual Seablite *Suada maritima*.

the normal form and in common with all ecads, it is not attached, rising and falling with the tide. It is a ball of curled fronds which interlock with other algae and salt-marsh plants, preventing them from being washed away. Ecads will be replenished by viable fragments of plants washed in by the tide. Zonation of ecads develops where they are abundant (typically, the west coast of Scotland) following the rocky shore pattern.

Higher plants

The Common Reed *Phragmites australis* is the tallest European grass at up to 3m (see Fig. 4.36). It replaces *Spartina* as salinity becomes very low at the head of the estuary, often producing a gradual transition as it invades the *Spartina* beds. Like *Spartina* it colonizes water-logged sediments with vigorous side growth to become quickly established. It can tolerate waterlogging by using air tissue in the plant, taking air down to the roots.

Eel or Sea Grasses *Zostera* species are important flowering plant species, not actually grasses, occurring around the coast with flattened leaves and tiny flowers pollinated by the water currents. The flattened leaves of *Zostera marina* are up to 1m long and 5–10mm wide but it is only found at the lowest levels of the shore and sub-littoral. The species found on mudflats and below the salt-marsh will be *Z. noltii* and *Z. augustifolia*, which are significantly smaller and more abundant. The creeping rhizomes send shoots up and downwards, stabilizing shifting mud. They can accrete extensive mud banks. The leaves have salt glands and can be a significant part of the diet of Brent Geese on migration.

Annual Seablite *Suada maritima*, a close relative of Glasswort, commonly occurs on salt-marsh and may be found with its relative once the marsh has become established. It can grow almost anywhere on the marsh up to the strandline.

See also *Ulva*, *Vaucheria*, *Calothrix*, *Pelvetia*, *Fucus* spp.

Fig. 5.21
Burrows and excavations of beetles.

Fig. 5.22
Bledius spectabilis, at 4mm in length. This female can spray a toxic mist onto parasitic wasps which enter the chamber to inject eggs into her eggs.

Fig. 5.23
Male *Bledius unicornis,* a small species approx. 2.5mm.

Fig. 5.24 *Bledius* burrow, arrowed, showing the side chamber with egg.

Animals of the lower salt-marsh

Depending on the circumstances a wide variety of organisms seen on sediment shores could be present in the mud around the pioneer zone, for example the Peppery Furrow Shell (see Chapter 4).

Insects

Hidden in this community are some of the most interesting and best examples of insects that have adapted to the marine environment forming dense and easily overlooked populations. The key problems to overcome are: tidal inundation and obtaining oxygen, the substrate, salt in the food and dispersal. To survive they have become highly specialized. An adaptation common to all is to be small, enabling them to survive in tiny crevices where air becomes trapped at high tide; another is a complete change in behaviour compared to related species on dry land. Salt can be extracted by Malpighian Tubules linked to the gut of insects but any process involving metabolism will be expensive in terms of energy. The main insect groups colonizing salt-marshes are the true bugs (Hemiptera), beetles and true flies (Diptera).

During May burrows appear in the sediment around the salt cliff with excavated debris around the entrance. They are produced by a number of different rove beetle species, the largest one being *Bledius spectabilis* at 4mm but most are significantly smaller. At low tide the tiny beetles run around the surface in search of food which is green algae. This is especially sought after rain when salt levels will be lowest. Food is stored near the top of the 10cm deep burrows, produced by the females. The entrance is narrow opening to a wide burrow with side chambers in which a single egg is laid, 24 overall. These are licked regularly to keep them free of fungus in this humid environment. Most importantly she aerates the burrow but the moment water seeps in with a returning tide she plugs the exit with stones to seal the chamber. On hatching, larvae are fed the alga but ultimately they leave and set up their own burrows before pupating and emerging as an adult. Very high densities of the burrows can occur, running into 1,000s per m². Few insects show the level of parental care found in the *Bledius* group and this is certainly an adaptation to the inhospitable habitat.

With such a plentiful supply of prey it is not surprising

Fig. 5.25
Pupa of a ground beetle predator found in the *Bledius* burrows, 3mm long.

Fig. 5.26
Bembidion littorale, 3mm long, beetle predator of *Corophium* and other beetles.

Fig. 5.27
Salt-marsh bug *Saldula pilosella* – a tiny predator, 2mm in length, top view.

Fig. 5.28
Salt-marsh bug *Saldula pilosella* – side view showing the proboscis underneath.

that ground beetle predators are here. *Dyschirius* and *Dicheirotrichus* are two commonly found genera. They move from burrow to burrow feeding on different stages in the life cycle of the prey. The former species has a very flexible 'waist' – ideal to negotiate the tight burrow entrance. They have their own burrows which can interconnect with those of *Bledius*. *Bembidion (Cillenus) littorale*, another common ground beetle, feeds on a wide variety of prey including small crustaceans like *Corophium*. All are very small, up to 4mm.

A group of true bugs that have adapted well to life here is the genus *Saldula*. Again, just a few millimetres in length they can be seen running across the sediment in significant numbers. With no fixed burrow to hide in at high tide they have adapted by being very fast runners and agile jumpers to avoid the incoming seawater. They jump on to vegetation and with their long sharp claws hold on tight, the streamlined body avoids the drag of the water. They can then tolerate periods of immersion until the tide drops, and are an active predator on other insects living here. The common froghopper bug, *Philaenus spumarius*, is a sap-sucking bug found on *Spartina*. It is tolerant of a wide range of environmental factors and although mainly on grasses it is found on 170 different hosts across most communities.

Salt-marsh

Fig. 5.29
Brent Geese feeding on the marsh in winter.

Fig. 5.30
Wigeon male (centre) with female (right).

Birds

The Brent Goose *Branta bernicla*, 60cm, with a black head and chest and a white patch on the side of the neck, is well adapted for marine life, found overwintering on salt-marsh; it nests in the Arctic migrating south for winter in the British Isles, where it starts feeding on *Zostera*. After about a month it moves onto *Ulva* and algal mats growing on the mud surface. This corresponds to the time of maximum growth of these plants. In the spring it changes to the higher marsh where it feeds on young salt-marsh grasses, e.g. *Puccinellia*. Salt-marshes are important feeding places for many overwintering birds mainly because the algae can grow throughout the year. In the absence of marine food they are known to move on to agricultural land. The Wigeon *Anas penelope* 50cm is a common duck on the lower salt-marsh in winter, feeding on *Zostera*, algae and fescue and often following behind the Brent Geese.

See also *Hydrobia*, *Corophium*, *Carcinus*, Shelduck and waders.

Salt pans

Across the entire salt-marsh are patches of bare mud of varying sizes. They often form where developing islands of vegetation merge. Some may become colonized but usually they fill with seawater and salt accumulates. Evaporation, during periods of dry weather and neap tides, increases the salinity. Rain will dilute the salt. In this way salinity varies to such extremes that plants find growth intolerable. Glasswort and Cord Grass may temporarily colonize but little else can cope with such variable salinity. At high tide animals may become trapped in them, depending on the size, like shrimps and fish. In times of rain salt pans become brackish and host temporary populations of breeding insects, especially mosquitoes and midges. There are varieties of insects like Water Boatman *Sigara* and water beetles more typical of pond life that have species adapted for the brackish life. Comparisons can be made with rockpools and like those, several more permanent populations exist. The small isopod crustacean *Lekanesphaera rugicauda* is a widespread species characteristic of flooded salt pans. It may attach to the surrounding vegetation or actively swim in the pool. It will be found in salinities down to 0.4 per cent and occurs in various forms including colour types (polymorphism), red, yellow and grey. The colour gene frequency depends on the salinity and temperature: yellow has a faster growth rate than grey under cold conditions and larger individuals have a higher chance of survival.

Hydrobia and *Corophium* are common in the surface mud of the flooded pans.

Fig. 5.31
A large salt pan. Note the *Spartina* colonizing on the left.

Fig. 5.32
Lekanesphaera rugicauda, a small isopod crustacean.

Salt-marsh creek community

Fig. 5.33
Creek community. Note the slumping of the side and recolonization by pioneers.

Problems and features

- The edges of the creek are unstable and prone to erosion; the ebb and flood of the sediment-loaded tidal water scours the borders of the creeks twice a day.
- Slumping of the edge will cause a step arrangement; if the mud is not washed away it may be recolonized by salt-marsh species.
- Daily scouring by the tide will prevent vascular plants growing on the steep sides.
- The tops of the edges are raised, being higher than the salt-marsh; this is called the levee.
- Drainage at the edge is high; obtaining water is a problem for organisms but waterlogging less so.
- Salt concentrations in the mud are high.
- If the creek becomes blocked, e.g. by slumping, a deep pool or channel pan develops.
- Creeks can make up almost a quarter of the area of a salt-marsh.

Fig. 5.34
Close-up of the bank showing thick mats of cyanobacteria.

Fig. 5.35 Narrow creek with dominant Sea Purslane.

Fig. 5.36 Sea Purslane *Atriplex portulacoides* flower.

Fig. 5.37 Sea Purslane with the red alga *Bostrychia scorpioides* beneath.

Fig. 5.38 Close-up of the surface of the leaf of Sea Purslane.

Creeks are a characteristic feature of marsh development. They ramify the surface and may occupy over a quarter of the area. Continual scouring by the tides will maintain them and their steep sides makes traversing the marsh difficult.

Sea Purslane *Atriplex portulacoides*

- A low growing, bushy plant; the elliptical leaves have a dense pile of velvet-like hairs which help to reduce water loss by transpiration.
- Characteristic species of the creek banks, where drainage is greatest.
- Sediment becomes trapped between lateral branches of the woody stems that lie prostrate and so adds to the accretion.
- To eliminate salt it is deposited in the leaves and then discarded, contributing to the detritus.
- Extensive woody rhizomes grow deep into the banks, giving some stability, and resistance to the scouring water in the creek.
- Intolerant of grazing or trampling.
- It may be affected by low temperatures in winter; it is rare in Scotland and Scandinavia.
- An epiphytic red alga *Bostrychia scorpioides* attaches to the base of the stem, obtaining shelter under the plant.
- Several fungi (moulds) are associated with the root system, forming mycorrhizae; this may help the plant in obtaining sufficient nutrients in a well-drained soil.
- It is susceptible to oil pollution whilst many other salt-marsh plants, e.g. *Puccinellia*, are tolerant.
- It is a refuge for many salt-marsh insects and spiders.

Vaucheria species

- A tiny, brown, filamentous alga which may grow in such profusion as to produce a thick, conspicuous layer on the mud surface with an appearance like felt.
- It colonizes the steep sides of creeks, where vascular plants are unable to attach, by using rhizoids. It also secretes a mucilage which binds the mud surface and reduces water loss from its cells.
- *Calothrix* and other cyanobacteria may be associated with *Vaucheria*, darkening the surface further.

Amongst the algal mats, covering the creek sides, is a micro-community of protists, nematodes, flatworms and microscopic crustaceans like copepods. Taking samples for examination under the microscope will show variation through the year. Where water accumulates thin diatom mats can proliferate in the winter.

Where slumping of the banks occurs, a range of species colonize depending on salinity and drainage including the grasses *Spartina*, *Puccinellia* and *Festuca rubra* as well as *Salicornia* and *Plantago maritima*.

Animals of the salt-marsh creeks

This may depend on the state of the tide as fish swim up the creeks at high tide and birds occupy them when it is clear. Whether small or large the creeks are like small estuaries and many of the estuarine organisms seen in the previous chapter can exist here. Notable species include *Gammarus duebeni*, an amphipod which survives burrowed under algae and debris at low tide. There is a cyclical change in the salinity of the water here and the amphipod is well adapted to regulate its blood concentration within narrow limits. Few other organisms can tolerate such extremes. *Corophium* is similar and lives in small burrows. Both are detrital feeders. The isopod *Lekanesphaera rugicauda*, which is common in salt pans, lives in the surface sediment and on algae, swimming freely at high tide. The larvae are less tolerant of low salinity.

Fish

The gobies and the Three-spined Stickleback *Gasterosteus aculeatus* swim up the creeks to feed on crustacea and are well able to cope with osmoregulation. The latter also feeds on copepods and ostracods. Juvenile Flounder live in the wider creeks and move away with age. Creeks are used by the Common Eel *Anguilla anguilla*, on their migration from fresh water to the sea, for feeding and acclimation, although eels are becoming increasingly rare.

Birds

Many of the species found in estuaries will occur here, such as the Shelduck and Little Egret. Mallard occasionally occur as well as wintering Wigeon consuming algal mats and shrimps. Waders like Curlew, Greenshank and Curlew Sandpiper will feed within creeks. The Redshank not only feeds in the creeks but nests on the levee, where it is slightly raised and drier than the surrounding marsh. If there is a very high tide the downy chicks are buoyant and float.

Terns hover over creeks, feeding on the fish that move in with the tide, and various gull species scavenge here on materials that wash into the creeks from the salt-marsh. Snipe can be found in large numbers when on autumn migration, feeding under the cover of the marsh and edges. A small brown bird, the Twite, overwinters on salt-marshes. Also known as a 'mountain linnet', it breeds in the north and Arctic on moorlands.

Fig. 5.39
Sea Purslane dominating the creek banks like a monoculture.

Upper salt-marsh community

Fig. 5.40
Upper salt-marsh community.

Fig. 5.41
Upper marsh – August.

Both the community view and general view (bottom left) were photographed in August, the peak flowering period. The latter shows the prolific Sea Lavender and Sea Aster on the upper marsh. Bottom right is a similar area photographed in April when Scurvy Grass flowers.

Fig. 5.42
Upper marsh – April.

Salt-marsh 137

Problems and features

- Partial flooding during spring tides causes drag which uproots plants.
- Low salt content in the soil (sediment).
- Shows a transition of salt-marsh into dry land.
- Strandline at the top of this region has deposits of organic matter and possible quantities of inorganic flotsam, e.g. plastic bottles, which have a shading effect on the plants.
- The most stable and constant habitat in the salt marsh.

Fig. 5.43 Thrift – *Armeria maritima*.

Fig. 5.44.1 Sea Aster *Aster tripolium*. Despite the daily covering by muddy water the flowers survive for weeks.

Fig. 5.44.2 Sea Aster *Aster tripolium*. 'Rayless' variety.

Sea Aster *Aster tripolium*

- There are several growth forms, depending on salinity, from a stunted form, 5cm in height, to 180cm types in optimum conditions (lime rich and low salinity).
- A short-lived perennial with two types of flower, those with rays of pale purple 'petals' (strictly speaking ray florets) and those which are rayless.
- Can be found throughout the marsh but seeds require fresh water for germination.
- Seed dispersal by wind is impeded as the fruits tend to clump together and fall to the ground; tidal water flooding the marsh then disperses them, which helps to prevent loss of seeds to the land.
- It is intolerant of shade.
- The leaves are often consumed by wildfowl.

Sea Plantain *Plantago maritima* (dead flowers present here, flowering in May)

- The narrow, fleshy leaves offer less resistance to water flow when immersed.
- It produces very dense roots.
- It is common in the upper and middle marsh.
- Shows great tolerance to a variety of stresses and forms part of several different communities, e.g. mountains and moorland.

Sea Lavender *Limonium* (species at the peak flowering period)

- A short, woody perennial, about 12cm high with lanceolate leaves which, combined with its small size, offers least drag amongst the plants here.
- It has a deep tap root.
- It has broad lavender-like flowers which can colour the salt marsh purple.
- Salt glands are found on the lower epidermis, excreting excess salt from cell sap, up to $0.5mm^3$ of salt per hour; it is the most salt-tolerant species in the upper marsh.
- Approximately 20 per cent of the root is air space, to overcome the absence of oxygen in the partly waterlogged soil.
- Chloroplasts in the cells are known to accumulate salt and may be responsible for a modified metabolism.

Thrift *Armeria maritima* (dead flowers present here, flowering in May)

- Common stress-tolerant plant able to cope with most maritime habitats, e.g. splash zone of rocky shore.
- It may form a dominant band of vegetation on the upper marsh where its pink flowers colour the marsh in early summer.

Fig. 5.45
Scurvy Grass *Cochlearia officinalis* flower surrounded by Sea Spurrey.

Fig. 5.46
Sea Spurrey *Spergularia* flower.

Fig. 5.47
Sea Milkwort *Glaux maritima*.

Fig. 5.48
Sea Rush *Juncus maritimus*.

- Salt glands for excreting salt are present on the leaves and it is therefore tolerant of high salt content.
- It is tolerant of grazing and this may be the reason for its abundance on some salt marshes with *Puccinellia*.
- A deep root system, where food storage occurs, gives it an added advantage of resistance over other competitors in the marsh.
- Its narrow leaves and squat nature reduce water current drag.

Red Fescue *Festuca rubra*
- A fine hair-like grass often found near the base of the common salt-marsh grass.
- Salt tolerant but becomes dominant at the top of the marsh with the optimum growth being above the strandline.
- Very tolerant of grazing and under such conditions may become dominant with *Armeria*.

Additional plant species of the upper salt-marsh

Scurvy Grass *Cochlearia officinalis* is not visible in the community photograph as it appears and flowers from April. Height is variable depending on the conditions, from a few centimetres to a bushy 50cm. It is not a grass but a member of the cabbage family with heart-shaped and succulent leaves. Also found in the upper marsh is Sea Spurry *Spergularia*, both the lesser and greater varieties. Sea Milkwort *Glaux maritima* is a short, creeping perennial and occurs in the highest and drier areas of the marsh. It is tolerant of both salinity (salt glands present) and low light levels (shade plant). The latter is possibly an adaptation to being near the strandline where it regularly becomes covered in debris. Orache *Atriplex prostrata* is often found amongst the strandline where the nitrogen content is high (see Fig. 6.6); seeds float and are dispersed by the tide. Sea Rush *Juncus maritimus* can be found around the strandline forming a distinct band on the marsh, up to 60cm. It consists of dense tufts which shade the ground below, slowing down evaporation from the soil. This region may be wetter than lower down the shore, allowing middle marsh species to grow here. It is not tolerant of a high salt content and the seeds only develop in fresh water although they can germinate under anaerobic conditions.

Algae
As well as diatoms thriving in the upper surface of the sediment, several species of larger algae can be found wrapped around the stems of the salt marsh plants. Many are just broken fragments of seaweed washed in by the tide but some use the tide for dispersal, such as *Ulva*. Becoming entangled in the marsh can be an advantage as it increases stability. Light for photosynthesis could

Fig. 5.49
Transition of salt-marsh into fresh water.

Fig. 5.50
Sea Club-rush *Bolboschoenus maritimus*.

be a problem for algae living underneath the tall marsh plants, so many species peak in early spring before marsh plants grow large.

Transition to a freshwater marsh

In some places, especially in areas of high rainfall, notably Scotland, Ireland and parts of Wales, the strandline may mark a transition into a freshwater bog. *Carex* (sedges) will be common amongst the *Juncus* (rushes). One widespread brackish species is the Sea Club-rush *Bolboschoenus maritimus* found in salt-marsh communities where fresh water dilutes seawater. In fact it is a good indicator of very low salinity and occurs high up the estuary where its range merges with that of the Common Reed. It also indicates high levels of mineral nutrients in the mud, which might be expected in the

Fig. 5.51
Grey Bulrush *Schoenoplectus tabernaemontani*.

strandline although this is not always the case. It may occur in non-saline conditions like sand dune slacks. In northern regions Common Flag Iris may replace Sea Club-rush. The Grey Bulrush *Schoenoplectus tabernaemontani* is a salt-marsh variant of the freshwater Bulrush. It is taller and with a blue sheen on the surface

140 Salt-marsh

Fig. 5.52
Grey Bulrush upper stem with flower.

Fig. 5.53
Naidid worm from the soil.

Fig. 5.54
Salt-marsh Wolf Spider *Pardosa purbeckensis*; note the strands of web.

compared to the Club-Rush, and is found in brackish mud where water runs on to the marsh. Very clear zones are visible.

Animals of the upper salt-marsh

Worms
The diverse group of polychaetes are found exclusively in the marine environment. In this community the more terrestrial forms are found, some highly adapted oligochaete worms. They are few in species diversity and are small, less than a centimetre in most cases. Tubifex worms live in the top layer of sediment and wriggling movements help to aerate the burrow. They can appear in huge numbers, particularly as they flourish in a variety of salinities, reddening the surface. Most oligochaetes are not so obvious here but small, white and delicate like the Naidids, which are more at home in fresh water, surviving in the algal turf and beneath the vegetation. With asexual reproduction they can bud off chains of segments to create new clones.

Arthropods
Hoverflies are abundant in summer, feeding on the pollen. Most of the animals of the upper marsh are terrestrial arthropods which have adapted to live in a habitat that floods daily. Those that show specific adaptations to living here include root aphids that have adapted to particular host species found on the upper marsh, like the Sea Aster, where they survive on the root system throughout the year. An aphid, *Lipaphis cochleariae*, and *Phaedon cochleariae*, a bright blue chrysomelid beetle (3mm long), feed specifically on Scurvy Grass, the latter falling prey to ground beetles. Dispersed by the tide across the entire marsh the small blue marine springtail *Anurida maritima* can turn up almost anywhere on the shore. Common on the rocky shore (see Figs 2.46–2.47), here it is a burrower. With a circadian rhythm to follow the tide, it emerges from a burrow shortly after the tide retreats. The greatest density occurs where the vegetation is least and near salt pans. High on the marsh it is restricted by competition with terrestrial springtails.

The Salt-marsh Wolf Spider *Pardosa purbeckensis* (0.9mm) is dark brown with pale patches on the carapace and small white dots on the abdomen. It runs rapidly over the surface of mud feeding on beetles, bugs and small crustaceans. With a returning tide the spider dives to the base of the vegetation where it stays with a trapped air bubble, sometimes held by strands of web, for up to several hours.

Birds
Snipe feed here during the winter, protected from sight in the vegetation, but otherwise shore species are not abundant, remaining along creek edges like the Redshank and Shelduck. Nesting is attempted by a few birds where there is no flooding, e.g. skylarks and meadow pipits on the raised areas.

See also *Littorina*, *Hydrobia*, *Carcinus*, *Corophium*, *Orchestia*.

Part 2: Ecology of the salt-marsh

General features

- A gradual transition and zonation of species occurs from the strandline to the lower salt-marsh, which is equivalent to the upper shore.
- Flowering plants dominate the shore with a secondary cover of small algae.
- A limited number of plant species are present and they are highly specialized, called halophytes ('salt tolerant').
- It is productive throughout the year, attracting birds in winter.
- The animal communities are principally terrestrial with marine species replacing them in the sparser vegetation of the lower marsh.
- As a hostile environment it is one of the most stressful of habitats for organisms to survive showing strong adaptations but with limited diversity.

The zonation of plants on the salt-marsh is primarily due to differing abilities to cope with salinity and waterlogging of the soil. Zonation of plants may also be due to seedlings' intolerance to salt, rather than adults'. Most halophytes develop tolerance with age. Animals display a gradual transition of terrestrial species in the upper areas to mud communities lower down, due to the salt content of the plants they graze upon. Several invertebrates are found here which are associated with one plant species. Where this plant has specialized to the stresses of the environment the animal has become unique. Lower salt-marsh species are detritivores. There is an interesting comparison with other seashore distribution patterns.

Summary of factors affecting salt-marsh species and zonation

Salinity
This varies over the area of the salt-marsh; salt is deposited within the sediment and therefore salinity of the soil is concentrated making it difficult for vascular plants to obtain water through the roots against an osmotic gradient. Salt pans show the greatest variation.

Waterlogging and oxygen
The tide may cover the plant with seawater but waterlogging of the sediment drives out oxygen and creates anoxic conditions. These are fatal conditions for roots. Vascular plants need to absorb minerals through roots (unlike the algae) and that requires energy, hence the need for oxygen for respiration.

Light and submergence
The seawater that submerges the marsh at high tide is very turbid due to the enormous quantity of detritus, which will seriously restrict light and photosynthesis. It will also restrict gaseous exchange around the leaves. Tidal movement has a dragging effect on the plants and this mechanical force can inflict tissue damage.

Rainfall and freshwater runoff
Drainage is poor on salt-marshes and seepage of water from the land as well as rain will change the salinity. This may affect the osmotic balance of an organism or the germination of seeds. It also allows colonization by freshwater species.

Fig. 5.55 Zonation: key plant species in order of their appearance from lower marsh (left) to upper marsh (right).

Fig. 5.55.1 Cord Grass.

Fig. 5.55.2 Glasswort.

Fig. 5.55.3 Sea Purslane.

Salt-marsh

Plant adaptations to the limiting factors

Tissue with a high osmotic potential
To absorb water through the roots a concentration gradient must be maintained so that water flows from the substrate into the plant tissue. Halophytes are the few specialized plants able to absorb and store very high levels of salt in their cells which maintains a concentration high enough for water to pass into them from the saline soil. This requires expenditure of energy as well as modified metabolism.

Salt glands
These are located on leaves (which tend to have the lowest osmotic potential) and consist of a few cells near the surface. They will differ between those halophytes which bear them. In most cases ATP (Adenosine Triphosphate) is used to pump chloride ions to the surface and the difference in the charge pulls sodium ions to the outside. This is an active excretion method.

Shedding leaves
This may be in addition to or instead of glands. In the autumn, salt is transported to leaves which are then dropped. Glasswort sheds salt at the end of the season but uses the stem as it does not have leaves. However, Sea Purslane is not seasonal and drops leaves whenever the salt content reaches an unacceptable level.

Succulence
This is comparable to cacti and is a way of tolerating high salt content in tissues by compensation with a high water uptake. Succulence also reduces drag, since the rounded profile gives a reduced surface area.

Air tissue
With anaerobic conditions in the soil, air is conducted down to the roots through aerenchyma tissue passing through the stem. *Spartina* contains over 70 per cent air space in the root and diffusion of air into the soil creates aerobic conditions around the root surface. This maintains an oxidizing layer which does not have toxic side effects.

Sclerenchyma
This needle-like tissue is found in most land plants but halophytes are high in these tough fibres and are able to resist the mechanical stresses of the tide when submerged. This is where *Spartina* gets the name Cord Grass, as the fibres coat the leaf surface (see Fig. 5.55.1).

Water conservation
Surrounded by salt water the plants need to conserve the pure water they do obtain. Halophytes have a lower number of stomata per unit area of leaf than most land plants. *Puccinellia* can curl leaves and *Spartina* has the stomata in pits to hold moisture.

Fig. 5.55.4
Sea Lavender.

Fig. 5.55.5
Sea Aster.

Fig. 5.55.6
Sea Rush.

Fig. 5.55.7
Sea Club-rush.

Fig. 5.56
The result of grazing by sheep on the salt-marsh. Note the salt-pans and creek.

Photosynthesis

Several halophytes have C4 metabolism. The difference with the more usual C3 is in the fixing of the CO_2. In C3 metabolism, phosphoglyceric acid (PGA) is the substance produced from the fixation. C4 plants (mainly tropical species) are those able to use an additional pathway. Here CO_2 reacts with phosphoenolpyruvate (PEP) to give oxaloacetic acid which can then be converted into aspartate or malate. This is within a cycle called the Hatch-Slack Cycle. The significance of this to salt-marsh plants is that (a) it requires less CO_2; (b) they can store these substances and hence store CO_2; and (c) it uses less water. The first of these helps the plant to photosynthesize when covered by water (reduced gaseous exchange occurs) and less water is used. In the second, storage of CO_2 means the completion of photosynthesis can take place at a different time to CO_2 absorption. That helps conservation of water as the stomata, if they have them, do not need to open in sunlight to bring in CO_2, this can be done at night.

Colonization and succession on salt-marshes

The zonation on the salt-marsh is a dynamic one involving a change in the communities with time, a process called succession. The speed of replacement by one community over another depends on several factors: the rate of supply of sediment; the degree of shelter afforded to the marsh; and the topography of the land. Complete succession from mud to a closed salt-marsh community may take between 200 and 500 years.

Pioneer phase

Algal growth on the sediment will help to stabilize the surface and allow the initial colonization of bare mud to take place. The actual pioneer species depends a little on the conditions. Cord Grass can be found on almost any salt-marsh but Glasswort needs more surface stability. The Common Salt-marsh Grass will do well but is not so salt-tolerant or dominant and may do better where grazing occurs. The two grasses are perennials and so can maintain their position. Creeping rhizomes of Cord Grass colonize rapidly and the plant may remain on its own for twenty-five years. During this time it is stabilizing the marsh and removing some of the salt, returning it to the sea via the active salt glands. Air is taken down to the roots and some diffuses into the soil, killing the anaerobic bacteria by the presence of oxygen and thus reducing soil toxicity.

Transition and establishment

By their actions the pioneers, so well adapted to the environment stress, improve the soil conditions. Gradually, other species that do not have these pioneering adaptations begin to invade spaces between the colonists. Sea Aster and Sea Lavender in particular slowly become established. They still require halophytic adaptations to survive but as things become crowded competition for nitrogen and light will weaken the pioneers. Salt-marsh Grass sustains itself by continued side growth. Pioneer species are typically not good at competing and are steadily eradicated by the better competitors. The vegetation changes to a general salt-marsh community. Grazing by domestic animals and the presence of fresh water will influence further changes. Tidal water draining from the marsh erodes sediment and forms the creeks which display the most dynamism, potentially destabilizing the marsh with each tide. The scouring effect will cause slumping of the banks which may in turn be recolonized encouraging a secondary succession to take place. Slumping can block creeks which then form into creek pans. Ultimately, these fill in with mud and, as in all salt pans, secondary succession returns them eventually to a full marsh community.

Climax community

Local conditions determine what might happen next as marine influence is reduced and eventually terrestrial conditions prevail. If accretion continues the height of the marsh moves out of the tidal range. Grasses in the marsh, particularly Red Fescue Grass, can become dominant to produce a grassland community. Small tree species such as willow or birch can invade, even oak and sycamore. However, by this stage changes are very slow to take place as the community has stabilized with substantially improved soil conditions. This stable community is now the climax of succession.

Around the strandline some sand dune and shingle species may occur. For example, Lyme Grass (*Leymus arenaria*) and Sand Couch Grass (*Elytrigia juncea*) – the former typical of the northern regions, e.g. Scotland, and the latter more southerly. Dense swathes of Shrubby Seablite (*Suaeda vera*) sometimes dominate the strand-line area if there is shingle present and lower down the marsh a similar species, the Annual Seablite (*S. maritima*) can grow.

Food and feeding relationships

Diatoms and algae abound in the surface sediment as do bacteria. Salt-marsh plants are productive but by virtue of their adaptations, e.g. thick cuticle and sclerenchyma, they are almost inedible whilst alive. As they decay so their nutritious state improves becoming an essential item as detritus in the coastal food web. Much of this detritus will be transferred to other shores, especially mud and sand. In turn, organic matter arrives from other ecosystems where it becomes trapped amongst the halophytes and then slowly rots. Land plants have been shown to form a third of salt-marsh detritus in some cases.

Fig. 5.57 Succession on the salt-marsh.

- Upper/General salt-marsh: Sea Lavender, Sea Aster, Sea Spurrey, Sea Plantain
- Creek: Sea Purslane
- Local Climax: Red Fescue, Sea Rush
- Transition: pioneers out-competed
- Pioneers: Cord Grass, Glasswort

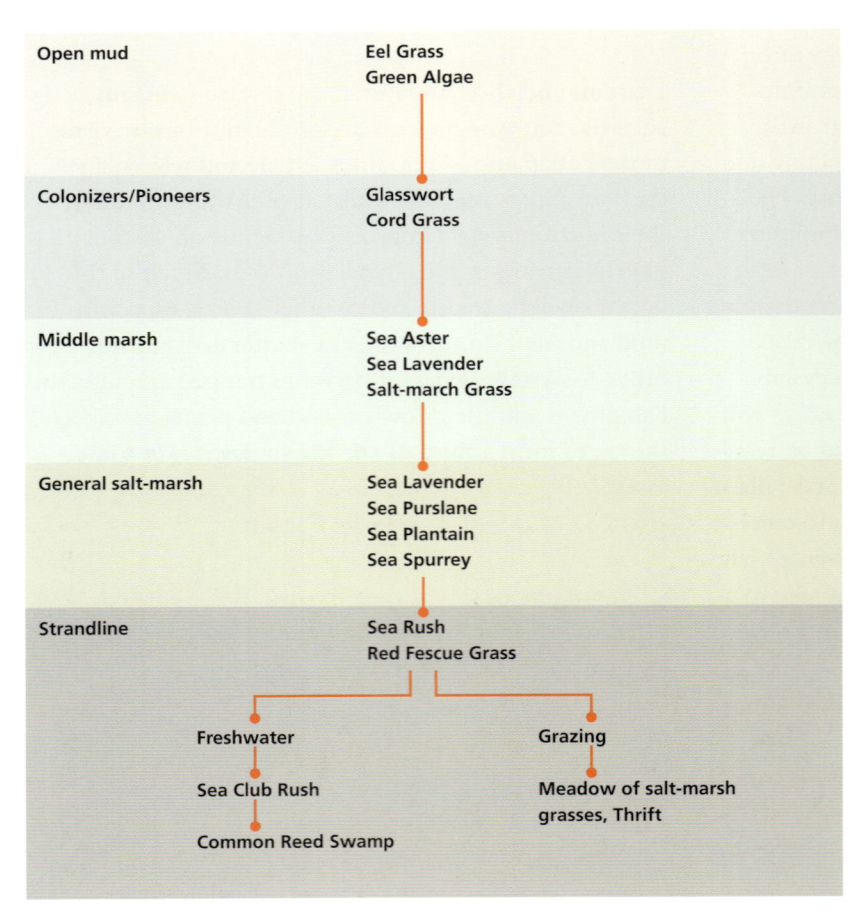

Stage	Species
Open mud	Eel Grass, Green Algae
Colonizers/Pioneers	Glasswort, Cord Grass
Middle marsh	Sea Aster, Sea Lavender, Salt-march Grass
General salt-marsh	Sea Lavender, Sea Purslane, Sea Plantain, Sea Spurrey
Strandline	Sea Rush, Red Fescue Grass

Freshwater → Sea Club Rush → Common Reed Swamp

Grazing → Meadow of salt-marsh grasses, Thrift

Fig. 5.58 Summary of succession within a salt-marsh – a halosere.

Fig. 5.59 Salt-marsh soil mites, important for decomposition.

146 Salt-marsh

Fig. 5.60
Upper marsh in May with Thrift and Sea Plantain in flower. The flying insects are St Mark's Fly *Bibio marci*.

Decomposition

As the plants decay their calorific value to animals actually rises, partly due to the growth of bacteria and fungi on the material. At the start there is a sudden loss in weight as soluble substances wash out. The sclerenchyma tissue that is such a substantial amount of the *Spartina* is high in lignin. It protects the leaves both from drag and being eaten. Lignin takes almost three times as long to decay as cellulose. As well as the micro-flora breaking up the leaf and stem litter there is considerable physical breakdown from tidal action. Once the particles have been made small they are more quickly decomposed by bacteria.

The consumers

Detritus is colonized and consumed by ciliate and flagellate protists. They mainly feed on the saprophytic bacteria. As the decay proceeds, consumption by crustaceans and molluscs increases the decomposition still further. This is because as they void the detritus as faeces it increases the nitrogen content, encouraging bacterial growth. The limited food and the abiotic conditions limit the biodiversity.

Chapter 6
SAND DUNES

Fig. 6.1
The Atlantic coast provides copious amounts of wind-blown sand to create large dune systems. Note the dark green embryo dunes next to the sandy beach.

Part 1: The communities

Introduction

Sand dunes occur above the high tide mark of sandy, sediment shores as their formation requires considerable quantities of wind-blown sand. Whilst not strictly a seashore (they are not found between the tides) they are very closely related. Many plants found on dunes also occur on shingle shores.

Substrate

The sand deposited on the beach and forming the dunes may be eroded rock (such as silica) or tiny fragments of shell. The amount of each will vary and a look under a hand lens may reveal complete, minute shells, some of which belong to the protists Foraminifera. The type of sand strongly influences the eventual development of sand dune communities. Even the smallest patch of dry sand above the high water mark will encourage the growth of some sand dune species.

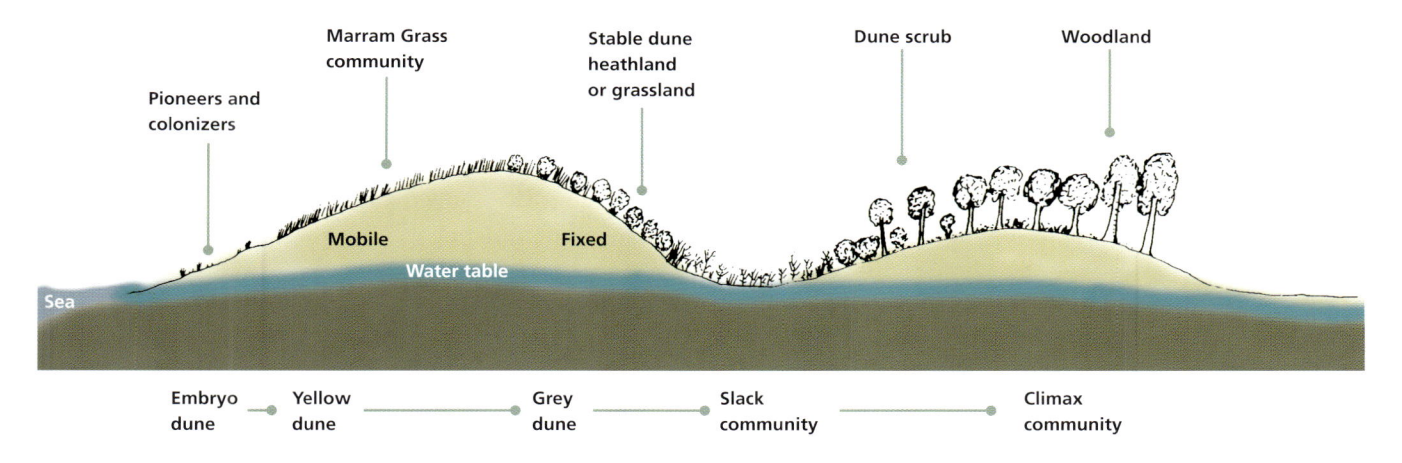

Fig. 6.2
Profile of a sand dune system.

Sand dune formation

The sand is carried inshore by currents and deposited at high tide. At low tide the water drains quickly on sandy beaches and the wind and sun will dry the surface, especially the upper shore. This dry sand is the source of material for the formation of the dunes. The amount is one of the factors in limiting the height and general size of the dune system. Wind is crucial in the development: as wind blows the dry sand up the beach any object projecting above the surface will be struck by the particles, which drop down and collect on the leeward side. In a short time objects are swamped and covered with sand to produce a bump on the beach.

Plants that can survive in this very harsh environment, e.g. Sand Couch, grow by rhizomes spreading out under the sand surface. As these plants become covered by sand it stimulates them to grow above it. More sand hits the plant and collects, and they respond with further growth upwards and outwards, gradually increasing the height and width of the hummocks. The final height depends on the amount of wind-blown sand. Nutrients to help plant growth come from detritus from the strandline. These early, small hummocks are the embryo dunes.

The communities

The earliest plant colonizers are the pioneer species and these help in developing embryo dunes, e.g. Saltwort. These species are gradually replaced by Marram Grass which increases the extent and stability of the dunes. With virtually no soil present and only sand visible these are called yellow dunes or mobile dunes. As stability increases more species colonize the dune, e.g. heather.

Fig. 6.3
Embryo dune formation where the wind-blown sand accumulates on the leeward side of the Sand Couch.

Over time an increase in organic matter develops into a dune soil, darkening the sand, producing a grey dune, also known as a fixed dune. This stability may be due to other grasses like the fescues. Areas near the water table or depressions in the dune become damp, even marshy. These are the dune slacks. After several hundred years, scrubland may develop into woodland, the climax community.

Problems/features of sand dunes

With soil at a minimum, water content is very low. The plants are called xerophytes and are adapted to conserve water: transpiration is slowed and they have extensive root systems with which to find water. The wind and salt only increase the problem of water loss yet further. The soils are very fragile and trampling by people and burrowing by rabbits can break through the soil, releasing fresh wind-blown sand to create blow-outs. These can cause massive erosion. Conditions are not so extreme as in a salt-marsh, however, and a higher biodiversity may be present.

Fig. 6.4
Lyme Grass *Leymus arenarius*. Note the cut grass, the action of rabbits.

Fig. 6.5
Prickly Saltwort *Salsola kali* binding the sand with Sand Couch *Elytrigia juncea* (behind).

Fig. 6.6
Sea Rocket *Cakile maritima* growing in the strandline. *Atriplex* is behind.

Embryo dune – the pioneer zone

Sand Couch *Elytrigia juncea*

- A smaller and finer grass than the Marram, 20–40cm.
- Tolerant of salt, it is the first grass to colonize the bare sand, initiating the building of the dunes.
- Its extensive rhizome system runs horizontally, sending up shoots above the sand, but the extent of underground vertical growth is limited to 40–50cm; hence it cannot compete with Marram in cases of greater amounts of wind-blown sand. The leaves are not very long and tend to droop over, making them poor collectors of sand.
- Root growth is rapid and vertical to reach wetter sand.
- Tolerant of occasional immersion in salt water.
- Tolerant of accretion rates of up to 30cm per year.
- Like Marram the stomata are sunk in pits. When the leaves dry hinge cells cause the leaves to roll up, closing the stomata and reducing water loss; the leaves also have downy hairs along them which trap moisture.
- There is a mycorrhizal association with the roots, which helps to obtain nutrients especially phosphorus.

Sea Rocket *Cakile maritima*

- A short, succulent annual plant.
- A member of the cabbage family; fruits are dispersed by the tide and it may form a dominant covering before the dunes start.
- It obtains many of its nutrients from decayed remains of items washed up on the strandline.
- It is a halophyte, but cannot tolerate submersion in seawater.
- The succulent leaves help tolerate a high internal salt content to enable water to be absorbed.
- It has extremely long roots for both anchorage and water.

Problems for plants

- Very unstable, with wind-blown sand.
- Very low water content.
- Salt is laid down with the sand but gradually removed by rainwater.
- Soil and humus non-existent; limited mineral ions although strandline may provide some nutrients.
- Extremes of temperature.
- Desiccating wind increases water loss.

Fig. 6.7
A small fly *Lipara lucens* lays an egg on Sand Couch, which stimulates a broad growth of plant tissue in which the larva feeds and develops. This swelling is known as a Cigar Gall.

Fig. 6.8
Sea Sandwort *Honckenya peploides*.

Prickly Saltwort *Salsola kali*
- Related to other halophytes like glassworts and seablites, this is a short, semi-prostrate annual pioneer plant.
- Growing low to the ground, its short, prickly leaves help to reduce water loss. Waxy cuticle also reduces water loss and the reduced size of the leaves helps against the drag of the wind.
- The succulent leaves and stem store water, helping it to tolerate a high internal salt content and enabling water absorption.
- It has a huge root system, both horizontal and vertical, which extends for several metres.
- It grows through sand if buried to produce embryonic dunes.

Lyme Grass *Leymus arenarius*
- 1–1.5 metres tall with a broad, stiff leaf.
- Often found with Marram and the Sand Couch as a dune builder.
- It is intolerant of high temperatures and is limited to northern Europe; in Iceland it is the dominant dune plant where Marram, a southern species, does not exist.
- The leaves can roll like the Marram in dry weather to enclose the stomata, reducing water loss.
- Unlike Marram the leaves are lost in autumn; this makes the dune less stable where it is dominant. Also it does not cope well with a covering of sand greater than 50cm and so is found more at the start of the dune system or if the dunes remain low in height.
- It is susceptible to rust and smut fungi, which can be seen as sooty deposit on the stem and leaves.

Orache species *Atriplex* sp. is common on shores where it is prostrate, has salt-glands and semi-succulent leaves. Sea Sandwort *Honckenya peploides* may produce carpets of low-growing clones on sheltered sand and shingle.

Marram Grass *Ammophila arenaria* (1m), is an upright grass which colonizes by an extensive rhizome system. Seeds scatter across the fore dunes in autumn and quickly germinate in the rain. It is intolerant of salt in the sand and does not colonize until rainwater has washed most of the salt away. It is one of the last species to colonize the embryo dune, but once it does the dunes very quickly gain height if wind-blown sand is available.

Yellow dune community – mobile dunes

Fig. 6.9
Yellow dune community.

Note: There is an overlap between the embryo and yellow dune communities.

Marram Grass *Ammophila arenaria*
- With a maximum height of 1m, it dominates the yellow dune.
- It is an upright grass which colonizes by an extensive rhizome system.
- Along the rhizome, leaves grow up to the surface whilst adventitious roots radiate out to collect water.
- If the leaves are covered by sand, buds at the bases produce shoots which break through to the surface and grow another tuft of leaves.
- Tracing back along the shoot the position of the last growth can be found (the node); the spaces between growth points is the internode. The length of internode varies with the depth of sand cover. In a bad winter the deposition of sand could be in metres and is reflected in the length of the shoot internode.
- The rhizome system penetrates deep into the dune which it has helped to create and with the lateral adventitious roots is able to obtain water.
- It is intolerant of salt in the sand.
- Transpiration is slowed by a thick shiny cuticle on the outer epidermis.
- Stomata on the inner epidermis are sunk into pits and surrounded by spines to reduce water loss; this is further enhanced by the presence of hinge cells that curl the leaf depending on the level of external humidity. The result is that in the sunshine the leaf is tightly curled around the inner epidermis but flat if it is raining.
- With Marram domination wind action over the dune reduces, which, in turn, reduces mobile sand and increases stability.
- With a change in the micro-climate the open community of Marram is colonized by other plants.
- In the absence of a new sand covering, the tussock of Marram gradually rots, contributing organic matter to the soil.

Problems for plants
- Unstable, with wind-blown sand; dunes are mobile.
- Very low water content.
- Some salt may be present but most will have been removed from the sand by rainwater.
- Soil and humus are non-existent; mineral ions are limited, although the strandline may provide some nutrients.
- Extremes of temperature.
- Desiccating wind increases water loss.

Fig. 6.10
Section through a Marram leaf showing the hinge cells, inner stomata and spines for water conservation.

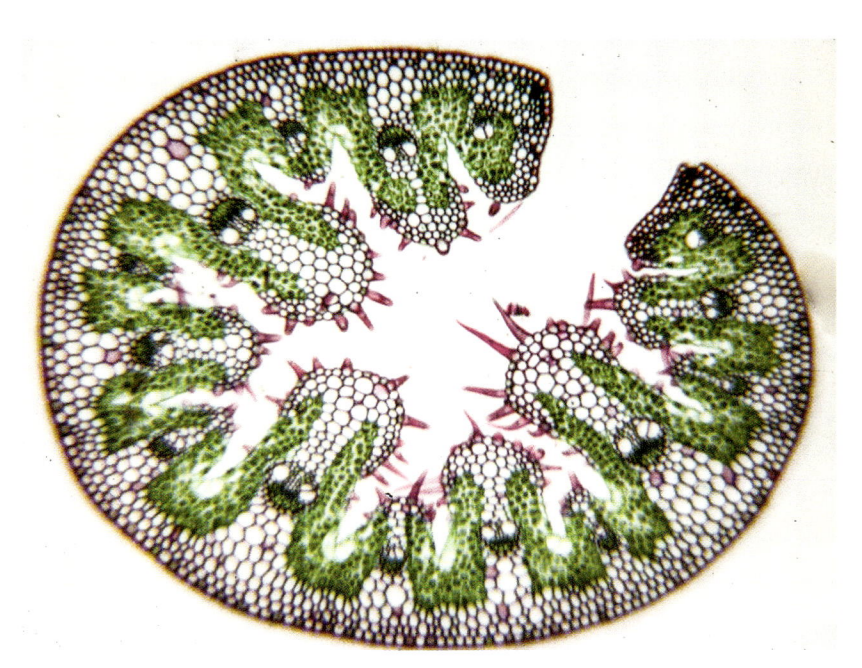

Fig. 6.11
Sea Holly *Eryngium maritimum*.

Fig. 6.12
Sea Holly showing the large tap root.

Sand Sedge *Carex arenaria*
- Invariably the individual plants are found arranged in lines; all are shoots from the same rhizome running about 15cm under the surface. A dense mat of sedge stabilizes the sand.
- It is intolerant of salt and a deep sand covering and so is more abundant where the dunes are more stable, in the grey dune.

Sea Holly *Eryngium maritimum*
- A low-growing perennial which is a member of the carrot family; blue umbel flower.
- It is a halophytic plant able to tolerate salty sand.
- With a tolerance for salt it can colonize before Marram grass.
- It has a fleshy tap root and is able to store water in it.
- It produces an extensive root system, up to 2m in length
- The leaves are leathery with a thick cuticle to reduce water loss; the grey-green bloom is due to a wax coating.
- The roots have a very high level of solutes to create an osmotic potential for water absorption from the sand.
- Like Marram it is able to grow out of a sand covering; the shoot lengthens and the internodes can be measured for the depth of sand.
- The flowers are especially attractive to insects.
- Tides and wind disperse the buoyant seeds.

Fig. 6.13
Portland Spurge *Euphorbia portlandica*.

Fig. 6.14
Sea Spurge *Euphorbia paralias*.

Fig. 6.15
Sea Bindweed *Calystegia soldanella*.

Sea Spurge *Euphorbia paralias* and Portland Spurge *Euphorbia portlandica*
- Both are similar although the latter species has keeled leaves.
- Succulence is a way of overcoming a high salt content in the tissues, necessary in maintaining a suitable osmotic potential.
- Thick waxy cuticles reduce water loss through transpiration.
- Deep roots facilitate anchorage.
- When covered by sand it stimulates growth which quickly brings them back above the surface; as sand covers the leaves so they die off, leaving a scar. Sand covering also stimulates stem branching and eventually they form clumps.
- Like other members of the spurge family they have a white, milky, poisonous latex sap which deters grazers. This means that energy invested in growth is unlikely to be lost to herbivores.

Sea Bindweed *Calystegia soldanella*
- A prostrate perennial, which grows amongst the dune grasses producing trumpet flowers (white with pink stripes) and kidney shaped, succulent leaves for water storage; shiny, waxy cuticle.
- Horizontal, creeping rhizomes spread the plant vegetatively, even when buried, and it is a favourite food of rabbits, which can severely limit its distribution.
- It is halophytic with a high salt content to maintain a very low osmotic pressure for water absorption.

Common Restharrow *Ononis repens*
- Mainly grows on alkali dune soils, where it is often prostrate and low-growing.
- Sticky, glandular hairs on the densely grouped leaves reduce water loss.
- A member of the Pea family, it therefore has nitrogen-fixing bacteria in root nodules.
- Rhizomes anchor the plant and stabilize the sand. The roots of this plant are long and deep enough to have arrested the plough, hence the name rest-harrow.
- Its prostrate growth form protects it from strong wind and the scour of the sand.

Fig. 6.16
Common Restharrow *Ononis repens*.

Fig. 6.17
Sand-hill Screw Moss *Syntrichia (Tortula) ruralis* subsp. *ruraliformis*.

Fig. 6.18
Mature yellow dune community before transition into grey dune.

Sand-hill Screw Moss *Syntrichia (Tortula) ruralis* subsp. *ruraliformis*

- The pale moss curls its pleated leaves against the stem in dry conditions, uncurling them when hydrated.
- This twisting and untwisting of leaves helps to dislodge loose sand grains.
- It is very tolerant of high temperatures, up to 60°C.
- It can shut down metabolic activity for months but will recover almost instantly when wetted.

Sand dunes 155

Fig. 6.19
Cinnabar *Tyria jacobaeae* moth caterpillars feeding on Ragwort.

Fig. 6.20
Cinnabar adult.

Common Cat's Ear *Hypochaeris radicata*
- A rosette plant; the leaves are pressed out flat on to the surface of the sand. Any water transpired from the lower epidermis will condense back into the sand.
- Beneath the rosette is a long tap root which stores water; lateral roots obtain water.
- It is able to tolerate a slight rise in the sand cover; tap root can keep the leaves supported until it has grown through the sand.
- Yellow flowers are borne on elongated stems, which can grow through the Marram tussock for pollination by insects.

Sheep's-bit *Jasione montana*
- A biennial flower which grows in tight-growing units to reduce water loss; long root system.
- Common in many coastal habitats; a relative of the Clustered Bellflower (Fig 6.28).

Ragwort *Senecio jacobaea*
- A common biennial of grassland, Ragwort may become prolific on the dune.
- After germination, the large leaves form a loose rosette on the sand in the autumn and winter when the dunes are at their wettest.
- In the second year of growth an extensive root system develops which is a necessary adaptation to survive the summer months.
- A tall yellow flower develops in the second year; dead flower heads remain until the following year and are conspicuous.
- The plant cells contain cyanide and few organisms eat the leaves. The yellow and black larva of the Cinnabar Moth *Tyria jacobaeae* does eat it; the adult colour is red and black and in both stages the colour warns of being distasteful to possible predators.

Fescue grasses *Festuca* species
- These fine-leaved grasses (reduced surface area for conserving water) further increase stability of the dune.
- Red Fescue is a pioneer grass as it can grow in nutrient-poor soils; other fescue species, e.g. Sheep's Fescue, come in when the soil quality improves.

Animals of the yellow dunes

Invertebrates
Insects and snails are the most abundant invertebrates on dunes although overall there is a paucity due to the limited and coarse vegetation. Harvestmen spiders feed on the visiting insects. The number of snails varies with the degree of calcium. Common Garden Snail *Cornu aspersum* (=*Helix aspersa*) can be very abundant, along with the extremely variable banded snails, although it should be noted that they are not always banded and the bands can be single, double or treble. Colour varieties depend on the vegetation. There are two species to consider, Dark-lipped Banded Snail *Cepaea nemoralis* and the White-lipped Banded Snail *C. hortensis*. Both feed on dead plant material and help in the recycling of the tough dune plants.

Vertebrates
Rabbits are abundant on dunes where burrowing is easy. Their droppings increase the soil humus content as far forward as the embryo dunes. They dig down to feed on the rhizomes, often cropping the leaves in the process. Gulls nesting on dunes increase the soil nitrogen.

Fig. 6.21
Dune Assassin Bug *Coranus woodroffei*. Found almost exclusively on dunes it is a voracious hunter of other invertebrates.

Fig. 6.22
Banded Snails showing some of the colour and pattern variants.

Fig. 6.23
Cochlicella acuta, a common sand dune snail, 10mm in length and actively eaten by sheep.

Fig. 6.24
Rabbits cut the Marram grass, chewing the softer bases. The remains plus their droppings help in the build-up of organic matter.

Fig. 6.25
Fulmar nesting in sand dunes, Outer Hebrides, Scotland.

Sand dunes 157

Grey dune community – fixed dunes with shell sand present

Fig. 6.26
Grey dune community: alkali soil.

Note: There is an overlap between the yellow and grey dune communities. The Marram is in decline here, and the thin soil is now covered in plants.

Marram Grass *Ammophila arenaria*
- Due to the lack of wind-blown sand the Marram begins to fail, tussocks break up to produce considerable leaf litter.
- Marram provides shelter and other plant species begin to grow beneath.
- Disturbance to the thin soil crust will release sand which would rejuvenate Marram (called a blow-out). This would start erosion of the dune and the cycle of dune formation would begin again.

Problems and features
- Very shallow and fragile soil with slight alkalinity.
- Very low water content.
- More sheltered and stable than the yellow dune with little or no wind-blown sand.
- Possible shading of smaller plants by Marram, both dead and alive.
- A wide range of species can live here especially if shell sand is present; most will be occasional colonizers, depending on localized regions and not specific to dunes. Just a few of the commoner species are given here.

Sand Sedge *Carex arenaria*
- This sedge colonizes after the Marram and is one of the most important plants of the dune for stabilizing the ground.
- Colonization is essentially by rhizomes; growth can be up to 4m per year.
- The rhizome grows approximately 15cm below the sand surface and runs in relatively straight lines, sending up tufts of leaves at the nodes.
- These tufts grow off the triangular stem in groups of three to give a 'star-like' appearance from above (typical of sedges).

Fig. 6.27
Sand Sedge *Carex arenaria* with the rhizome partially uncovered to show strong tip. Arrows mark the clone plants at the nodes.

Fig. 6.28
Clustered Bellflower *Campanula glomerata*.

- The tufts reduce wind speed at the soil surface; this and the 'weave' of rhizomes, as they criss-cross the dunes, help in increasing stability.
- The asexually produced tufts of leaves develop a flower; they can be seen in straight lines, showing where the rhizome is buried beneath.
- This rapid colonization will produce clonal groupings so that most likely the individuals seen in a small area are genetically identical.

Wild (Dune) Pansy *Viola tricolor* subsp. *curtisii* (see Fig. 6.48)

- The plant is fairly prostrate to the sand surface with the flowers held above it. They are a variable species in colour and form; many flowers are self-pollinated. Despite the colour variation particular dune systems will have a dominant colour form. This is down to genetic isolation as although the dunes may look extensive each flower patch may be some distance from the next.

Mouse Ear Chickweed *Cerastium* species

- This is an annual plant whose seeds germinate in the autumn when water is plentiful; this produces an abundance of seedlings in the spring.
- To survive the desiccation it dies early in summer, surviving in seed form.

Additional plant species

Once the grey, alkaline dune becomes established it will be more reminiscent of dry grassland and waste ground communities.

Large-flowered Evening Primrose *Oenothera erythrosepaia*, a medium to tall biennial plant with reddish patches on the stem.

Biting Stonecrop *Sedum acre*, a low growing, creeping plant which colonizes patches of the shallow soil and consolidates the stability of the soil surface. There are bright, erect, yellow flowers. Found mainly on alkaline soil, it is capable of living in very dry conditions and is a succulent.

Clustered Bellflower *Campanula glomerata* indicates lime is present. Common well into autumn, it is a hairy perennial up to 40cm tall with spear-shaped leaves.

Other species commonly encountered are the tall, blue Viper's Bugloss, Lady's Bedstraw, Thyme, Helleborines, Bee and Pyramidal Orchids and Yarrow.

Grey dune community – fixed dunes with silica sand

Ling *Calluna vulgaris*
- A bushy heather which produces large numbers of tiny seeds (wind dispersed), enabling quick colonization.
- Germination requires a wet soil and the seeds usually start to develop in autumn. Rapid growth ensures a suitable overwintering plant; growth slows in summer months.
- Seeds need light for germination and young plants develop in open places on the dune. The seeds remain viable for many years and only when the shading effect of Marram declines will the Ling begin to grow.
- After twenty to thirty years the bush begins to collapse, exposing the centre with deep leaf litter; young birch trees may become established here.
- Conservation of water is important: leaves have a very reduced surface area and are clumped together. Stomata are opened and closed according to the turgidity of the plant, rather than set in pits like in other heathers, giving greater control.
- The roots have an association with a fungus called *Phoma*. This assists Ling with its mineral needs, e.g. nitrogen, by localized decomposition.
- As the Ling ages its woody stems become colonized by lichens.

Fig. 6.29
Grey dune community: acid soil.

160 Sand dunes

Fig. 6.30
Ling *Calluna vulgaris*: close-up of the tightly packed leaves (reducing waterloss) and delicate flowers.

Crowberry *Empetrum nigrum*
- A prostrate and creeping plant that resembles the heather family and is a close relative.
- Shiny black berries appear in September after passing through green, pink and purple colours.
- Short leaves reduce water loss but it is not as well adapted as the heathers and is found on dunes and heaths in the north, where higher rainfall occurs.

Problems and features
- Very shallow and fragile soil.
- Very low water content.
- More sheltered and stable than the yellow dune with little wind-blown sand.
- Possible shading of smaller plants by Marram, when both dead and alive.
- Silica sand and any shells incorporated into the dunes are whole: calcium is very low, minerals are leached out by rainwater and the soil becomes base poor. The result is an acid soil, pH 3.5–5: this is a specialized niche for organisms and is typically heathland.

Lichens
- Lichens make up an important part of a heather community; up to thirty species may be present.
- They are especially common when rabbits are present.
- Lichens can completely cover the surface of the sand making an important contribution to sand stabilization.
- The fungal component is able to absorb and hold water for long periods.
- Dozens of species grow on fixed dunes and they show a distinct zonation.
- As the Ling ages, so they gradually colonize the woody stems.

Mosses
- Mosses grow on the sand surface, increasing their cover with stability.
- Not tolerant of shading.
- Grazing by rabbits may cause a decline in mosses.
- By growing in very tight cushions, excessive water loss is reduced.

Sand Sedge *Carex arenaria* is found on most dune systems and is not associated with any one plant community or soil.

Fig. 6.31
Bell Heather *Erica cinerea*.

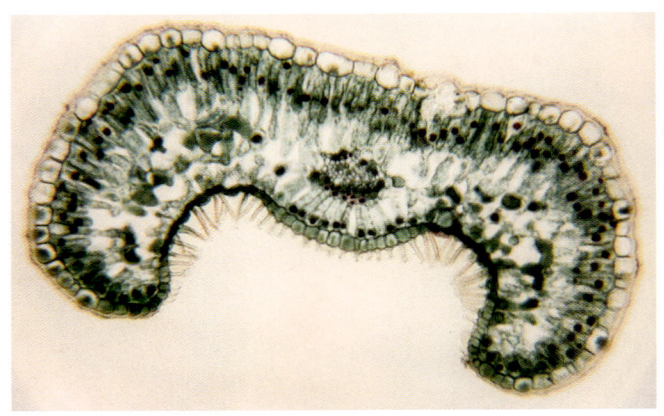

Fig. 6.32
Bell Heather leaf in section showing hairs underneath, reducing waterloss.

Additional plant species on acidic grey dunes

Bell Heather *Erica cinerea*
- A woody shrub up to 0.7m high with small, bell-shaped flowers.
- Well adapted xerophyte with needle leaves; the stomata are set in pits and covered by spines.
- A southerly species; it replaces the Crowberry.
- It is evergreen and this reduces the need for high soil mineral content.
- Pollination is carried out by insects; thrips, common inside the flower, are the most effective.
- If fertilization does not occur, the stigma and stamens lengthen to enable wind pollination. It can-self pollinate.
- Survives very dry conditions, even more so than *Calluna*.
- Intolerant of grazing and shade.

Common Gorse *Ulex europaeus*
- These become established after the heathers.
- Although not part of the community, they may invade the heath; upon taking hold of an area it will destroy the heathland, shading out the *Calluna*.
- Leaf litter is very acidic, adversely affecting species living close by.
- Roots have nodules with nitrifying bacteria, improving nitrogen uptake.
- Leaves are reduced to spines which limit transpiration and offers protection from herbivores.
- The yellow flowers open early in the year and have a strong, sweet smell, attracting insects, especially the tiny thrips.
- Seeds are released from the pods with a noisy crack.
- Seeds are dispersed by ants; by grasping the extended peduncle (stalk) they can carry them to nests where the elaiosome (high in fats) is removed but germination can still take place. Ant nests and trails are often in lines and this is reflected in gorse bush distribution.
- Dwarf Gorse *U. minor* flowers in late summer, along with the heathers, unlike the Common Gorse, and tends to be prostrate. Western Gorse *U. galli* is intermediate in size between the two.

Bracken *Pteridium aquilinum*
- Upon invading a heath it may shade out other species, becoming dominant with the *Calluna*.

Animal species on acidic grey dunes

Heather Beetle *Lochmaea suturalis* feeds on *Calluna* and may lead to defoliation. A small, rounded brown beetle, it pupates in the raw humus below the plant. Fox Moth *Macrothylacia rubi* larvae feed on heathers, hibernating in the autumn and resuming in spring before pupating. Adults fly by day and night.

Slack community – damp alkaline slacks

Fig. 6.33
Slack community: alkali.

Fig. 6.34
Silverweed *Potentilla anserina*.

Note: There is an overlap with the grey dune communities.

Creeping Willow *Salix repens*
- The creeping stems produce a prostrate form over the surface.
- It will dominate the slack and can grow into dense bushes.
- An extensive root system (up to 10m total length) assists in obtaining nutrients from the poor soil.
- The prostrate stems will also take root.
- It recovers well from erosion or minor sand coverings and therefore colonizes the slacks early in the succession process.
- Any wind-blown sand reaching the slack will accumulate around the willow, forming small hummocks; this results in a drier habitat and other plants can move in to colonize.
- It cannot survive a permanently waterlogged soil and its distribution is therefore limited.

Problems and features
- These are the flat 'lows' behind the dune system.
- Closeness to the water table and condensation at night produces a damp soil.
- During winter the water table rises, giving temporary flooding.
- The soil is stable but low in nitrogen and phosphorus, as earlier leaching would have removed them.

Sand dunes

- Dry areas allow tall vegetation; the wetter it becomes the more prostrate it grows.
- A dense leaf litter forms beneath; much humus is generated by the willow.
- The fluffy patches are the seeds.

Fig. 6.35 Larva of Six-spot Burnet Moth *Zygaena filipendulae* about to pupate on Marram.

Fig. 6.36 Six-spot Burnet Moth *Zygaena filipendulae*.

Fig. 6.37 Sea Buckthorn *Hippophae rhamnoides* is a thorny shrub found on damper ground of some dunes. The berries are important in winter for birds.

Silverweed *Potentilla anserina*
- A fine mat of hairs gives the leaf its shiny, white surface.
- Its runners creep over the surface of the soil entangling with the willow.
- It is typical of damp grassy places and its presence here reflects the occasional flooding that must occur.

Marsh Pennywort *Hydrocotyle vulgaris*
- It has a distinct circular leaf with the petiole arising from the centre.
- Typical of damp places it is a prostrate creeping perennial; a sign here of occasional flooding.

Creeping Bent Grass *Agrostis stolonifera*
- Unlike the grasses already seen it does not have a rhizome – instead, it possesses stolons, which penetrate through the prolific willow roots.

Sedge *Carex* species
- In the wet soil several species can be found below the willow and overlap with the Sand Sedge.
- Rhizomes disperse underground, shooting upwards and develop into new plants.
- Glaucous Sedge *C. flacca* favours calcareous damp grassland and may be dwarfed in the undergrowth.
- Common Sedge *C. nigra* is common on most damp grassland.

Birdsfoot Trefoil *Lotus corniculatus*
- The yellow flower is usually tinged with red.
- A creeping, prostrate perennial plant with an extensive root system for obtaining nutrients.
- It is not unique to dunes but widespread in grasslands generally.

Common Daisy *Bellis perennis*
- A common species on damp dune grassland.
- Its flattened, rosette leaves tolerate grazing and conserve water.

Dark-lipped Snail *Cepaea nemoralis*
- Commonest snail on dunes, most abundant in the damper regions.
- An example of genetic polymorphism, where several colour forms are present: yellow, pink, brown and striped.

The larva of Six-spot Burnet Moth *Zygaena filipendulae* feed on the *Lotus* plants and during August the adults emerge from the pupa, attached in a cocoon to Marram leaves. They are day-flying and may occur anywhere on the dunes.

Slack community – damp acidic slacks

Note: There is an overlap with the grey dune communities.

Cross-leaved Heather *Erica tetralix*
- This is the only heather to tolerate waterlogged soil.
- Normally grows in a rounded bush but when shaded it becomes more sparse.
- The bell-shaped flowers are paler pink than *Erica cinerea* and are held in a small cluster at the end of the single stem.

Various Rush and Sedges species grow throughout the slack.

Bog mosses *Sphagnum* species
- A characteristic feature of acid bogs, these hold water like a sponge (even during dry summers), supplying other species which live in it.
- A succession of bog mosses develop: the first in standing water followed by ones growing above in progressively drier conditions; this creates a hummock which in turn will be colonized by heathers and grasses. When almost 1m high it may collapse and the succession starts again (an example of cyclic succession).
- They are important in the establishment and development of the slack.
- After death the acidic and waterlogged (anoxic) conditions will prevent decomposition and matter accumulates to form peat.

Fig. 6.38
Slack community: damp acidic.

Problems and features

- These are the flat 'lows' behind the dune system.
- Closeness to the water table may lead to some patches of standing water, resulting in waterlogging.
- Stable soil, but very low in nitrogen and phosphorus as earlier leaching would have removed them.
- Permanent water removes oxygen and reduces decomposition, limiting the establishment of many plants and animals.

Fig. 6.39
Extensive slacks may become flooded during winter and in some cases form permanent water bodies.

Fig. 6.40
Common Sundew *Drosera rotundifolia* leaf, growing amongst mosses. The sticky-tipped tentacles enable it to obtain basic mineral ions by catching insects as the soil is of such poor quality.

Willow *Salix* species
- Several types of willow will grow, all of which attain a height of 5–10m, restricting the light reaching the ground and thereby reducing other plants beneath.
- Many are tolerant of the permanent waterlogging.

Additional species of dune slacks

Alder *Alnus glutinosa*
- Their root nodules fix nitrogen, which may be used by other plants in the community.
- Their presence in a slack depends on the intensity of rabbit grazing; in a flooded community it is too wet for rabbits. If myxomatosis reduces rabbit density on drier slacks the growth of Alder can occur and even when the rabbit population recovers the tree continues to develop.

- The seeds float (water dispersed) and need light to germinate; hence, they are found on the edge of the slack where there is less shade.

Common Reed *Phragmites communis*
- May develop large stands in slacks.

Animal species on acidic wet slacks

Mosquitoes breed in the stagnant pools and these are consumed by the damselflies and dragonflies, a common sight on flooded dune slacks. A number of amphibians breed here and the rare Natterjack Toad is typically found in these conditions in both acid and alkali pools.

Fig. 6.41
Pyramidal Orchid *Anacamptis pyramidalis* on alkali dunes.

Fig. 6.42
Wax cap fungus *Hygrocybe punicea*. Fungi are important to help in the breakdown of the tough dune plants.

Part 2: Colonization and succession of sand dune communities

General trends

- There is a zonation of vegetation inland from the sea.
- This zonation is not static but is gradually changing as one community replaces another over time: succession.

Features of succession

Pioneer zone
The pioneer species can tolerate a wide range of environmental stresses. Sea Rocket and Prickly Kale will colonize bare sand near the strandline, obtaining much of their mineral ions from organic matter washed up on the beach. Although tolerant of salt they cannot cope with being buried too deep by the unstable, wind-blown sand. But Sand Couch Grass can and soon will develop embryonic dunes as the sand collects around it.

Yellow dune
Marram colonizes when the salt has leached away, and shades out the other grasses. It thrives on wind-blown sand. Its rhizomes can grow to amazing depths and its ability to conserve water soon makes it the dominant species above the high tide mark of sandy shores. Lyme Grass may be co-dominant in northerly, cooler climes but it cannot tolerate high temperatures or covering by too much sand. Marram causes the dune to continue growing as long as wind-blown sand is abundant and not a limiting factor, with some dunes reaching 30m in height. These will be in more exposed areas, typically facing the Atlantic. As dunes become taller it will change the abiotic conditions, particularly the wind profile, and depending on the degree of wind and sand the growth slows. Wind blowing off the peak of the dune may create levels of turbulence behind, which encourages erosion, and any removal of sand near the water table causes a slack to develop. The increased stability on the dune spells its death: the lack of wind-blown sand eventually causes the break-up of the Marram tussocks, although rhizomes continue growing underground from stored food.

Grey dune
As stability increases, so does soil quality. To start with this was no more than the inorganic sand but with time debris from the plants and rabbit droppings help develop a shallow soil. This organic matter changes the colour so it becomes darker. Overall, the soil is still very thin, possibly just a few centimetres, and will be fragile and easily damaged by animal activity. Behind the dune peaks there will be protection from the wind and the sand surface warms up encouraging the germination of seeds. A rise in temperature, shelter and the presence of organic matter encourages plant diversification so those not so well adapted to the harshness of the early dune environment quickly increase in number. If shell sand is present

Fig. 6.43 Flooded slack beneath high dunes. In the background is a blow-out.

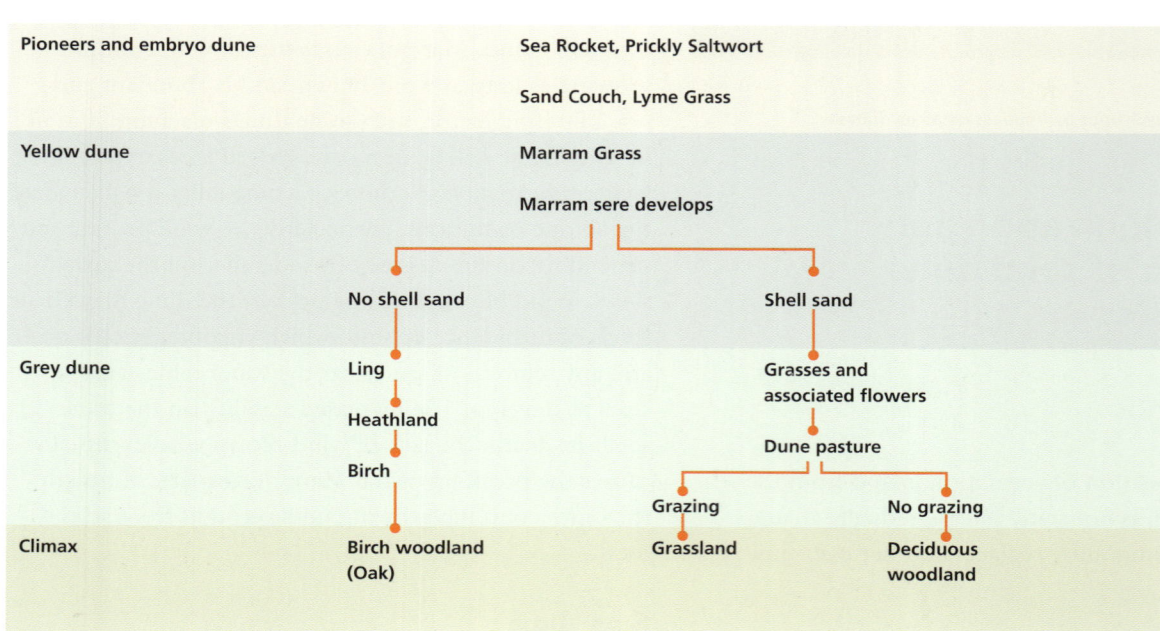

Fig. 6.44 Summary of succession within sand dune communities.

Pioneers and embryo dune	Sea Rocket, Prickly Saltwort
	Sand Couch, Lyme Grass
Yellow dune	Marram Grass
	Marram sere develops
	No shell sand / Shell sand
Grey dune	Ling / Grasses and associated flowers
	Heathland / Dune pasture
	Birch / Grazing — No grazing
Climax	Birch woodland (Oak) / Grassland / Deciduous woodland

the dunes remain alkaline and lime-loving; downland plants and animals appear. This is the most biodiverse community, sometimes with large numbers of orchids present. On sheltered coasts the sand will be inert silica with shells washed up intact. As the dunes build so the shells remain in their original state with the calcium locked inside. The result is that the dune becomes acidic and very poor in minerals, resulting in a low diversity. A heathland community is the result.

Slacks

Where the dunes hollow out to be near the water table, water content increases and a different community forms. If it is acidic the dry heath becomes a wet heath and eventually a bog where it reaches water. In alkaline conditions it is like a damp meadow with plants like the Marsh Helleborine. On some coasts with large systems local topography can lead to the formation of freshwater lakes behind the dune ridges, e.g. Studland, Dorset, or Ythan, N. Scotland. These can cause substantial flooding of the slacks.

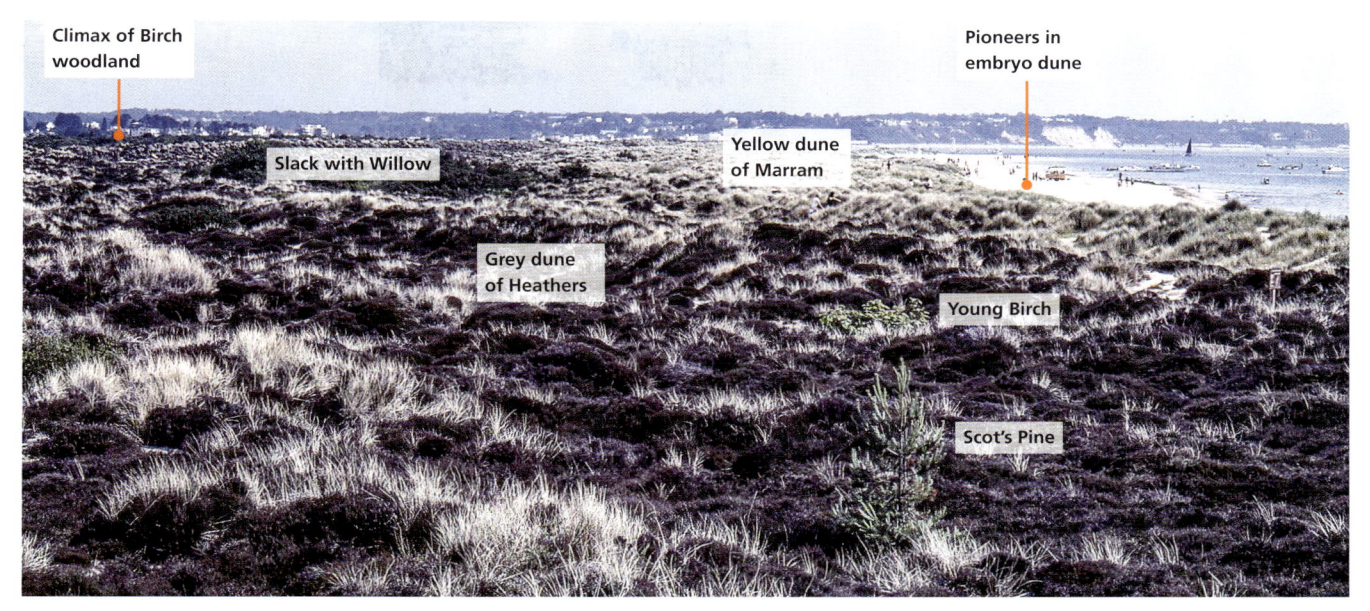

Fig. 6.45
Example of a succession process on acid dunes, Dorset, UK.

Each community in this succession is called a sere and a cross section across the dune will reveal several distinct seres until one becomes stable and remains, the climax community. This will depend on local conditions. In acidic systems the heath will be colonized by Birch and Scots Pine, possibly Oak and then Beech so that a mixed woodland occurs.

Ecological succession

Succession is the gradual change in populations and communities with time – in this case several hundred years. As succession occurs the following features take place:

- The height and differentiation of the communities increase with age.
- Development of the soil takes place with time, including an increase in depth, humus content, water holding capacity and formation of soil horizons (layering, seen in a soil profile).
- Productivity increases with the development of the soil and communities.
- The communities begin to affect the micro-climate around them as succession progresses, e.g. the wind action, temperature.
- The diversity of species changes from a few at the start to many later when the environmental stress has lessened and fewer specialized adaptations are necessary for survival.
- There is a gradual replacement of one community by another but the speed slows with age, e.g. Marram may remain dominant for thirty years, Ling for fifty years and Birch for hundreds of years.
- The stability of the community increases with age. Marram and the soil at the start is unstable and easily breaks down with erosion; as time goes on blow-outs become less likely as the soil increases in depth.

Fig. 6.46
A large blow-out producing large amounts of mobile sand.

Blow-outs and conservation

The soil is like a thin skin over the surface of the sand. Once broken, erosion starts with the hole enlarging to release more and more sand. Eventually the blow-out, as it becomes known, can be 40m across, decimating a large area of dune. As the rhizomes and roots are exposed they soon die, releasing their grip on the sand, increasing the destabilization. The release of so much sand stimulates the regrowth of Marram and the process of succession starts again. For centuries humans have understood Marram's value in this respect and it has long been law in the Hebrides, where crofters owe their living

Sand dunes 169

Fig. 6.47
View of crofts on machair, Barra, Outer Hebrides.

to the machair, to replant a tussock of Marram when a break in the surface was seen. Today, many dunes have replanting programmes and people are asked to walk on duck-board paths to reduce erosion by trampling.

Machair vegetation and soil

On the north and west coast of Scotland the extreme wave action smashes shells to produce sand dunes almost entirely of shell sand. The result is a dune system which develops as before but results in a pasture land as a climax community. The calcium carbonate levels reach 90 per cent although other minerals, e.g. nitrates, are lacking. Windy conditions may spread the dunes inland, covering blanket bogs and moorland, and climbing up the sides of headlands. For centuries it has been used by crofters for grazing their cattle and sheep. Minor cultivation in the growth of barley and rye has taken place. Grazing has not been intense and use of pesticides is unusual, resulting in a wealth of wildlife. Dominated by the yellow Lady's Bedstraw and red Wild Thyme, machair is a refuge for the Corn Marigold (killed off elsewhere by pesticides) and a rare bird, the Corncrake. Slacks behind the dunes will also be alkaline. With the high rainfall, machair lochs develop, filled with Bog Bean and reeds as well as being rich in fauna.

Fig. 6.48
Machair dune with Wild (Dune) Pansy *Viola tricolor* subsp. *curtisii* in the foreground.

170   Sand dunes

Chapter 7
SHINGLE

Fig. 7.1
The extensive shingle beach at Dungeness has ridges and troughs. The latter is of a finer shingle which is colonized by Sea Kale *Crambe maritima*. The larger the stones, the more difficult it is for plants to grow.

Fig. 7.2
Thrift is a coastal plant on cliffs, splash zone, salt-marsh, dunes and shingle.

Introduction

Shingle beaches are the poorest of all maritime habitats. Between the tides shingle is virtually devoid of life as the substrate rolls around, preventing attachment or shelter. Above the high tide line instability and rapid drainage is still a problem and requires well-adapted plants to colonize. Few plant species can survive.

Shingle 171

The substrate

It is typically composed of rounded pebbles with a gradation of size down or along the shore. The size will influence which species are able to colonize and develop. There is considerable overlap with sand dunes species. If wave action is limited then a layer of sandy material is deposited over the shingle or may be blown here from nearby dunes. Silt, sand and organic matter will increase the chance of plant invasion as the spaces between the stones fill and improve stability.

Fig. 7.3
Sea Kale *Crambe maritima*, an important early colonizer.

Fig. 7.4
Sea Mayweed *Tripleurospermum maritimum*.

Problems and features

- Mobile shingle; heavy pebbles will crush organisms.
- Rapid drainage produces low water and mineral content.
- Large air spaces.
- Saline conditions.
- Localized conditions determine the principal plant species.

Shingle beach formation

The build-up of shingle comes from long-shore drift, which is the movement of materials along the coast by the oblique action of waves. Four types of shingle beach can be recognized:

- A fringing beach, e.g. at the strandline of a sandy beach.
- A shingle bar crossing a bay, e.g. Chesil Beach in Dorset, UK.
- A curved spit, the end of which may change as more material collects.
- Forelands, which continue to build new tracts of land, e.g. Dungeness in Kent, UK.

Three main features affect the formation:

- The strength and direction of wave action.
- The size and quantity of pebbles.
- The range of tidal movement.

Problems and features of shingle

It is unstable and mobile. Often a storm creates a bank of shingle and, just as suddenly, breaches it. With large spaces between the pebbles and stones drainage is rapid, leading to a poor nutrient status and a lack of water. Seawater may percolate through shingle, increasing salinity, and in any low ground behind a shingle ridge water will be brackish and lakes may form. Behind spits salt-marsh develops so that communities can merge together. Only when sheltered will shingle become colonized and then only by a very limited group of pioneers. Colonization and succession follows a pattern like sand dunes except the number of species is far less as they adapt to extreme stress. Care should be taken on shingle beaches as they can be steep, unstable and liable to collapse; swimming here is dangerous.

Shingle pioneer zone

Sea Kale *Crambe maritima*, a member of the cabbage family and one of the first plants to colonize shingle, is a tough-looking perennial with thick stem bases and a woody root to withstand the pressure of the moving shingle. The fleshy, crinkled edge leaves are purplish, succulent and hang low to conserve water. Nutrients are obtained by an extensive root systems from decayed, washed-in seaweed. The corky fruit allow the dead flower heads to float and be dispersed by the sea.

Fig. 7.5
Curled Dock *Rumex crispus*.

Fig. 7.6
Yellow-horned Poppy *Glaucium flavum*.

Fig. 7.7
A rosette plant, Ox-tongue, showing the extensive tap root to reach and store water.

Fig. 7.8
Sea Sandwort *Honckenya peploides* is at home on shingle as well as embryo dunes.

Sea Mayweed *Tripleurospermum maritimum* has slightly fleshy leaves which are deeply and intricately divided into thin lobes. This hairless herb has scentless, white flowers. The Spear-leaved Orache *Atriplex prostrata* has tiny flowers. Both species are characteristic shingle pioneers. Also with white flowers is Sea Campion *Silene uniflora*. Like all these species found near the strandline they are tolerant of well-drained areas and particularly abundant where nitrogen content has been increased by deposited organic matter. Deep, probing roots reach water whilst aerial parts of the plant sprawl over the surface which helps to reduce water loss and stabilizes the shingle surface. Humus collects below the prostrate plants, providing a raw soil which encourages Sea Plantain, Cat's Ear and others to grow upon it. The Sea Beet *Beta vulgaris* subspecies *maritima* has succulent dark green leaves and can be a dominant species in the strandline.

The distinct Yellow-horned Poppy *Glaucium flavum*, produces long, curved seed pods with thousands of tiny black seeds. It has semi-succulent, thick waxy leaves and is tolerant of high salt levels. Small plants colonize in the autumn developing over winter at the back of the strandline. Sea Sandwort *Honckenya peploides*, a low, creeping perennial of sand dune and shingle, has a deep root system and dense leaf arrangement to reduce water loss. It can be an extensive cover over the surface stabilizing the ground. Along with Prickly Saltwort *Salsola kali* they survive coverings of sand and gravels. Thrift *Armeria maritima* is related to the Sea Campion and is also a cliff species able to tolerate salt spray and dry conditions. It forms cushions that help to bind the shingle surface, conserving water.

Shrubby Seablite *Suaeda vera* is 1–1.5 metres tall and common in the east of England, where dense bands form just behind the shingle ridges. Here it may be swamped by mobile pebbles and pushed flat. Tough, woody stems survive to produce new stems and roots from these prostrate branches. Repetition of this gradually spreads the plant across the shingle, adding humus, soil and stability. Seeds are sea dispersed and grow deep tap roots on germination.

Fig. 7.9
Common Restharrow *Ononis repens*.

Fig. 7.10
Sea Beet *Beta vulgaris* subspecies *maritima*.

Fig. 7.11
Flowering plants on fine shingle. Viper's Bugloss (blue); Yellow-horned Poppy (young, pale green plants); pink and white Valerian (pink and white); Ox-tongue (yellow).

With the increasing stability and humus formation provided by the pioneers other salt-tolerant species become established like the Red Fescue *Festuca rubra*, one of the first grasses to appear. Rhizomes provide rapid colonization and narrow leaves reduce surface area to conserve water. A common salt-marsh and sand dune species, it soon establishes tracts of pasture as it is grazed by rabbits. Other grassland species appear, like Birdsfoot Trefoil *Lotus corniculatus*, which create dense patches over the grassy shingle. This, like the Common Restharrow *Ononis repens* found here, has root nodules which fix nitrogen, enriching the soil. Over time typical grassland species arrive like Creeping Buttercup *Ranunculus repens*, Milk Thistle *Silybum marianum* and Curled Dock *Rumex crispus*. With pioneers making poor competitors they diminish under the onslaught of the invaders and the community changes.

On shingle bars it is not always possible to see the climax community as they are too narrow and unstable. Foreland shingle may display a more complete successional sequence with Broom. Like other heather species discussed on acid dunes, as they age they die from the centre, producing a protected soil in the middle which trees may colonize.

Animals of shingle
There are few characteristic species of shingle although one, rare individual should be mentioned: the Scaly Cricket *Pseudomogoplistes vicentae* is found in a few UK locations under the stones. An unusual species in many respects as males are rarely found and individuals grow slowly and survive overwintering on the warm shores.

Seabirds
Although few feed here they may nest on stable shingle. Chicks are well camouflaged, such as the Ringed Plover and Oystercatcher and merge with the shingle. Black-headed Gulls and terns use secluded shingle banks for their colonies.

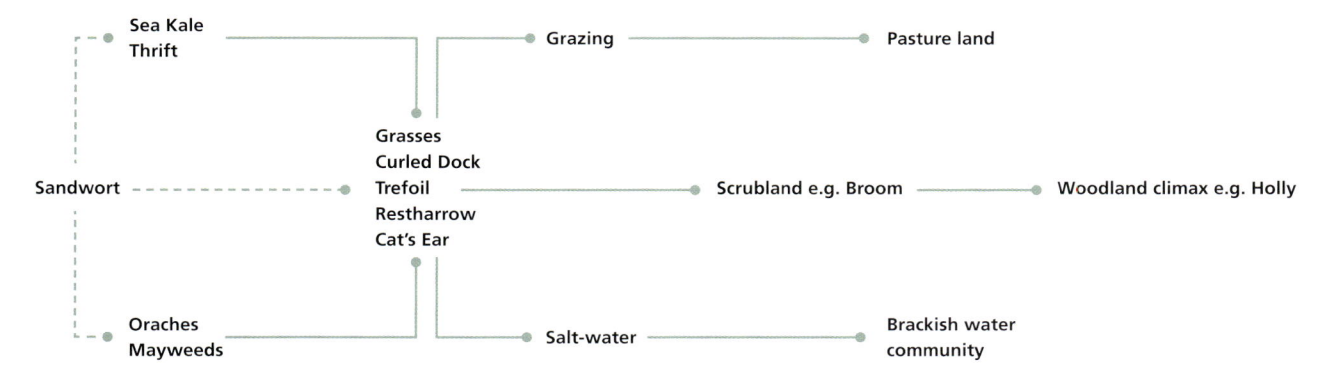

```
Sea Kale
Thrift                          Grazing                              Pasture land


                        Grasses
                        Curled Dock
Sandwort                Trefoil             Scrubland e.g. Broom      Woodland climax e.g. Holly
                        Restharrow
                        Cat's Ear


Oraches                                                               Brackish water
Mayweeds                                    Salt-water                community
```

Fig. 7.12
Summary of succession on shingle. Colonization is shown on the left, with succession moving to the right of the diagram.

Fig. 7.13
Scaly Cricket
Pseudomogoplistes vicentae.

Fig. 7.14
Sea Bindweed *Calystegia soldanella* with smaller leaves on shingle than sand dunes.

Shingle 175

Chapter 8
THREATS AND CONSERVATION

Fig. 8.1
Coastal vessels can be a risk as they come near to the land. Shipwrecks are surprisingly common and escaping fuel oil is a dangerous contaminant.

Introduction

The threats to the marine environment are so immense they can only be touched upon here. These threats and the conservation efforts being made are constantly changing, with considerable information available online. The size of this chapter should not, therefore, reflect the importance of the topic, in fact the reverse.

Pollutants

The seas of the planet have long since been used as our dumping ground. The enormity of oceans may seem infinite. The dumping of raw sewage, probably the earliest example of humans contaminating the seas, has long been recognized as a major health hazard to ourselves as well as reducing oxygen levels and killing fish.

The National Research Council in 2002 estimated that an average of 1.3 million tonnes of oil hydrocarbons enter the sea per year, although the possible range is enormous. Oil pollution from high-profile tanker spills is around 8 per cent, with 46 per cent natural seepage.

Fig. 8.2
Sea Empress soon after hitting rocks at the entrance to Milford Haven, February 1996.

Fig. 8.3
Plastic pellets or nurdles found on almost every shore in the world.

The single spills like that from the *Exxon Valdez* in Alaska, March 1989 (38,800 tonnes of crude) and *Sea Empress* in Pembrokeshire, February 1996 (72,000 tonnes) prompted stricter standards for shipping crude around the world. Single-hulled tankers finally started to be phased out in 2010. However, the actual amount of oil pollution is very difficult to estimate accurately and it continues. Oil not only contaminates wildlife, but as people attempt a clean-up chemical dispersants are used. These may themselves be toxic although much of the problem is that it makes it easier for marine life to absorb and ingest the oil, killing them.

Plastic is a global problem. Not just the plastic bottles and packaging ending up on beaches but the basic raw plastic resin microplastics, called nurdles. Most are accidentally released into the marine environment. There was a major spill off Hong Kong in 2012 which covered miles of beaches, some looking like snow. Nurdles are found washed up on shores worldwide and are known to release toxic chemicals, e.g. benzine, dioxins and Aldicarb, both there and in the seawater. They are also consumed by marine organisms.

Fig. 8.4
Wireweed *Sargassum muticum*, an alien species, arrived in the UK in the late 1970s but has become a common sight in the south and west where it out-competes other seaweeds due to its rapid growth.

Highly documented is the effect of anti-foul paint, particularly the ingredient tributyltin (TBT). Extremely toxic, it has been painted onto the underside of boats to kill marine organisms that would otherwise attach and grow. However, the chemical leaches out into the water and has been responsible for reducing mollusc populations. Dogwhelk populations showed a massive decline during the 1970s and 1980s. Some recovery has occurred by species mutation and a ban on the chemical usage. TBT has a reproductive effect (imposex) by simulating sex hormones. Other chemical releases into the environment have had similar effects on salmon.

Large estuaries are often the sites for industrial units like power stations, which require large quantities of water for cooling generators and machinery. Heated water when discharged raises the temperature of the estuary, reducing local populations and encouraging alien species, e.g. the American Clam and a leathery sea squirt, *Styela clava*, originating in Korea.

Mariculture is the specific culturing of fish and shellfish under marine conditions. Whilst it reduces the need for fishing there are side effects. A large concentration of fish will generate waste whilst overcrowding encourages disease. To combat this, cultured organisms are fed antibiotics and other chemicals all of which end up in the marine environment. New pollutants appear all the time. In southern England, spring 2013, more than 4,000 seabirds were affected by polyisobutene (PIB) spills. Guillemots were most affected.

Climate change, invasive and alien species

It is unclear exactly what will be the result of increased greenhouse gases on seashores. There is grave concern over the increase of carbon and changes to hydrogen ions in seawater, which could ultimately make the sea acidic and profoundly alter the chemistry of marine ecosystems. Rising temperature will change community composition as northern, cold water species are replaced

Fig. 8.5
Pirri-pirri bur grows on sand dunes and is a non-native from New Zealand. The large hooks catch in clothing and spread easily, producing a negative impact on native species.

Fig. 8.6
Trawling in large estuaries for shellfish such as scallops. This damages the seabed destroying sessile organisms.

Direct action on the shore

Over fishing will always have a negative side to populations but it is often the way that fish stocks are collected that can cause the problems. Bottom trawling, e.g. for scallops, can destroy entire benthic communities. The effect can be seen at low tide on mudflats where beam trawls decimate surface layers. Bait digging seems innocuous. Sediment shores are dug-over for lug and ragworm to be used as fishing bait. For an individual's needs this will have minimal impact; the problem arises when this is done on a commercial basis, daily. The shore sediments become so mixed that ultimately all diversity is lost and become a monoculture of ragworm, which as a disturbance tolerant scavenger is able to cope. Trampling can be very damaging to delicate systems and will vary according to the habitat, typically reducing diversity. Interestingly, over-trampling on salt-marsh may have the reverse effect. The woody stems of the prostrate Sea Purslane can suffocate the growth of most salt-marsh species. However, it is not resistant to trampling which allows other species to come in. Trampling in spring when salt-marsh seeds are germinating and young plants developing may decimate populations back to bare mud.

Salt-marsh succession is nature's land reclamation and this can be encouraged to produce large tracts of agricultural land. Mudflats are seen by some planners as a lifeless area waiting for development. A sea wall, drainage and plenty of concrete with pile-driving will soon convert it to dry land.

by southern species as their distribution moves northward. This has already been noted in a number of planktonic organisms. With larval stages surviving the northerly currents colonization of new shores is inevitable. The number of alien species is highest in terrestrial and freshwater environments as a result of accidental human introduction. However, over 100 non-native species are known on UK shores. The brown alga *Sargassum muticum* arrived in France from the Pacific attached to oysters and by 1973 began to colonize rockpools on the Isle of Wight. It has now distributed around the coast as far as west Wales. Initially it swamped native species and dominated the pools although decades on it has reached somewhat of a balance. Some like Carpet Sea-squirt *Didemnum vexillum*, also from the Pacific, are recent invaders (2008). It too is a rapidly growing species, smothering all local life where it lives disrupting resident communities. This is the typical result of an invasive species and can devastate local communities.

Marine conservation

It has often been said that we know more about the surface of the moon than our own seas and shores. As recently as 2013, an unusual marine habitat was discovered in a Scottish sea loch. Metre-high mounds of mud in Argyll's Loch Sween made by organisms called mud volcano worms; sea pens covered a huge area of seabed near Loch Linnhe and south of Arran; ocean quahog clams were widely recorded in abundant numbers. Quahog clams are the world's longest living molluscs – one found in Iceland was over 400 years old. The discoveries formed part of the work to develop a network of Marine Protected Areas (MPAs), possibly thirty-three sites around the coast of Scotland. Ultimately, it is only through protected areas, by designated government agencies or administered by voluntary groups like the Marine Conservation Society, that survival of our shores will occur.

Controversial is the formation of No-take Zones. These are places for no commercial fishing or destructive activities to take place. Single species conservation is a very limited approach as organisms invariably need an intact ecosystem to survive. 0.01 percent of UK waters are No-take Zones, one is the area around Lundy Island. After five years of restrictions being in place mature lobsters have risen six-fold. Scarlet and gold star corals, pink sea fans, sea urchins and octopus have increased. The principle is that by using these zones as nurseries with no removal or damage the marine organisms multiply and then migrate out of the zone where they can be fished. After decades of use in New Zealand the efficacy of this system has been proven beyond doubt and has the commercial fisheries on board. This is not the case in the UK. The UK government announced it will create twenty-seven new Marine Conservation Zones (MCZs) to protect wildlife in the seas around the English coast, helping seahorses, coral reefs and oyster beds to remain safe from dredging and bottom-trawling. However, the government's own science advisers recommended the creation of 127 MCZs to halt the rapid decline of fish, lobsters, oysters and seahorses. Marine conservation still has a long way to go.

The Council of Europe Ministers officially adopted the European Code of Conduct for Coastal Zones, an initiative of the European Union for Coastal Conservation, which launched the idea in 1993. The documents can be viewed on their website.

Why conserve?

Seashores are some of the most beautiful and spiritual places on earth. They are some of the most biodiverse environments and as a result of human overcrowding on land represents one of the few remaining vestiges of wilderness left in the UK. Algae and plankton are one of our hopes for the future of the planet as a carbon sink to reduce climate change and the highest rate of primary production (food). For all the aesthetic reasons for maintaining our coasts it is what we do not know as much as what we do that may save humanity. One of the gravest threats to human health is drug resistance by bacteria. Our range of antibiotics is running thin. Anthracimycin is a compound that has just been extracted from a marine micro-organism found in sediments in California. To discover a genuinely original antibiotic is rare and this one seems to be effective at killing MRSA and anthrax. The compound's unique chemical structure may result in a whole new class of antibiotic medicines.

In researching new threats to our security, biodiversity is essential – it may seem a purely selfish perspective on conservation but it helps, along with the ecosystems services approach, to put a price tag on our priceless seas and shores. They must be protected at all costs or humanity will disappear.

Fig. 8.7
Human impact on eel grass beds.

GLOSSARY

Some terms used in this book are listed below.

Active transport (re. algae): energy is expended to move minerals through a membrane (see also diffusion).

Autotroph: organism with the ability to produce food energy from basic materials, e.g. green plants and photosynthesis.

Benthos: the community of organisms inhabiting the sea floor.

Chromatophore: pigment-containing cell.

Cilia: short, hair-like organelles on the outside of cells used for movement.

Conceptacle (re. algae): depressions in the frond where gametes are produced.

Detritus: microscopic fragments of organic matter.

Ecad: An organism whose form has been affected by its environment (e.g. unexpectedly low salinity due to a supply of fresh water).

Ecdysis: the process of shedding the exoskeleton in arthropods (e.g. crab).

Diffusion (re. algae): the passive movement of minerals through a membrane from a high concentration to a lower one (see also 'active transport').

Epiphyte: a plant using another organism as substrate for attachment (not a parasite).

Epizoite: an animal living on another organism but not a parasite, e.g. barnacle attached to a crab's carapace.

Light compensation point: when the rates of photosynthesis and respiration in a plant are equal so there is no net change in carbohydrate.

Littoral: living on the seashore; as a region, it is between high and low tides.

Metamorphosis: change in form during the life cycle from embryo to adult.

Mycorrhiza: a symbiotic association with a fungus on the roots of higher plants.

Nematocyst: sting cells of Cnidarians e.g. anemones and hydroids.

Node: the point on a plant stem from where the leaves grow. **Internode** refers to the space between successive nodes.

Osmotic potential: a solution's capacity to absorb water through a semi-permeable membrane.

Perennial: a plant that continues to grow from year to year.

Prehensile: an adaptation for gripping and holding.

Primary production: the production of chemical energy in organic compounds by living organisms.

Radula: a membranous strip with rows of chitonous teeth, used in feeding; a characteristic of gastropod molluscs.

Rhizome: a horizontal stem growing under the soil, sending shoots up, roots down.

Runner: a horizontal stem growing above ground, rooting at nodes.

Sere: communities in succession e.g. originating from sand dunes – xerosere, originating from rock – lithosere.

Siphon (re. molluscs): two muscular tubes which enable bivalves to obtain oxygenated water and food from surface (inhalent siphon) and deposit waste (exhalent siphon).

Succession: a sequence of communities which develop over a period of time; see Sere.

Taxis: the locomotional response of an organism to a stimulus, e.g. sea slaters move away from light.

Thallus: a simple plant body with no differentiation into roots or stem e.g. alga.

Transpiration: the loss of water by evaporation from plants, usually from leaves.

REFERENCE AND FURTHER INFORMATION

Books

Ballantine, W.J. *A Biologically-defined Exposure Scale for the Comparative Description of Rocky Shores* (Field Studies, 1961)

Barnes, R.S.K. *The Brackish-water Fauna of Northwestern Europe* (Cambridge University Press, 1994)

Bunker, F., Brodie, J., Maggs, C. and Bunker, A. *Guide to Seaweeds of Britain and Ireland* (Marine Conservation Society, 2010)

Dring, M. *The Biology of Marine Plants* (Cambridge University Press, 1991)

Fish, J.D. and Fish, S. *A Student's Guide to the Seashore*, 3rd ed. (Cambridge University Press, 2011)

Green, J. *The Biology of Estuarine Animals* (Sidgwick and Jackson, 1968)

Hayward, P. *Animals on Seaweed* (Richmond, 1988)

Hayward, P. *Animals of Sandy Shores* (Richmond, 1992)

Hayward, P. *Seashore* (Collins, 2004)

Hayward, P., Nelson-Smith, T. and Shields, C. *Collins Pocket Guide: Sea Shore of Britain and Europe* (Collins, 1996)

Hayward, P. And Ryland, J. *Handbook of the Marine Fauna of North-West Europe* (Oxford University Press, 1995)

Larink, O. and Westheide, W. *Coastal Plankton – Photo Guide for European Seas* (Verlag Dr Friedrich Pfell, 2011)

Lewis, J.R. *The Ecology of Rocky Shores* (Hodder and Stoughton, 1964)

Little, C., Williams, G. And Trowbridge, C. *The Biology of Rocky Shores*, 2nd ed. (Oxford University Press, 2009)

Newell, R.C. *Biology of Intertidal Animals* (Marine Ecological Surveys, 1979)

Piper, R., *Animal Earth* (Thames & Hudson, 2013)

Ranwell, D.S. *Ecology of Salt-marsh and Sand Dunes* (Chapman and Hall, 1972)

Websites

www.marlin.ac.uk
The website of the Marine Biological Association covers many aspects of the marine environment and offers help with identification. There are a number of useful PDF downloads, e.g. non-native species.

www.field-studies-council.org/publications
There are a number of identification guides to suit all levels including the very specialist identification books published under the Synopses of the British Fauna published by the Linnaean Society and the FSC. Check out the Field Studies Journal tab as many free downloads are available, e.g. Ballantine's Exposure Scale.

www.nhm.ac.uk
Natural History Museum: general interest with help in identification of species.

www.gastropods.com
Guide to marine snails.

www.mcsuk.org
The Marine Conservation Society.

Appendix 1

CLASSIFICATION OF THE ORGANISMS USED IN THE BOOK

The biodiversity of creatures living on the seashore is immense and understanding this range can be assisted by categorizing them into similar types. The Swedish botanist Linnaeus was the first to attempt some form of classification in the eighteenth century and the system he devised forms the basis of what scientists use today. The practice of classification is called taxonomy and looks at similarities and differences in the characteristics of organisms. Today this may mean DNA analysis. A taxon is a group of similar species placed together using these characteristics. A hierarchy of taxa is necessary to gradually breakdown the huge biodiversity of organisms present in the world into smaller and smaller units. The sequence of these are, in descending order: domain, kingdom, phylum, class, order, family, genus and, finally, species. Linnaeus gave us the binomial system of providing two parts to the species name, *Homo sapiens* in the case of ourselves.

The classification of the Common Limpet would be:

Domain	Eukaryota
Kingdom	Animalia
Phylum	Mollusca
Class	Gastropoda
Order	Patellogastropoda
Family	Patellidae
Species	*Patella vulgata*

The first part is the genus and the second the specific name. However, taxonomy is dynamic, constantly changing as new analyses are made and new species found. Probably by the time this book is published some of the scientific names given in this book will have changed. For example, the Blue-rayed Limpet has had its name changed a number of times in recent years as taxonomists have moved it between several genera. For many years it was *Patina*, then was moved to *Patella* and in a blink of an eye became *Ansates*. In this books if there has been a recent name change, the previous one is given, often in parenthesis. Within the species level subtle differences can occur such that a third name may be given, a sub-species. For example, Wild Pansy *Viola tricolor* subsp. *curtisii*. Problems can occur with classification higher up the chain so that major taxons can be subdivided. In the Gastropoda example above it is divided into sub-classes with limpets in the Prosobranchia, which means the gills are in front of the heart. Sub-class Opisthobranchia, such as sea slugs, have the gills located behind the heart. In some cases a number of species may be aggregated into a 'super-species' level, like the Rough Perwinkle and some tar lichens, whereby the abbreviation **agg.** is added at the end of the species name.

It is impossible to go into the detail of taxonomy here, but knowing the relationships between different groupings is useful when studying the life in any habitat, especially the seaweeds and animals found on the shore. More information can be found on the internet but unfortunately it is a very confusing story. The main problem is that not everyone agrees on where to place difficult groups. Once it was thought there was just the plant and animal kingdoms but for some decades this has expanded to five, six, eight or even more kingdoms. Much depends on structures within the cell. Archaebacteria are very primitive, early forms of bacteria and are separated from all other life. Most bacteria covered in the book and cyanobacteria are contained within the kingdom Monera. Algae, like the range of seaweeds found on the seashore, are a major headache. Once cyanobacteria, that can photosynthesize, were classified as algae (called blue-green algae) but are now squarely kept with bacteria.

Fig. 11.1
Algae in the lower shore have the greatest diversity displaying most colour forms

Algae were traditionally placed in the plant kingdom (along with mosses, ferns and flowering plants) as they superficially appear like them; some people still put green algae in that taxon. But what is a green alga? Certainly we can divide the algae by colour: reds – the Rhodophyta; browns – the Phaeophyta; and the greens as Chlorophyta. Then we have the diatoms and dinoflagelates. The latter are usually put with algae and yet they have some characteristics of animals. Problem groups including all algae and the single-celled animals like Amoebae (called the protozoa) were lumped into one kingdom called the Protoctista, often reduced to the term Protista. This is really a kingdom of convenience and most taxonomists are unhappy that such an increasingly diverse range of organisms should be together. Some would prefer the algae to be given kingdom status or, because of their cell variation, multiple kingdoms.

The final anomaly are lichens, which are defined as a symbiotic association between an alga and a fungus. In the case of *Lichina pygmaea* it is both a fungus and cyanobacterium. Fungi are a separate kingdom and so lichens could therefore be a combination of three kingdoms. As a consequence, it has been generally agreed that lichens are named by the host fungus and would then be in the kingdom of Fungi. The fungus *Stigmidium ascophylli* is found as a symbiont on the brown seaweeds *Pelvetia* and *Ascophyllum*. They are not referred to as lichens as the algal component is the dominant part. These seashore algal-fungal associations are termed mycophycobiosis.

The Animal kingdom is vast but, possibly due to the degree of research time spent on the organisms, is an easier taxon to understand. The 'tree' given in the following two pages attempts to show the main groups of organisms to be found on the seashore and a guide to their lineage and origin.

Appendix

Fig. 11.2
The lineage and classification of seashore organisms mentioned in this book.

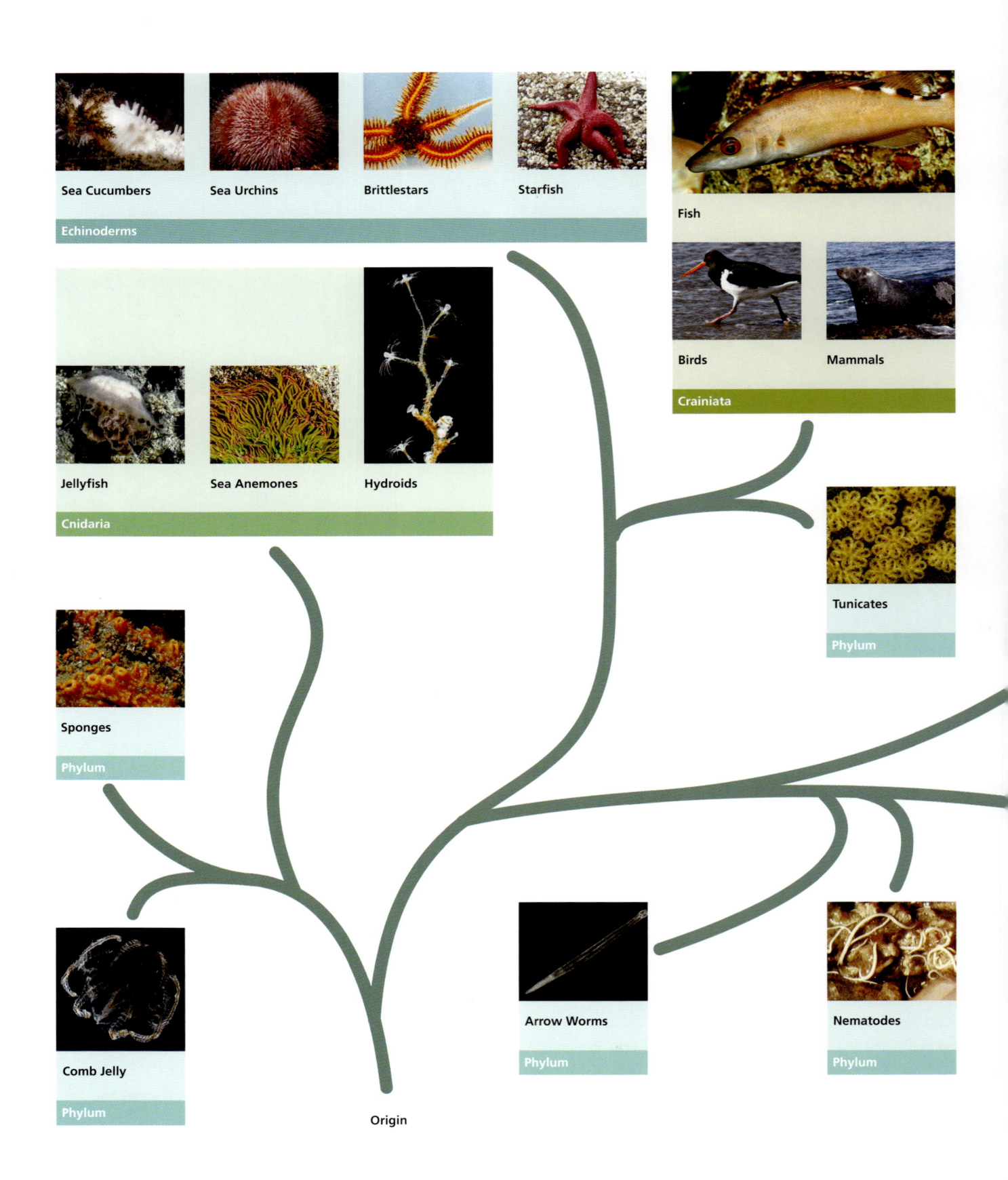

| Sea Cucumbers | Sea Urchins | Brittlestars | Starfish |

Echinoderms

| Fish |
| Birds | Mammals |

Crainiata

| Jellyfish | Sea Anemones | Hydroids |

Cnidaria

Tunicates

Phylum

Sponges

Phylum

Comb Jelly

Phylum

Arrow Worms

Phylum

Nematodes

Phylum

Origin

186   Appendix

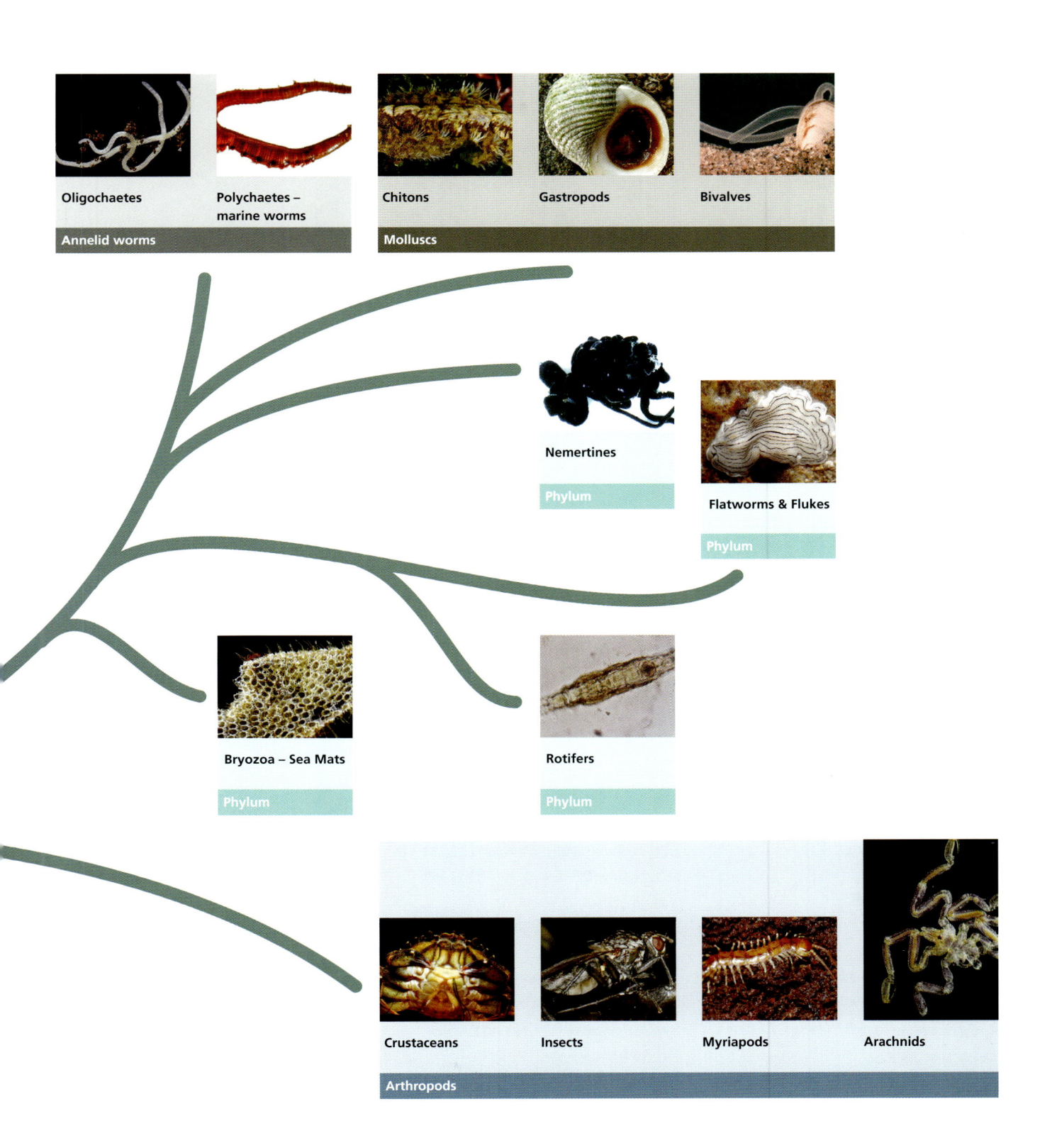

| Oligochaetes | Polychaetes – marine worms | | Chitons | Gastropods | Bivalves |

Annelid worms

Molluscs

Nemertines

Phylum

Flatworms & Flukes

Phylum

Bryozoa – Sea Mats

Phylum

Rotifers

Phylum

| Crustaceans | Insects | Myriapods | Arachnids |

Arthropods

Appendix **187**

INDEX

Pages in **bold** type indicates that this is the main entry for the subject.

abiota 8, **10**, 14, 64, 73, **74**, 76, 80, 82, 113, 124, 167
Acanthocardia echinata 99
Acanthochitona crinatus 82
accretion 122, 128
Achelia 69
Acholoë squamosa 105
Acrocnida brachiata 105
Actinia equina 22, **44–45**, **47**, 57, 75, 77
Aeolidia papillosa 22, **60**
aerenchyma 124–126, 130, 143
Agrostis stolonifera 163–164
Alaria esculenta 66–67, 77, 79
Alder 166
algal mats 129, 136
alien invasive species 178
Alnus glutinosa 166
Ammophila arenaria **149–153**, 157–158, 160, 167–168
Anemone, Beadlet 22, **44–45**, **47**, 57, 75, 77
Anemone, Daisy 102
Anemone, Gem 52
Anemone, Snakeslock 16, 47, 81, 83
Anemonia viridis 16, 47, 81, 83
Anguilla anguilla 136
Annual Seablite 130, 145
Anoplodactylus 69
Ansates (Patella) pellucida 20, 66, **68–69**
Anthyllis vulneraria **27–28**
anti-fouling paint 52
Anurida maritima **43**, 141
Aplysia punctata 59–60
Arenicola marina 25, **97–98**, 116–119, 179
Armeria maritima **27–28**, 32–33, 35, **137–138**, 171, 173, 175
arrow worms 88
ascidians/tunicates 20, 22, **68**, 71, 80
Ascophyllum nodosum 14–15, **44–46**, 72, 75, 84, 129–130
Aster tripolium 123, **137–138**, 140, 143, 145–146

Asterias rubens 65, **70**
Asterina gibbosa 61
Asterina phylactica 61
Astropecten irregularis 105
Atriplex portulacoides 123–124, **135**, 136–137, 140, 142–143, 146, 179
Atriplex prostrata 139, 151, 173, 175
Audouinia 102
Aulactinia verrucosa 52
Aurelia 89

Bacillaria paxillifer 86–87
bacteria 18–20, 30, 95–96, 107, 114–115, 119, 128, 145, 147, 180
bait digging 108, 118, 179
Ballan Wrasse 62–63
Ballantine's Exposure Scale 79
Baltic Tellin 99, 109, 117–118, 121
Banded Snail **155–157**, 163
Banded Wedge Shell 103
barnacles 14, 22–23, 32, 38, **41**, 44, 52, 70, 72, **75**, 76–79, 81, 83, 90
beetles 131
Bell Heather **162**, 165
Bellis perennis 163–164
Bembidion littorale 132
Beta vulgaris subspecies *maritima* 27, 173–174
biodiversity 72–73, 94, 123, 147, 149, 180
biofilm **17–20**, 23, 40, 48, 79
biota 8, **13–16**, 20, 76, 80
bioturbation 118
Birdsfoot Trefoil 163–164, 174
Biting Stonecrop 158–159
Bledius spectabilis 127, **131–132**
Bledius unicornis 131
Blenny 62, 83
Bloody Henry 70
Blow-out 169
Bog mosses 165
Bolboschoenus maritimus **140**, 143, 146
Boot-lace Weed 64, **66–67**
Bostrychia scorpioides 135
Botryllus schlosseri 68, 71

Bracken 162
Brent Goose 130, **133**
brittle star 71, 83
Bryozoan 20, 22, 54–55, 59, 61, 66, 84
Burrowing Brittle-star 105
Buttercup 174
Butterfish 62

Cakile maritima **150**, 167–168
Calanus 89
Calliostoma zizyphinum 65, **68**, 73
Calluna vulgaris 149, **160–162**, 168
Caloplaca **33–34**, 35
Calothrix 40, 136
Calystegia soldanella 154, 175
Campanula glomerata 159
Cancer pagurus 45, **48**
Candy-stripe Flatworm 108
Carcinus maenas 44, **48**, 50, 75, 82, 84, 104, 111, 115, 117
Carex arenaria 153, 155, **158–159**, 161
Carpenter's Rule 86–87
Carpet Sea-squirt 179
Cat Worm 102–103
Catanella caespitosa 38–39, 74
Cat's Ear, Common 155–156, 158, 173, 175
Cepaea **155–157**, 163
Ceramium 46, **51**, 83
Cerastium 159
Cerastoderma edule 99, 118, 120
Ceratium 87
Cereus pedunculatus 102
Chaetognatha 88
chart datum 11
chemosynthesis **20**, 119
chiton 20, 82
Chondrus Crispus **44–45**, 50, **54–56**, 65, **67**, 68, 82, 83
Chorda filum 64, **66–67**
Chrysaora hysoscella 85
Cigar Gall 151
Ciliata mustela 62
ciliates 18, 88, 107, 147

Cinnabar Moth 156
Ciona intestinalis 71
Cladophora rupestris **51**, 53, 59
Clava 59
Clavellina lepadiformis
climate change 88, 178
Clingfish 49, **62–63**
Clunio maritima 41, **53**
Clustered Bellflower 159
Cochlearia officinalis 137, **139**–140
Cochlicella acuta 157
Cockle Shell 99, 118, 120
Codium fragile **57**, 59
Collemopsidium 41
Comb Jelly 85
Compass Jellyfish 85
competition 13–15, 29, 45, 55, 64, 73–75, 116, 120–121, 127
copepods 84, **88–90**, 107, 112, 116–117, 136
Coral Weed 21, 53, 55–56, 70, 80–82, 84
Corallina officinalis 21, 53, 55–56, 70, 80–82, 84
Coranus woodroffei 157
Cord Grass 9, 123, **125–130**, 133, 136, 140, 142–147
Corkwing Wrasse 62
Cormorant 29, **31**, 83
Cornu aspersum 155–156
Corophium volutator 111, 117–119, 120–121, 133, 136
Corystes cassivelaunus 104
Cowrie 68
Crab, Broad-clawed Porcelain 53, 83, 91
Crab, Common Shore 44, **48**, 50, 75, 82, 84, 104, 111, 115, 117
Crab, Decorator 20–21
Crab, Edible 45, **48**
Crab, Hairy 66, **69**
Crab, Hermit 83
Crab, Long-clawed Porcelain 53
Crab, Stone 20, 22, **60**, 65, 69
Crab, Velvet Swimming 22, **60**, 69
crabs 20, 22, 23, **48**, 50, 52, 79–80, 83, 118
Crambe maritima 171–172, 175
Crangon crangon 100, 118, 133
Creeping Bent Grass 163–164
Creeping Willow 163
Crenilabrus melops 62
Crepidula fornicata 110
Crithmum maritimum 27–28
Cross-leaved Heather 165
Crowberry 160–161
Curled Dock 173–175
Curlew 97–98, 113, 120–121
Curlew Sandpiper 136

Cushion Star 61
Cushion Star, Brooding 61
Cuvie 19, **64–66**, 76–79
cyanobacteria 18–19, 26, 35, 40, 72, 134, 136
cypris 90

Dabberlocks 66–67, 77, 79
Daisy, Common 163–164
decomposition 8, **23**, 147
diatom 18–19, 58, **85–88**, 92, 95–96, 107, 119, 129–130, 139, 145
Dicheirotrichus 132
Didemnum vexillum 179
Dinoflagellata 87
Dogwhelk 44, 49, **52**, 54–55, 77, 79, 83–84
Donax vittatus 103
Doris pseudargus 59, 69
drag 126–127, 138, 143, 151
Drosera rotundifolia 166
Dulse 54, 65, **67**
Dune Assassin Bug 157
Dunlin 120
Dyschirius 132

ecads 124, **129–130**
Echinocardium cordatum 104–105, 119
echinoderms 70, 80, 83, 92, 104
Echinus esculentus 70
ecosystem **8**, 10, 23, 36, 119, 123
Ectocarpus 46
Eel Grass 9, 64, 98, 123, **130**, 133
Eel, Common 136
Eider Duck 52, 121
Elysia viridis 59–60
Elytrigia juncea 145, **149–152**, 167
Empetrum nigrum 160–161
Encrusting Red Algae 44, **54–56**, 65, 81
Ensis ensis 103, 115, 119
environmental gradient 12, 26, 72
Ephyra stage 89
epi-fauna 84
epitokous planktonic phase 93
Erica cinerea **162**, 165
Erica tetralix 165
Eryngium maritimum 153
estuaries 94, 96, 99, 106, 111, 113, 116, 122
Euglena 107
Eulalia clavigera **58–59**, 68
Euphorbia paralias 154
Euphorbia portlandica 154
Eurydice pulchra 100
Evadne 89
Evening Primrose 158

faecal soup 119
feeding mechanisms 83
Festuca rubra 27, **136–139**, 145–146, 155–156, 174
fish 22, 31, 80, 83, 118, 136
flatfish 99
flatworms 107–108, 136
flounder 111–112, 136
flukes 42, 84
foraminifera 107, 148
Fox Moth 162
Fucus ceranoides 78, **106–107**
Fucus serratus 44, **54**, **56**, 68, 72, 78, 80, 82
Fucus spiralis 17, **38–41**, 72, 75, 77, 79, 107
Fucus vesiculosus 14–15, 20, **44**, **46–47**, 50, 72, 74–79, 84, 107
Fulmar 29, **31**, 157
Furbelows 66–67

Gaidropsarus mediterraneus 62
Gammarids 111, **117**, 136
Gannet 31
Garden Snail 155–156
Gasterosteus aculeatus 112, 136
Gibbula cineraria 65, **68**, 73
Gibbula umbilicalis 44–45, **50**, 68, 73, 80
Glasswort **123**, **125–129**, 133, 136–137, 141–142, 146
Glaucium flavum 173–174
Glaux maritima 139
Goby, Common 112, 118, 136
godwits 113, 120
Gorse, Common 162
Grantia compressa 55
Green Branch Weed **51**, 53, 59
Green Sponge Fingers **57**, 59
Greenleaf Worm **58–59**, 68
Greenshank 136
Grey Atlantic seals 23
Grey Bulrush 140–141
Grey Sea Slug 22, **60**
Guillemot **29–30**, 178
Gull, Great Black–backed 29
Gull, Herring 29
Gull, Lesser Black–backed 29
Gutweed **39**, 41, 50, 54, 74–75, 77, 107, 119, 123, 129, 139

Halichondria panicea 55, **57**, 65
Halidrys siliquosa 81, 83
halophytes 122, 124, 143, 145, 151, 154
Haustorius arenarius 103–104
Heart Urchin 104–105, 119
Heather Beetle 162

Hediste diversicolor 102, **108**, 112, 115–121, 179
Hemiptera 131
Henricia oculata 70
Heron 120
Himanthalia elongata 15, **55–57**, 77–79, 81
Hippophae rhamnoides 164
holdfast 17, 19, 64–66, 68, 71, 98
holoplankton 88
Honckenya peploides 151, 173, 175
Hydobia ulvae **109–110**, 111, 113, 120–121, 133
Hydractinia 83
Hydrocotyle vulgaris 163–164
hydroids 20, 22, **58–59**, 70, 80, 83
Hymeniacidon 44–45, **54–55**, 57
Hypochaeris radicata 155–156, 158, 173, 175

Idotea 60–61
Iguana, Marine 76
imposex 52
Inachis 115
indicator species 14, 79, 140
Irish Moss **44–45**, 50, **54–56**, 65, **67**, 68, 82, 83

Jasione montana 155–156
Juncus maritimus **139–140**, 143, 146

Keeled Tube Worm 54, **58–59**
Kidney Vetch **27–28**
King Ragworm 108, 119
Kittiwake **29–30**

Labrus bergylta 62–63
Laeospira corallinae 21
Laminaria digitata 19, 54, **64–66**, 72, 76–79
Laminaria hyperborea 19, **64–66**, 76–79
Lanice conchilega 90, 101–102, 119
Lasea rubra 43
Laver 42
Laver Spire Shell **109–110**, 111, 113, 120–121, 133
Leathesia 46,
Lekanesphaera rugicauda 100, 111, **133**, 136
Lepadogaster purpurea 49, **62–63**
Leymus arenarius **150–152**, 167–168
lichen **33–35**, **40**, 72, 77–79
Lichina confinis **34–35**,
Lichina pygmaea 35, **40, 43**
light 16, 42, 55–56, 67, 74, 92
Light Bulb Ascidian 71
Ligia oceanica 42
Limacia clavigera 69
Limonium 123, **137–138**, 143, 145–146

Limpet, Blue-rayed 20, 66, **68–69**
Limpet, Common 20–21, 38–39, **44–45**, **48–49**, 54, 68, 76–79, 81, 83
limpets 14, 19
Ling 149, **160–162**, 168
Lipaphis cocheariae 141
Lipara lucens 151
Lipophris pholis 62, 83
Lithophyllum 44, **54–56**, 65, 81
Lithothamnion 44, **54–56**, 65, 81
Little Egret 113, 121, 136
Littorina fabalis 45, **50**
Littorina littorea 21, 44, **49–50**, 73, 76, 81, 84, 90, 92, 99, 101
Littorina obtusata 17, 44–45, **50**, 73, 83
Littorina saxatilis 20, 32, 38–39, **42**, 73, 78
Lochmaea suturalis 162
Lotus corniculatus 163–164, 174
Lugworm 25, **97–98**, 116–119, 179
Lyme Grass **150–152**, 167–168

machair 170
Macoma balthica 99, 109, 117, 118, 121
Macropodia 20–21
Macrothylacia rubi 162
mangrove 123, 128
mariculture 178
Marine Bristletail 36
Marine Pseudoscorpion 43
Marine Springtail **43**, 141
Marram Grass **149–153**, 157–158, 160, 167–168
Marsh Helleborine 168
Marsh Pennywort 163–164
Masked Crab 104
Mastocarpus stellatus 16, 45, **67**, 79
medusa 89
megalopa larva 91
Melaraphe neritoides **34–35**, 73
meroplankton 88
Microphallus 42
midge, marine 41, **53**
Milk Thistle 174
minnows 112
mites 146
Moon Jellyfish 89
Moon Shell 99
Mouse Ear Chickweed 159
Mussel 20, 22, **52**, 70, 76, 79
Mya arenaria 109, 116–119
mycorrhiza 127, 135
Myrianda 93
Mytilus edulis 20, 22, **52**, 70, 76, 79

Naidid worm 141
nauplius 90–91
Neathes virens 108, 119
Necora puber 22, **60,** 69
nematode 136
nemertines 108
Neoamphitrite figulus 98
Neobisium maritimum 43
Neomysis 111
Nepthys hombergi 102–103
niche **14–15**, 29, 76, 80
no-take zones 180
Nucella lapillus 44, 49, **52**, 54–55, 77, 79, 83–84
Nudibranchs 20, 22, 59–60, 68
nurdles 177
Nymphon 69

Oarweed 19, 54, **64–66**, 72, 76–79
Obelia 58, 89
Ochrolechia parella **32–34**
octopus 83
Odontella 87
Oenothera erythrosepaia 158
oil pollution 35, **176**
Ononis repens **154–155**, 158, **174–175**
Ophiothrix fragilis 71, 83
Opossum Shrimps 111
Orache 139, 151, 173, 175
Orchestia gammarella 100
Orchid 159, 167
Osilinus lineatus 51
Osmundea pinnatifida 17, 44, **46–47**, 56, 75
over-fishing 179
Owenia 102
Ox-tongue 173–174
Oystercatcher 20, 37, 49, 52, **62–63**, 121, 174
oysters 110, 180

paddleworm 68
Palmaria palmata 54, 65, **67**
Parablennius gattorugine 62
parasitism 84
Pardosa purbeckensis 141
Patella intermedia 68–69
Patella ulyssiponensis 68–69, 77, 79
Patella vulgata 20–21, 38–39, **44–45**, **48–49**, 54, 68, 76–79, 81, 83
Pawsonia saxicola 71
Peachia hastata 102
Peacock Worm 108, 119
Pelvetia canaliculata **38–41**, 72, 75, 77, 79, 129
Pepper Dulse 17, 44, **46–47**, 56, 75
Peppery Furrow Shell 109, 117–118, 131

Periwinkle, Edible 21, 44, **49–50**, 73, 76, 81, 84, 90, 92, 99, 101
Periwinkle, Flat 17, 44–45, **50**, 73, 83
Periwinkle, Rough 20, 32, 38–39, **42**, 73, 78
Periwinkle, Small **34–35**, 73
periwinkles 19, 73
Petrobius 36
Phaedon cochleariae 141
pheromone 56
Philaenus spumarius 132
Pholis gunnellus 62
Phoma 160
photosynthesis **16–17**, 26, 34, 55–56, 59, 74, 81–82, 85–86, 92, 96, 119, 124, 126, 140, **144**,
Phragmites australis **130**, 140, 166
phycobilins **55–56**, 67
Phyllodoce lamelligera 68
phytoplankton 85–88
Piddock, Oval **25**, 75
Pilumnus hirtellus 66, **69**
pipe fish 83
Piri-pirri bur 179
Pisidia longicornis 53
plankton blooms 87, **92–93**
Plantago maritima 35, 123, **136–138**, 146–147, 173
plastic pollutants 177
Platichthys flesus 111–112, 136
Pleurosigma 107
Pluteus 92
Polinices 99
Polydora 90, 92, 118
Pomatoceros triqueter 54, **58–59**
Pomatoschistus microps 112, 118, 136
Porcellana platycheles 53, 83, 91
Porphyra umbilicalis 42
Portland Spurge 154
Potentilla anserina 163–164
Prasiola stipitata 36
Prawn *Palaemon* 82–83
Prickly Saltwort 149, **150–151**, 168, 173
primary production **16–20**, 36, 85, 96, 113, 180
Procerodes littoralis 108
Prostheceraeus vittatus 108
protist 18, 72, 87, 107, 119, 136, 147, 148
Psammechinus miliaris 70
Pseudomogoplistes vicentae 174
Pteridium aquilinum 162
Ptychocyclis 88
Puccinellia maritima **125–129**, 133, 135–136, 145–146
Puffin 28, **29–30**,
Pycnogonum litorale 69

quahog clams 180

rabbits 20, 27, 29, 156–157, 161, 166–167
radula **20–21**, 48, 83
Ragworm 102, **108**, 112, 115–121, 179
Ragwort 155–156
Ramalina siliquosa 32–34
Ranunculus repens 174
Razor Shell, Common 103, 115, 119
Razorbill **29–30**
Red Fescue 27, **136–139**, 145–146, 155–156, 174
red tide 87
Redshank 113, 120–121, 136, 141
Redthreads 102
Reed, Common **130**, 140, 166
Restharrow, Common **154–155**, 158, **174–175**
Ringed Plover 113, 120, 174
Rock Samphire 27–28
Rockling, Five–bearded 62
Rockling, Shore 62
rockpool 18, 25, 55, 75, **80–82**, 179
rotifer 18
Rumex crispus 173–175

Sabella pavonina 108, 119
Sabellaria alveolata **25**,
Saccharina latissima **64–66**, 79
Saccorhiza polyschides 66–67
Sacculina 84
Saldula pilosella 132
Salicornia **123**, **125–129**, 133, 136–137, 141–142, 146
Salix repens 163
Salsola kali 149, **150–151**, 168, 173
salt glands 124–125, 130, 138–139, 143, 145
salt pan 124, **133**, 142
Salt-marsh bug 132
Salt-marsh Grass, Common **125–129**, 133, 135–136, 145–146
Sand Couch Grass 145, **149–152**, 167
sand eels 30
Sand Gaper 109, 116–119
Sand Mason 90, 101–102, 119
Sand Sedge 153, 155, **158–159**, 161
Sand Star 105
Sandhopper **36–37**, 42, 100, 116
Sargassum muticum 178–179
scale worms 58, **68**
Scaly Cricket 174
Schistidium 34
Schoenoplectus tabernaemontani 140–141
Scilla verna 27–28
sclerenchyma 143, 145, 147

Screw Moss **155**, 158
Scrobicularia plana 109, 117–118, 131
Scurvy Grass 137, **139**–140
sea anemones 8, 22, 58, 83
Sea Aster 123, **137–138**, 140, 143, 145–146
Sea Beet 27, 173–174
Sea Belt **64–66**, 79
Sea Bindweed 154, 175
Sea Buckthorn 164
Sea Campion **27–28**, 173
Sea Club-rush **140**, 143, 146
sea cucumber 71
Sea Empress 177
Sea Gooseberry 85
Sea Hare 59–60
Sea Holly 153
Sea Ivory 32–34
Sea Kale 171–172, 175
Sea Lavender 123, **137–138**, 143, 145–146
Sea Lemon 59, 69
Sea Lettuce 51, 81, 84, 107
sea mat 20, 22, 54–55, 59, 61, 66, 84
Sea Mayweed 172–173, 175
Sea Milkwort 139
Sea Oak 81, 83
Sea Plantain 35, 123, **136–138**, 146–147, 173
Sea Potato 104–105, 119
Sea Purslane 123–124, **135**, 136–137, 140, 142–143, 146, 179
Sea Rocket **150**, 167–168
Sea Rush **139–140**, 143, 146
Sea Sandwort 151, 173, 175
Sea Slater 42
sea slugs **58**, 68
sea spiders 69
Sea Spurge 154
Sea Spurry 139, 146
sea squirts 22, **71**, 83
Sea Urchin, Edible 70
Sea Urchin, Green 70
sea urchins 20
seabirds 22, **27–31**
Sea-gherkin 71
seahorses 180
seaweed flies 36–37
Sedum acre 158–159
Senecio jacobaea 155–156
sewage 176
Shag 29, **31**
Sheep's-bit 155–156
Shelduck 113, 121, 136, 141
Shrimp, Common 100, 118, 133
shrimps 23

Shrubby Seablite 145, 173
Sigara 133
Silene uniflora **27–28**, 173
Silverweed 163–164
Silybum marianum 174
Six-spot Burnet Moth 164
Slipper Limpet 110
Snipe 136, 141
Spartina 9, 123, **125–130**, 133, 136, 140, 142–147
species richness 84
Spergularia 139, 146
Sphagnum 165
Spiny Cockle 99
Spiral Worm 21
Spirobis 54–55
Sponge, Bread Crumb 55, **57**, 65
Sponge, Orange 44–45, **54–55**, 57
Sponge, Purse 55
sponges 22, 57, 70, 80, 83
Spring Squill **27–28**
star ascidians 71
starfish 52, 83
Starfish, Common 65, **70**
Stickleback, 3-spined 112, 136
strandline 19, 116, 123–124, 139, 167
Striatella 18
Strigamia maritima 36
Suada maritima 130, 145
Suaeda vera 145, 173
Suberites 83
succession 14, 17, 124, **144–146**, 149, 165, **167–169**, 172, **175**, 179
Sugar Kelp **64–66**, 79
sulphide layer 107, 109, 114–116, 119, 124–125
Sundew, Common 166
supply-side ecology 76
symbiosis 16, 34, 40, 83
Syntrichia ruralis subsp. *ruraliformis* **155**, 158

Talitrus saltator 100
Tar Lichen, Black 32–34, **38–40**
Tar Lichen, Green 38, 44–45
Tellin Shell 99, 116, 118, 120
Tellina fabula 99
Tellina tenuis 99, 116, 118, 120
Tephromela atra **32–34**,
terebellid 98
Thalassiosira 85–86
thermocline 93
Thongweed 15, **55–57**, 77–79, 81
Thrift **27–28**, 32–33, 35, **137–138**, 171, 173, 175
tidal rapids 80

tides **10–12**, 80, 94, 113, 123, 141
tintinnid 88
Tomopteris helgolandica 88, 92
Tompot Blenny 62
Topshell, Common or Toothed 51
Topshell, Grey 65, **68**, 73
Topshell, Painted 65, **68**, 73
Topshell, Purple 44–45, **50**, 68, 73, 80
topshells 19, 51, 68, 73
trampling 179
trawling 179
Tri-butyl tin (TBT) 52, 178
Tripleurospermum maritimum 172–173, 175
Trivia monacha 68
Tubifex worms 141
Turnstone 63
Twite 136
Tyria jacobaeae 156

Ulex europaeus 162
Ulva lactuca 51, 81, 84, 107
Ulva species **39**, 41, 50, 54, 74–75, 77, 107, 119, 123, 129, 139

Valerian 174
Vaucheria 136
veliger 90
Verrucaria maura 32–34, **38–40**
Verrucaria mucosa 38, 44–45
Vertebrata lanosa 46
Viola tricolor subsp. *curtisii* **158–159**, 170
Vipers Bugloss 159, 174

waders 113, **120–121**, 136
wave action **12–13**, 20, 40, 46, 48, 55, 74, **76–79**,
Wigeon 133, 136
Wild (Dune) Pansy **158–159**, 170
Wireweed 178–179
Wolf Spider 141
Wrack, Bladder 14–15, 20, **44**, **46–47**, 50, 72, 74–79, 84, 107
Wrack, Channel **38–41**, 72, 75, 77, 79, 129
Wrack, Horned 78, **106–107**
Wrack, Knotted 14–15, **44–46**, 72, 75, 84, 129–130
Wrack, Serrated 44, **54**, **56**, 68, 72, 78, 80, 82
Wrack, Spiral 17, **38–41**, 72, 75, 77, 79, 107

Xantho 20, 22, **60**, 65, 69
Xanthoria 16, **32–34**,
xerophyte 149, 162

Yellow Horned Poppy 173–174

Zirfaea crispata **25**, 75
zoea 91
zonation/zones 14, 26, 29, 34, 41, 73–74, 76–79, 80–81, 94, 114–116, 124, 130, 140, 142, 144, 161, **167–168**
zooea larva 48,
zooplankton 88–92
Zooxanthellae 81
Zostera species 9, 64, 98, 123, **130**, 133
Zygaena filipendulae 164